Nothing Never Happens

Experiential Learning and the Church

By John D. Hendrix

SMYTH&HELWYS
PUBLISHING, INCORPORATED · MACON, GEORGIA

Smyth & Helwys Publishing, Inc.
6316 Peake Road
Macon, Georgia 31210-3960
1-800-747-3016
©2004 by Smyth & Helwys Publishing
All rights reserved.
Printed in the United States of America.

The paper used in this publication meets the minimum requirements of
American National Standard for Information Sciences—
Permanence of Paper for Printed Library Materials.
ANSI Z39.48–1984. (alk. paper)

Library of Congress Cataloging-in-Publication Data

Hendrix, John, 1935-
Nothing never happens : experiential learning and the church / by John D. Hendrix
p. cm.
Includes bibliographical references
ISBN 1-57312-421-4
1. Bible—Study and teacing
2. Experiential learning—Religious aspects—Christianity
I. Title.
BS600.3 .H46 2003
268—dc22

2003023929

Diagram of Seven Doorways from *Seven Pathways of Learning: Teaching Students and Parents about Multiple Intelligences*, by David Lazear, 1994. Reprinted with permission of Zephyr Press, Chicago.

Sections of Chapter 10 appeared as "The Seed, The Sower, and The Soil: Toward a Primitive Curriculum," in *Baptist History and Heritage*, vol. 26 (Nashville: Historical Commission of the Southern Baptist Convention and the auxiliary Southern Baptist Historical Society, July 1991), 43-52.

Contents

To the students, administration, and faculty of
The Southern Baptist Theological Seminary
in Louisville, Kentucky, 1984–1995;
and to the people of Northside Baptist Church
in Clinton, Mississippi, 1996–2002.

Preface

I have no idea when all of this began. I suppose the first stirrings came in the middle of the 1960s (1963–1966) at the New Orleans Baptist Theological Seminary with John Price Jr., Harold Rutledge, Clyde Walker, Lewis Scholle, and Stanley Watson and with Myron Madden, Don Cabaniss, and Dale Wright during my weekly excursions to Baptist Hospital. My earlier theological training at Midwestern Baptist Theological Seminary (1958–1962) with Morris Ashcraft, Ralph Elliott, Roy Honeycutt, John Howell, Hugh Wamble, Bill Morton, Alan Gragg, and Clifford Ingle rooted me in working with and loving the biblical text. They also blessed me with an insatiable hunger for learning and an understanding that I did not have an adequate process for communicating that learning. Sometime during those eight years, I began seeing myself as an experiential educator, and when we drove across that long Lake Pontchartrain bridge headed for Nashville in fall 1966, Lela and I knew we were vastly different from the two people who married in August 1958.

Looking back on my eighteen years at the Baptist Sunday School Board (1966–1984), I would now describe myself as a reflective practitioner involved in active experimentation. At least, that's how the "experientialists" Donald Schon and David Kolb would describe it. This experimenting required an enormous amount of long-suffering and patience by those people who impacted me the most—James Sullivan, Annie Ward Byrd, Philip Harris, Lloyd Householder, and later Roy Edgemon and Art Criscoe. Lela reminds me that we didn't unpack the good dishes for six years, thinking any moment we would be on the move looking for another job. I remember a weeklong journey through the Baptist churches of Michigan when I was sent there to introduce new member training materials. Instead, I experimented with "action parables," and the state Church Training director had to retrace my steps and do the job I failed to do. The "two mountains where God lives" in Baptist life (Ridgecrest and Glorieta) became my laboratories for experiential learning, and I became much more comfortable using these processes with the people from the churches.

Although my faculty colleagues at the Southern Baptist Theological Seminary (1984–1995) were playfully suspicious of my teaching style, I never questioned their loyalty and commitment to me. However, those energizing students in classrooms who were ready to try anything finally helped me bring a little more preciseness to a rather chaotic process. I owe a great debt to doctoral students I supervised (or were they supervising me?): Susan Shaw, Linda Givens, Ed Richardson, Bob Brocious, David Cassady, David Adams, Libby Cunningham, Mark Price, Lawanda Smith, and Jerry Bowling. I must also mention a vast number of Ph.D. students who were required to take my summer course in teaching principles and methods. I remember those summers with great fondness, and my imagination says that those students might still be doing active experimentation with some of the events of the classes.

This may or may not be my last writing for publication, so I must mention people and churches who became mentors and emotional guarantors—Loren S. Goings, Bill and Marilyn Oberkrom, Harold and Eva Marie Evans, Ernie and Bonnie White, Jim and June York, Avery and Ann Lee, Henry and Clo McGill, and Jim and June Hatley. Some are gone, but they still whisper in my ears, particularly during my years as a pastor.

The churches include Mt. Washington Baptist Church, Kansas City, Missouri; First Baptist Church, Versailles, Missouri; First Baptist Church, Blue Springs, Missouri; First Baptist Church, Bolivar, Missouri; St. Charles Avenue Baptist Church, New Orleans, Louisiana; Immanuel Baptist Church, Nashville, Tennessee; Bellevue Baptist Church, Nashville, Tennessee; Walnut Street Baptist Church, Louisville, Kentucky; Duport Road Baptist Church, Monrovia, Liberia, West Africa (charter members); Crestwood Baptist Church, Crestwood, Kentucky; Ballardsville Baptist Church, Ballardsville, Kentucky; Northside Baptist Church, Clinton, Mississippi; and Alta Woods Baptist Church, Jackson, Mississippi. I can't imagine a more diverse group of Baptist churches, but there has always been one there when we needed one. Someone asked my old friend Jerry Brown how I was doing as interim pastor of Bellevue Baptist Church in Nashville. Jerry responded, "Well, he's doing all right. He's one-third teacher, one-third shepherd, and one-third crazy." That's the best thing I've ever heard said of me, and I've tried to be faithful to that perception and hope that some of it comes through in this book. Most of the people in the churches, with a few exceptions, have affirmed those parts of me with grace and good humor. If my grandchildren (Madison and Savannah Johnson and Hank, Jake, and Bailey Ann Hendrix) are ever interested in reading some of this, they may think there is a little more to Papa than "crazy."

A mile and a half from our home in Clinton, Mississippi, is the historic Mississippi College (founded in 1826). No matter where I go, there are people with ties to this school, an intricate system of connections that is apparently worldwide. Martha Hutson in history and education and Stan Baldwin in neuroscience have commented, critiqued, and corrected this manuscript. I express gratitude and appreciation to them.

I wrote the book in two phases, eight years apart. I originally drafted a manuscript at the Glorieta Conference Center, near Sante Fe, New Mexico—a good place and a good place to write—during a six-month sabbatical from Southern Seminary in spring and summer 1994. My intention was to write a textbook for my classes in Christian teaching and experiential education. When I left Southern Seminary in December 1995, I had no students and no classroom. My cohorts at Smyth & Helwys Publishing, David Cassady and Mark McElroy, with their own brand of craziness, reminded me of that fact. "And besides, whatever possessed you in thinking that you were an academic in the first place?" they queried. That made me mad, but of course, they were right. So the manuscript was not cracked open again until my retirement from the pastorate at Northside Baptist Church in 2002, although it floated through a couple of other publishers' hands. Sections of it have been rewritten, and sometimes I wonder who that person was who wrote in 1993–1994. Although much of it has been reshaped, the original structure remains the same—two introductory chapters and four chapters on the experiential movements of experience, exegesis, reflection, and application. The final four chapters apply the model to leadership, preaching, cross-cultural studies, and curriculum development. I now hope it is more who I am and less what others looking over my shoulder might expect of me. Thanks to David and Mark for staying with me when I didn't deserve it, but I stayed with them when they didn't deserve it, either!

So there they are—people and places that left their imprint on me for more than fifty years, and I can find them all in and between the words and lines of this book. It is somewhat ironic that I have encouraged people to write since my earlier days with the Baptist Sunday School Board, but my own writing has been a lonely venture; it's not why *don't* you write a book, but why *did* you write a book. There are two exceptions. R. Clyde Hall continually encouraged me to write, but he was always in a bind and asking me to bail him out. Still, he kept me writing for many years in Nashville. Of course, Lela, my wife, is the one. Lela is an experiential educator in her own right, and her doctoral work at Vanderbilt University in Nashville provides her with educational foundations that continue to stimulate me. Her perceptions and encouragement matter the most. She has been cleaning up my messes for forty-five years, including whatever she could do with this manuscript.

Finally, six months after I retired from the pastorate, the editor of the *Clinton News* called and asked what I was doing. I said I was trying to finish a book and working a part-time job for my friends who own the Hemphill Souse and Sausage Kitchen in Jackson. The editor responded, "That is very interesting. Tell us more about your work with souse and sausage." And that's about the way it is with my writing.

John D. Hendrix
Clinton, Mississippi
August 2003

Introduction

"The best thing for being sad," replied Merlyn, beginning to puff and blow, "is to learn something." This is the only thing that never fails. You may grow old and trembling in your anatomies, you may lie awake at night listening to the disorder in your veins, you may miss your only love, you may see the world about you devastated by evil lunatics, or know your honour trampled in the sewer of baser minds. There is only one thing for it then—to learn. Learn why the world wags and what wags it. That is the only thing which the mind can never exhaust, never alienate, never be tortured by, never fear or distrust, and never dream of regretting. Learning is the thing for you.[1]

This is a book about learning theory and biblical interpretation. Learning is the better way for us (perhaps the best way), the one journey that never disappoints and never fails. We may lose the whole world, but learning will continue to sustain us. In our hunger for learning, we join God in a great endeavor; in our distaste for learning, we soon discover a distancing from God. Trying to write this chapter has often felt like participating in a town meeting or a church business meeting. Sometimes loud voices want to dominate the discussion. At other times, more quiet reflective discourse surfaces. There are moments when all the voices speak at once and other moments when silence seems to be the only thing that helps. Learning is that way for me.

My romance with the Bible began with a series of mini-epiphanies that seemed to run parallel with developmental and situational crises. I've told these stories often, and they have changed as I have changed, but the original chronicles are firmly in place and are reconstructed through memory and imagination.

My first encounter with a biblical text came when I was fifteen. Baptist Hill was a primitive Baptist camp set deep in the Ozark hills near Mt. Vernon, Missouri. It was named Baptist Hill, I suppose, because it jutted up out of a pasture land, in the middle of a winding gravel road that led to a small hilltop area with cabins and bunk houses, a mess hall, a swimming pool with cold spring water, and the famous open-air pavilion. Every evening we would go to the pavilion for "preaching." We would sit on the back rows, flirting with the girls and pretending not to listen. However, I heard every word and experienced a growing restlessness of spirit. The preacher was Clyde T. Francisco, an Old Testament professor from the seminary in Louisville, Kentucky. The evenings were hot and muggy with hundreds of funeral fans flashing in the air, reminding us that we were dealing with life-and-death issues. In Missouri we would say it was "close," words hanging in the air because there was no room for them to escape and no breeze to carry them. The text on Thursday evening was "Clay in the Potter's Hand" from Jeremiah 18. The preacher offered a simple outline I have never forgotten. God has a purpose for your life, but, like the clay, you can resist and spoil God's purpose. Still, God reworks us in a way that "seems good for God to do." That "Baptist Hill" was not exactly a mountain, but hearing the word of God was a Sinai experience for me at an experiential level for the first time. I have never forgotten that sermon and have tried to preach it many times with much less effect than on that hot steamy night in July 1950.

My second encounter with a biblical text came during the first semester in the birth of a new seminary. Midwestern Baptist Theological Seminary opened for the first time in September 1958. We met in a makeshift classroom in the historic Calvary Baptist Church in Kansas City, Missouri. I sat on the back row of Old Testament introduction with four college classmates. We had the warm feeling that we were all engaged in a pioneer effort of starting a new seminary. The professor was Ralph Elliott, and he was introducing the biblical text in Genesis 1–2. In some ways, the atmosphere was similar to the Baptist Hill experience eight years earlier—thick and heavy, with some students hardly breathing. Elliott introduced two stories in Genesis 1 and 2 that came from two different periods in Israel's history, with different names for God and different stories to tell. "Study the text," he said. Although the classroom had a certain heaviness, lights were going off in my head and I imagined a breeze blowing across my body as if someone had suddenly opened all the windows in the room. I walked out of class exhilarated and laughing. But to my surprise, my four classmates had an opposite reaction. They were angry, promising one another not to go back the next day. Of course, they did, but their words were similar: "If you believe that, then before long, there will be nothing left." In the days to come, I felt that danger with the ambivalence of something lost and something found. It was a critical moment and I sensed that I had to let the text say what it wanted to say and not what I had already decided it should say. I was walking into a whole new world of biblical studies, but our valued friendship was never quite the same. This microscopic event led eventually to the dismissal of Ralph Elliot at Midwestern

Seminary and became a forerunner to the denominational crisis that pitted friend against friend for decades.

The biblical encounters seemed to come quickly in those early days of a new seminary. Two semesters later in spring 1960, I walked into another class titled "Old Testament Theology," taught by another new professor, Roy Lee Honeycutt. This was a small class in a small classroom, and Roy was a robust figure, filling the whole classroom with his presence. His voice was strong, courageous, and bold. He seemed like a throwback to another age, an Old Testament prophet in a buttoned-down suit, and before the class was a week old, the word "covenant" came flowing out of his mouth. It was the same voice that entranced and electrified me as a new professor at my first Southern Seminary convocation in Fall 1984. It was the same robustness of spirit that I saw reappear in his covenants with students, faculty, and administration and in his attempts at covenant with seminary trustees. I'm sure he would be embarrassed if I called him a contemporary Jeremiah, living daily with fervor and sadness. He would not for a moment take credit for making Jeremiah 31:31-33 a text that has stayed with me almost daily for forty years. He would probably say it is coincidence that what he said about covenant had anything to do with the forming of a Covenant Community in Nashville, Tennessee, in 1970, and subsequently the shaping of a community by the same name in Louisville, Kentucky, in 2000, by Lela's and my son, Jud. That seems to be the way it is with covenants—sustaining relationships over long periods of time, reaching out in unpredictable directions, and binding hearts with unbreakable ties. I tell you these stories to show that my first three life-changing encounters with Scripture came indirectly from people at Southern Seminary in the 1950s. I wonder what was happening there?

My fascination with the learning process as it relates to the study of Scripture began on a Sunday morning in fall 1965. In the emotional terror of trying to make my life more transparent to others, life seemed to go into a moratorium, as if waiting for something to happen. The word came in the form of a sermon by Myron Madden titled "The Gospel and the Self." It seemed as if I were hearing a biblical text for the first time or in a way I had never heard it before. I remember being amazed that these words were in the Bible. They spoke so clearly of my dilemma, somehow putting into words the feelings and intuitions I could not name for myself. I felt as if I had been invaded by a strange world, although I had read biblical texts most of my life. I remember going home that Sunday afternoon and looking for the text. Again, there were surprise and shock in finding it.

Out of curiosity I returned to my files, looking for my New Testament seminary notes. Sure enough, there it was, a whole page of commentary on 1 Thessalonians 2 taken five years earlier. But the exegesis of the text had left not the faintest memory or any sense that I had heard those words before.

What happened to me that day could not be described as an orderly, well-developed learning experience. It was chaotic, contradictory, and confusing. That "hearing" began a conversation with myself, the biblical text, and, finally, with other people. Although those days marked the turning point in my understanding of Scripture, not even my closest friends and loved ones had any sense of the inner core of conversation that was taking place between the biblical text and myself. There was much more to learn about 1 Thessalonians.[2] The romance with that book had only begun. First Thessalonians became the mirror from which I could reflect on the deeper dimensions of the self. I knew myself in a way that I never had before. Along with that feeling was a new appreciation for the power of the biblical word. If that text could create a convictional experience, then any text had the same potential. A pebble had dropped in the vast lake of biblical interpretation, but the rippling effects were to impact my reading of Scripture from that point forward.

The fifth event came during the cold, depressing winter months of 1972. Lela and I took a short journey from Nashville, Tennessee, to Louisville, Kentucky, in search of personal renewal. Findley Edge invited us to a retreat led by Gordon Cosby of the Church of the Savior in Washington, DC. Gordon spoke only twice—thirty minutes at the beginning of the retreat and thirty minutes in closure. The remainder of the retreat was spent in corporate silence. After thirty-six hours of silence, he had only one question: "What do you know now that you didn't know before?" He used a simple but powerful teaching methodology of an advanced organizer (thirty-six hours of silence) to speak thirty minutes about giftedness and bodiness.[3] I have thought about his leadership many times since then. How could a man lead an entire retreat and speak only in two thirty-minute periods? This experience led me on a five-year love affair with Ephesians 4:11-16 focused on the themes of equipping, giftedness, spiritual formation, and the nurturing and numerical growth of the church. Ephesians 4:11-16 continued to generate new ideas and became the primary foundational planning document of the Church Training Department of the Baptist Sunday School Board for several years.

After doing weekly sermon preparation for several years and never being quite satisfied with how it was going, my thoughts kept going back to a design I found during a curriculum seminar at Southern Seminary in 1993. The plan was a simple integration of biblical studies for all ages in Sunday school and worship following the *Revised Common Lectionary*.[4] Again, I was not prepared for what happened. Sermon preparation became a new challenge and offered new energy. There were times when the biblical development of the lectionary initially did not make sense to me, but the more I worked with it the more confluent (flowing together) it became. Church life took on a quieter, more trusting climate.

Even though we were involved in a building program with significant changes in the life of the congregation, most of us seemed to be looking and walking in the same direction. I could see it in their faces. "We know where you are and where you're coming from," they seemed to say. An undercurrent of "knowing" seemed to wash through us. There was the surprising look of recognition on the faces of children, turning to parents in wide-eyed wonder that "Big John is saying something I already know." Thus, I confronted the most profound of all learning experiences—we learn what we already know. I remember the first service in the new sanctuary and the tugging to leave the lectionary for a Sunday and do something specific for that day. But a contrary voice kept whispering that the lectionary would have a word for us. From my perspective, it had a lot to say.

It's a long journey from a primitive Baptist camp in the hills of Missouri to a worldwide lectionary of biblical texts—but no longer than the journey from heart to head and back again. In a sense, that is the longest journey we will ever make. One way to make that journey is through stories, and there are common threads that tie these stories together. They all come out of crises, either personal or organizational. They all come as a surprise with the biblical text somehow slipping in from the edges and corners amid seemingly unrelated daily activities and events. The biblical encounters are events in themselves, catching up and overshadowing other significant situations and taking on lives of their own. They are all text-specific, centered on rather small blocks of biblical texts. They provide themes that have stayed with me through fifty years of ministry—Old Testament stories, covenants, giftedness, and "sharing the gospel and self." They are all initiated by hearing and primarily through preaching and teaching, although small group expressions play a dominant part. They all result in expressions of internal surprise to the point of astonishment. Finally, all these "experiences" lead to quiet musings of gratitude and giving thanks. "This is the word of the Lord. Thanks be to God."

The Word of the Lord. . . Thanks Be to God

An old Hebrew litany proclaims thanksgiving to God even if God were to do one thing and nothing more. One act of God would be enough to give thanks. A slice of the entire litany goes something like this:

> How thankful must we be to God, the All-Present,
>   for all the good He did for us.
> Had he helped us forty years in the desert
> And not fed us manna
> It would have been enough for us!

Had he fed us manna
And not given us the Sabbath
It would have been enough for us!
Had He given us the Sabbath
And not brought us to Mount Sinai
It would have been enough for us![5]

There is much more to the litany, as there are many more biblical encounters for most of us. But would one encounter be enough if it brought us to giving thanks? While in Africa, we heard of an old tribal legend that spoke of a people with a hole in the top of their heads. There were times when the hole would open up, providing more light, air, and insight. Memory, imagination, and reflection keep the hole in the head ajar and the window to the soul cracked open. Without any concentrated effort on our part, understanding increases. We experience deep loss and there is room for something new. It does no good in trying to keep the hole in the top of the head open. In moments of almost total distraction, the word of the Lord comes slipping in. Thanks be to God.

The word of the Lord is something to be heard; someone is speaking to us, not sending us emails and memos. Finally, as adults, we are read to again, much like we were as children; it's too bad that the only place I am now read to is in church. Our response is gratitude and thanksgiving because gratitude creates new possibilities, opens new doors, and keeps the hole in the head ajar. Maybe everything that really matters begins with gratitude. Let's reverse the order. "Thanks be to God . . . the word of the Lord."

If you do too much of this, it will drive you crazy, but reflect on the following. When you read or hear a biblical word, phrase, or text, here are some possibilities. Whatever is read or heard explodes into tiny fragments that are picked up by millions of cascading cells and converted to form a path to the brain. There, in some sort of mysterious sequence, the words or phrases are developed into scenes that are instantly compared with stored words and pictures you already know. The whole process is like taking a house or table apart splinter by splinter, moving it by an eighteen-wheeler to a different location, and putting it back together splinter by splinter in such a way that you still recognize it as "house" or "table." All this happens in less than a second. All this may be going when you listen to classical or easy-listening music; track baseball scores from the night before; feel certain emotions like mad, glad, sad, or scared; process the pain in your right hip from a run earlier in the day; and wonder how the brain can possibly do all of this at the same time and still put it together in a way that makes sense.

When we finally realize how beautiful this whole process is, we wonder how we could possibly be interested and fascinated with anything fictitious or bizarre again, and how there could ever be anything in movies, television, or the Internet that could match this spectacular event going on in our heads. Finally, we may come to the highest levels of thinking-feeling processes—the initiation of gratitude and thanksgiving. All that can be said is "Thank you." "Therefore I have uttered what I did not understand, things too wonderful for me, which I did not know" (Job 42:3). "Such knowledge is too wonderful for me; it is high, I cannot attain it . . . I praise you, for I am fearfully and wonderfully made" (Ps 139:6, 14).

After reading these accounts, you might think I am one of those people who lives every day immersed in Scripture. Well, I am not. There are days, even weeks, when I don't crack open the biblical text, although the ruminating on texts continues daily. Reading for me has always been selective, preparing a lesson or sermon, until that moment of surprise when a word, phrase, story, or teaching catches me unaware and tells me once again "this text is about me."

NOTES

[1] T.H. White, *The Once and Future King* (New York: G.P. Putnam's Sons, 1939), 185-86.

[2] See John Hendrix, *To Thessalonians with Love* (Nashville: Broadman Press, 1982).

[3] An advance organizer "scaffolds" an experience in a specific direction by providing concepts, principles, and generalizations—"introductory material presented ahead of the learning task and at a higher level of abstraction and inclusiveness than the learning task itself." This is a term introduced by David Ausubel in *Educational Psychology: A Cognitive View* (New York: Holt, Rinehart, and Winston, 1968), 148. See "Advance Organizers" in *Models of Teaching*, Bruce Joyce and Marshal Weil (Englewood Cliffs NJ: Prentiss-Hall, Inc., 1986), 70-88.

[4] The *Revised Common Lectionary* was published in 1992. "Lectionary" is a schedule of biblical readings for each Sunday from the Old Testament, the New Testament letters, and the Gospels. The readings vary according to the seasons of the Christian year—Advent, Christmas, Epiphany, Lent, Easter, and Pentecost. The schedule involves a three-year cycle, and the first three letters of the alphabet are used—A, B, C. The schedule begins again with Year A. Each new Christian year begins on the first Sunday of Advent, four Sundays before Christmas Day.

[5] From *Passover Haggadah*, Rabbi Nathan Goldberg (New York: KTAV Publishing, 1984).

CHAPTER ONE

Experiential Learning: Cycles and Polarities

> I seem to be a person who falls easily into contrary views. It's always happening that I talk to one person and find what she says convincing, and then talk to someone else with a contrary view and find her equally convincing (except where she says that the first person was wrong.) The same thing happens to me in my reading. Even "thinking for myself," I characteristically start off believing X and then drift into believing not X—but wanting to hold on to both.
>
> Perhaps it's because my brain is accustomed to accepting conflicting data and somehow dealing with it but not reconciling it: I started out cross-eyed and childhood surgery left me with two good eyes which happen to look outward in different directions.[1]

This chapter attempts to introduce some of the theory behind experiential learning and biblical interpretation. Experiential learning refers to concrete participation in the daily processes of living rather than categories of information. It is often a "double-visioned" (some would say cross-eyed) perspective seeking to bring together educational and biblical perspectives. Learning and biblical interpretation are the same thing and can be separated only for the sake of discussion.

Experiential learning differentiates from rational, cognitive theories that emphasize abstraction. Experiential learning seeks to develop a holistic, integrative perspective on learning that combines experience, perception, cognition, and behavior.[2] At times this process runs smoothly with some sense of order and sequence. At other times the process is "messy," with leaps, paradoxical jumps, and movements in opposite directions. Learning is perceived as a four-stage cycle of concrete experience as a basis for observation and reflection (perception). These observations are gathered into beliefs (cognition) from which new implications for action (behavior) can be deduced. This movement through experience, perception, cognition, and behavior has both cyclical and polarity implications.

Learning emphasizes and enhances all four modes of the process. The process often runs smoothly, but it is not always a simple journey. Tension is inherent in movement from mode to mode. Some kind of learning model is always used on the study of Scripture. A circular process suggests entering the conversation at various points. Exegetical study may precede change or specific action, but action and change may precede study, and exegesis becomes as helpful in interpreting change as it is in initiating it.

Any learning theory should bring us closer to the natural ways people learn—the spontaneous processes of everyday life. We are accustomed to thinking that learning is a logical, step-by-step, sequential experience. Bible study and teaching are affected by this thinking. How many times have we heard, "Follow these four easy steps in Bible study"? Although the format may vary, there is usually a process of building up the body of information, concepts, and principles and applying them to life. Read the text. Explain the text. Apply the text.

Learning hardly ever follows these steps in everyday life. We do not plod step by step in linear sequential fashion, nor do we solve problems through cognitive, orderly processes. More often we use intuition, play games with ourselves and others, and take leaps of fantasy and imagination, intentionally ignoring logic. Learning, like life, runs in cycles and seasons, peaks and valleys, comings and goings, high tides and low tides. Life is formed by cycles of experience. Let us agree to be suspicious of steps in learning and follow the more natural leadings of cycles and the contraries of polarities. Steps presume hierarchies and levels of achievement, which present grave dangers to the humble reading of biblical texts. We will no longer be able to say that teaching and learning are a planned, sequential series of steps that lead to ends known in advance and realized through efficient teaching. The clearer and simpler the steps, the more artificial the process seems. Instinctively, we catch truth "on the way," a momentary glimpse that lacks smoothness and symmetry, more awkward and angular as it breaks through to us.

Cycles

Cycles are experienced in the daily routine of life—A.M. and P.M.; morning, afternoon, and evening; spring, summer, fall, and winter. Ultimate meanings for Christians are revealed by the concrete acts of God in time. Christ was put to death on a specific day "at about the sixth hour," related to the Passover festival of the year, and he rose on the third day. All this is in the same cycle of time in which we live—the time in which we are born, grow up, earn a living, age, and face death. The early church was aware of these movements and focused on morning and evening prayer, Christmas and Easter cycles, and other seasonal experiences. We may be less aware of learning cycles, but they appear spontaneously in daily living.

The Bible depicts little of our clock-watching and time schedules. Biblical people experienced time more holistically. No one counted seconds, minutes, or even hours. Early Christians apparently learned to count hours from the Romans. Time units were based on the observation of experience, appropriately called "watches" (Exod 14:24; 1 Sam 11:11). Time ran in cycles—the coming, going, and returning of the sun, and the monthly reoccurring of the full moon. By far, the most important unit of time was the day, the basic unit of experiential life. However time was counted or measured, biblical people seemed to know that God was not controlled by time or sequences of events. God met people in each moment of experience, offering each new moment as a possibility for learning and knowing. Thus the psalmist prays that God will "teach us to count our days that we may gain a wise heart" (90:12).

All learning processes occur in time sequences. How events are planned within a period of time is an unconscious but nevertheless crucial aspect of learning. The more popular process is to follow well-defined mechanical and efficient steps in a staircase model that is always upward, finally arriving at some position or platform on which one can firmly stand. But the natural processes of learning are more circular, rhythmic, and periodic. What was once experienced reappears in a different form. What goes around comes around. We have the sense that we have been this way before, stepping into a stream that is familiar, yet with a different temperature and flow. This brings us to the simplest but perhaps most profound of all learning theories: we learn what we already know.

The seasons of the soul have their own way of doing things. The events of the soul seem to be circular and repetitive with different themes and nuances. We move in circles, coming back to where we started, turning and twisting, repeating, recollecting, reconstructing, reforming, and reliving. Daydreaming and remembering draw the past into the present. We drift out of the present to revisit people and places of our past. We root like plants, blossom and fade like flowers, hoping that we are perennial. We sway with the wind currents, respond to the cycles of sun and moon, and discover that we are more and more like the earth in which we live, move, and have our being.

Life does not seem to offer clear ways and straight paths. We tend to wander. We recycle family in strange and odd ways. I see the ways of my father and mother in the things I do, and I see the same patterns in my son and daughter. Maybe we expand the cycles a little, but we continue to repeat the same themes. Communities of people that seem to be more primitive pay closer attention to the cycles and seasons in learning and ritual. Instead of growing and developing, perhaps we simply keep turning over and over, oscillating, as the old gospel spiritual suggests, "Like a wheel in a wheel, way up in the middle of the air."

Experiential Bible study takes seriously our natural, spontaneous ways of living. In the cycles of daily experience, we consistently, either consciously or unconsciously, ask ourselves, "How do I feel about that?" "What really happened?" "What is this experience teaching me?" "Is there something about this experience that will be helpful tomorrow, next week, or even next year?"

Experiential Bible study uses a circular concept of learning and suggests practical ways of using it. Learning occurs when something we experience grabs us as it relates to a biblical text. We then draw meaning from the text, look back at the experience in a reflective manner, draw personal insights, and risk those insights in a practical way. This process is often experienced in our ordinary living. Experiential Bible learning can be defined as a relatively stable but permanent change in people that results from experience, biblical exegesis, reflection, and application. In "slang" (easily remembered terminology), the four movements are "Hook," "Book," "Look," and "Took."

Diagram 1: Experiential Bible Study Model

EXPERIENCE

A point of *interest,* related to the learner's *experience,* expressed in an unusual way, which gives *immediacy* to the content.

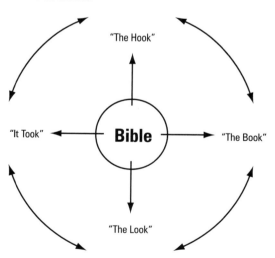

APPLICATION

A short, straight "punch" to motivate learners in the *practice* of Scripture, with gives *involvement* with the content.

"The Hook"

"It Took"   **Bible**   "The Book"

"The Look"

EXEGESIS

An accurate, precise *exegesis* of a biblical word, passage, or theme that proclaims the *principles* of the Scripture and *informs* the content.

REFLECTION

The biblical content *reflected* on and held "in solution" with *needs, life situations,* and *personal biography,* which provides *intimacy* and *intensity* with the content.

In spite of different labels, most learning cycle theorists use concepts to describe how people learn and ultimately manifest a change in behavior. Jones and Pfeiffer have developed an experiential learning cycle of experiencing (activity), publishing (sharing reactions), processing (patterns and dynamics), generalizing (principles), and applying (planning).[3] Kolb, Rubin, and McIntyre designed a learning model around concrete experiences (demands of the real world) and observations or reflections on experience. This leads to the formulation of abstract concepts and application, or "testing concepts in new situations."[4]

James E. Loder has developed five movements that are descriptive of a transforming event.[5] The first movement is a "rupture" in what is known, which creates an inner conflict and a need to set things right. The second movement is an interlude for scanning—a time of waiting and wondering, looking over the terrain of one's situation, and searching for possible solutions. The third movement is the constructive act of imagination—an insight, intuition, or vision that impacts with convincing force and leads to the transformation of the ruptured situation. The fourth movement is characterized by release and openness—a release of energy that has been "bound up" and a freedom to move in new directions. There is a "sigh of relief" that often brings a wave of new insights. The final movement is an interpretation of the solution into behavior that is a gain over the original conditions. In summary, transformational knowing is carried on conjointly as imagination and personal intuitions interact with reflective or theoretical knowledge.

All learning models suggest that we are stronger in some of these processes and weaker in others. There is also the suggestion that skills in all phases of the learning cycle are required for effective learning. Therefore, movement and momentum are involved in learning.

Look back at the diagram of the experiential Bible study model. The horizontal line (exegesis-application) in the model represents the individual, systemic, ordered, coherent "organizing" of life. In following this line, we analyze, abstract, direct, think, plan, verbalize, reason, sequence, and figure it out. It is willful and powerful, always wanting to take over, without knowing that destroying the balance sabotages the whole. The vertical line (experience-reflection) seeks balance and wholeness. It represents the irrational, unpredictable, spontaneous "bursting" of life. In following this line, we imagine, intuit, vision, dread, feel, relate, gesture, sense, and get the picture. Real learning comes in the blending of both parts and whole.

What happens when all the parts come together in the study of the Bible? We can only venture a guess. Learning is a thinking, feeling process of bringing our whole selves to the biblical text. When the thinking, choosing, rational process connects with the intuitive, emotional, and relational process, the sparks are ignited. We transcend the ordinary. Through the power of the Holy Spirit, we experience revelation and are changed and perhaps transformed. We test both our experience of Scripture and our interpretation of Scripture in Christ's body, the church, waiting for confirmation that "it has seemed good to the Holy Spirit and to us" (Acts 15:28).

Learning may start anywhere and go in any direction. This dynamic makes the learning process imprecise and chaotic. Still, the model does provide boundaries, and learning breaks down if all four areas are not entered at some time. The Bible lives at the center of the process and is "text specific." The "ways of knowing" move around and through the center. The biblical core informs and transforms all the ways of knowing. The Living Word operates within the process and outside the process, working within and breaking in, making all things new.

All models are inadequate, but they at least provide a framework for learning. Since transforming kinds of learning are unpredictable and capricious, a model provides structure. The model cannot explain transformation, but it does provide handles for processing it. By placing learning in a framework, we are freed for an intensity of involvement. Yet there is more. The model provides a structure for the Holy Spirit to embody. We do not control the Holy Spirit with a framework. Rather, we provide God's Spirit with an arena to fill up with grace. By building a frame, we offer the Spirit something to work with, knowing all the time that the wind of God's Spirit blows where it will.

Let's look at the model in a different way. Take an eight- to ten-inch-long slip of paper one inch wide and draw a line from one side to the other. Call the line "thinking and doing." In our model, it is the horizontal line of exegesis and application. Turn the sheet over and draw another line. Call that line "sensing and feeling." In our model, it is the vertical line of experience and reflection. The two sides represent two separate and distinct ways of knowing and understanding Scripture. Now twist the paper and join the ends. You now have one unending line, joined and blended together in unity. The cognitive (thinking) and the affective (feeling) are confluent (flowing together). This is another way of picturing a process of learning that can bring us into a transforming relationship with Scripture.

The Emmaus Road experience is a way of introducing the transforming nature of the experiential learning cycle and a way of applying it to biblical interpretation.

1. What is going on here? (*Experience*)
2. If you want to know what is going on, you need to know what went on before. (*Exegesis*)
3. "Did not our hearts burn within us?" (*Reflection*)
4. Returning to Jerusalem. (*Application*)

Continuing to take cues from James Loder, I have used the Emmaus Road experience in Luke 24 to develop a six-movement process of transformational or convictional knowing. Convictional knowing is event-oriented when experience, imagination, and intuition come together with the theoretical and practical.

1. Conflict. Conflict begins in an unsettling, unusual experience where the known world becomes unfamiliar. There is a "rupture" in normal life where balance and equilibrium are lost. The disciples experienced the pain and disillusionment of the death of Jesus, but with some dim awareness that God was doing something. This hope stubbornly persists.

2. Contemplation. A time of talking and discussing follows. The contemplative move is the naming of experience, a deeper indwelling into their own lives, giving the experience air and ventilation. At this point, a stranger enters the conversation and begins a dialogue. "What are you discussing with each other while you walk along" (Luke 24:17)? Discussing means "to throw in turn, a ball, from one to another, a beautiful picture of conversation as a game of words."[6]

3. Conceptualization. Those "slow of heart" (slow to understand or comprehend) are reminded of all the Law of Moses and the prophets, a recalling and remembering of the cognitive underpinnings. Jesus interprets (form of word *hermeneus*) himself. He explains and makes clear how he sees himself from the Old Testament Scripture.

4. Choosing. Choosing is a decisive point of risking alternatives. Through an intuitive act the disciples constrain Jesus (a forceful, bodily compelling) to stay with them. The transforming moment (insight) comes in the breaking of bread when feeling, thinking, watching, and doing come together and configure. Jesus is not known in exegesis. He is known in the breaking of the bread.

5. Commitment. The disciples commit to an unthinkable risky act of returning the same seven miles back to Jerusalem in the dark. But now the road is seen in a new way. The past is interpreted in new light. "Didn't our hearts burn within us?" Life is lived forward (walking to Jerusalem), but understanding comes in looking back in the light of new insights.

6. Confirmation. The disciples think they will tell what they have learned, but instead they are told by others that Jesus is alive. They "rehearsed" (a form of the Greek word for exegesis) what had happened to them on the road and those who heard responded with "Yes!" The community confirmed the experience. A new community is created of people who "know" the same things. The disciples found themselves back at the same place with the same people, thus completing the cycle. But they were strangely different.

Experiential learning is a cycle of interpretation. It describes how we interpret our world, our Scripture, ourselves. A learning cycle wraps around us in ways that avoid distancing from the biblical text and separating knowing and doing. We believe in order to understand and understand in order to believe. Paul Ricoeur saw all of these aspects in his characterization of hermeneutics: "Hermeneutics seems to be animated by this double motivation, willingness to suspect, willingness to listen, vow of rigor, vow of obedience."[7]

Hermeneutics—Learning to Speak Plainly

In Greek mythology, Hermes was the god of invention and travel, speech, writing, and learning, and the messenger of the other gods. Hermes is pictured as wearing winged shoes and a hat and carrying a winged staff. The word was to be carried quickly, without hindrance. From this mythical figure, we get our word "hermeneutics"—a complex discipline that often denies the root meaning of the word "to speak plainly."

Hermeneutics is the attempt to articulate and express thought in such a way that understanding comes. Hermeneutics is an art in the service of understanding. It takes seriously the "fog index" of interpretation. God's word is to go forth and accomplish something. It is sent on a mission and does not return empty-handed (Isa 55:11). God's word is sent forth in the world with wings and it runs swiftly. It hastens quickly through the earth. It causes ice to melt and waters to flow (Ps 147:15-18).

What is meant by saying that words are carried on wings? Biblical interpretation should be fluent, smooth, vivid, graphic, and even eloquent. If words are carried on wings, they will be inspirited with thoughts that have breath and life. Words that are sent forth and run swiftly strike home, glowing with light and warmth, like a fire burning in the soul. Words can do anything the speaker wants: make contact, state facts, invoke anger or laughter, distort, charm, or seduce. Words can be used to confuse. Then more words must be added to cover up words. The flood of verbiage drowns us in a lack of clarity. This results because people refuse to speak plainly with words that have lightness and buoyancy so when they fly through the air and hit us, they leave an impact.

Every hint of the word in the New Testament carries with it the meaning of plain speaking. In John 1:38, Jesus converses with the disciples and simply asks, "What are you looking for?" In the conversation with the blind man in John 9:7,

Jesus speaks plainly: "Go, wash in the pool of Siloam." The church's hermeneutic began when the stranger was approached by the disciples on the Emmaus road— "Then beginning with Moses and all the prophets, he interpreted to them the things about himself in all the scriptures" (Luke 24:27). In 1 Corinthians 12:10, that which has been spoken vaguely by others needs the clarifying interpretation of the hermeneut. First Corinthians 14:28 warns that, when the hermeneut is not there to speak plainly, others should remain silent.

If speaking plainly is the task of hermeneutics, why do we have complexity? Much hermeneutical theory is an overload of multiple files of information, a language of complication and increased technical sophistication. Hermeneuts become servants of a theory rather than servants of communication and understanding. We can follow all the hermeneutical principles and rules and still not create genuine understanding. Common understandings are like those that exist within close-knit family groups. What is said is understood through shared experiences and attitudes. The ultimate end of hermeneutics is understanding.

Polarities

Polarity models come from gestalt concepts and thought. Gestalt theory says that there are opposite counterbalancing poles of action. These opposites attract and knowledge of each pole increases the range of learning possibilities. The aim is to achieve a rhythmic movement from one pole to another as in the swing of a pendulum. Swinging between the poles creates energy. Being stuck in the middle puts us in a barren land that holds us captive. Experientially, we sense learning to be a momentary insight grasped in pieces and fragments, lacking symmetry and wholeness, and, at best, awkward and messy. Learning is that way because life is that way. There is always an adventuresome, spontaneous quality to all interpretation.

Polarities suggest some resolution of conflicting ways of viewing the world. There is a conflict between my world and the world of biblical experience. There is a conflict between what I see and what I do. Paulo Friere's work with the dialectic nature of learning is incorporated in "praxis," which is reflection upon the world in order to transform it. Essential to praxis is a process of naming the world, which is both active (naming causes transformation and change) and reflective (our choice of words gives meaning to the world around us).[8]

The coming together of polarities throws everything into balances and counterbalances and is closer to the gathering of insight. Insights seemingly invade our being, sometimes in quiet meditation and silence, other times in vigorous activity and exercise. They go just as quickly as they come, and many of the insights into Scripture are lost in a fleeting moment. If we take polarities seriously, Bible study is never a simple journey. There is tension inherent in every movement. Kurt

Lewin discovered that learning is best facilitated when there exists a contrary tension between immediate concrete experience and the more analytic attachment of analysis. Cycles tend to run more smoothly and sequentially. Polarities are harsher, with risky leaps that jump the tracks. Polarities are opposite properties, movements in opposite directions—north and south, east and west, left and right. When people are working with polarities, they frequently say, "The other side of the picture," "The flip side of the coin," or "On the other hand." Many of the insights achieved simply emerge. They are found in the bouncing back and forth between the poles rather than being preconceived and effectively attained. Christian faith is full of powerful polarities—law and gospel, Christ as true man and true God, the Christian as saint and sinner. We will never get over the difficulty in combining these opposites and holding them all with dogged tenacity.

Once or twice a week, I participate in an activity that appears to be restricting. The room is totally enclosed with four walls and a high ceiling. There are no windows, and the only door fades into the back wall. There is nothing in the room. Only painted lines break the monotony of walls, floor, and ceiling. Do you feel the restrictions? If it is a prison, the answer is yes. But what if the room is a racquetball court? Now the limitations are exciting, intense, and exhilarating. The confining walls make movement enormously challenging. So it is with unpredictable learning provided by a framework of polarities. Let us describe several ways that polarities can be defined by their values in learning.

Comprehension and Apprehension

The dynamic relationship between comprehension and apprehension lies at the center of experiential knowledge. These two polarities present opposite modes of grasping experience—one through the direct apprehension of immediate, concrete experience and the other through the indirect comprehension of symbolic experience.

Comprehensive knowledge is well-known. We are able to analyze, critique, evaluate, and discern differences between concepts. Most scholarly methods of Bible study are based on comprehension. Comprehensive knowledge is an objective social process, a tool of culture with a complex network of words and symbols. The most extreme form of comprehensive knowledge is the belief that all knowing must ultimately be based on empirical or logical data.

The process of apprehension is closer to appreciation and is less recognized and understood. Appreciation is the process of attending to and even being fascinated with one's experience—those experiences that interest us and capture our attention. It is a personal, subjective process that cannot be known by others except by the communication of our immediate experience. Wonder and beauty are examples of appreciation that comes from sense experience.

Appreciation is a process of affirmation. Unlike criticism, which is based on skepticism and doubt, appreciation is based on belief, trust, and conviction. To appreciate is to embrace. In Bible study there is the tendency to "trust" comprehension and to view with suspicion the intuitive, subjective process. Used rightly, the process of comprehension is capable of selecting and reshaping apprehension in ways that make experience more profound and powerful. When comprehension and apprehension come together in Bible study, the Scriptures have the power to redescribe human experience.

Assimilation and Accommodation

Assimilation is a process of taking in the word and appropriating it as nourishment. The process is fluid—a way for the word to become food for the soul, to be chewed up, swallowed, and digested so its energy flows in our veins and is absorbed in our tissue. Assimilation brings a sense of sufficiency and satisfaction that our hungers have been fed. Bible study is seen as a gratifying experience. In preaching, teaching, and curriculum development, the word is "tailored" to meet needs and is molded and shaped for contemporary life. It is made palatable through pictures, stories, charts, and graphs. The Bible "in the language of the people" is a process of assimilation, an intentional, aggressive work with the text to bring it up to date and make it attractive to the contemporary world. In other words, we act upon the word.

Accommodation is a process of letting the word act upon us. We make adjustments to the demands and complexities of a text that comes from a different time and place. We are bent into the shape of Scripture rather than shaping Scripture to meet needs. We rearrange and orient ourselves to this strange world of the culture and language of the Bible, bringing our lives into accord with its demands. Often this feels like a giving way, a yielding, bending, and surrendering that takes on obedience and submissiveness. We shape our lives to fit its patterns, in a sense getting our lives to catch up with the flow of the biblical text rather than demanding that the text catch up with us.

Convergence and Divergence

The task of biblical interpretation lies on a continuum between convergent and divergent thought. Convergent thought relates to a way of thinking that is in concert with information. There seems to be a single correct answer or solution to a question or problem. Exegesis demands convergent thought. The tense of a verb, the syntax of a sentence, the type of literature, and the cultural context of a letter are examples of convergent thinking. The technical and precise aspects are preferred.

Convergence brings Scripture together toward a focus on specific problems and practical application. Convergent thinking is governed by logic, focusing on specific exegetical tasks. Orderliness and efficiency in working with concepts are valued. There is controlled expression of emotion. Convergent thinking is not likely to be convinced by anything but reasoned discourse and is characterized by careful lesson planning, central Bible truths, and focal passages. There is a concern for what fits and what comes together in an orderly way. That which intersects, connects, parallels, cross-references, and comes to the point is valued.

Divergence organizes everything through imagination, meaning, and value. Observation and reflection are more important than thinking and action. The search for meaning generates insight, brainstorming, imagination, and feeling. Rather than looking for parallels, divergence looks for contrasts with what is remote, distant, non-central, and what seemingly appears peripheral. Like seed, the word is dispersed, broadcast, sowed randomly, and extended in diverse and unpredictable directions. Like seed, it grows unsystematically and appears in unexpected places. Instead of focusing, it digresses, going off on tangents.

The greater strength of divergent thinking lies in imaginative ability and awareness of meaning. Divergent ability generates alternative ideas and processes such as brainstorming and metaphorical thinking. Both in reflection and application, creative thought is most evident and most required. Why do some people approach the word in a highly analytic and logical manner while others are more adept at inductive, imaginative processes? Why are some interpreters creative, while others follow conventional patterns only? How do we account for different learning styles among interpreters? All of these questions share in common the notion that there is some kind of tension, or polarity, between the objective, the analytic, the rational and the subjective, the sensitizing, and the intuitive.

Brain Hemispheres

Clasp your two hands into fists and imagine cramming them into your head. There you have a left- and right-sided brain, about the size of your two fists, the color of dirty snow, and the substance of cold grits with a lightning storm flashing through it. At least, that's how my brain sees mine!

Scientific research suggests that the left hemisphere of the brain is suited for analytic approaches to problem solving. The right hemisphere operates more creatively and globally in conceptual organization. The famous studies by Nobel Prize winner Roger W. Sperry on the function of split-brain patients in

California help demonstrate the subtle psychological differences between the two cerebral hemispheres. The left hemisphere was logical, convergent, and analytical; the other was intuitive and divergent, helping the person experience his or her world in terms of gestalt, or whole. Walter Wink's popular book *Transforming Bible Study* suggests a right-brain process in interpreting Scripture.

A review of the research data indicates conflicting findings for the notion of functional specialization in the brain. Both sides of the brain are involved in the various human functions, including thought. However, people may differ according to a predominant style of processing information.

The process of biblical interpretation requires the use of the whole person. In some phases of the interpretative process, the left brain functions (logical thoughts are prominent), as in the exegesis of the text. The rules of grammar are logical and there is not much room for divergent thought. The latter stages of interpretation in reflection and application are certainly not beyond logic, but require more of the function of the right brain. The ability to grasp the whole picture in relationship to a particular doctrine or issue in Scripture requires this kind of thought. Theory building in systematic theology is an example of such divergent abilities to see the whole as well as the part. The essential unity and authority of a Scripture ensure that the part is not divorced from the whole. Biblical interpretation that is true to its source, the Scripture, is not a "half-brained" procedure.

Learning Styles

Growing out of experiential learning theory are the concepts of learning styles. Learning styles are stable and enduring patterns of human personality that seem to arise from genetics and the environment. We don't need to know in detail all the learning complexities of people, but it is important to teach with the assumption that a diversity of learning styles exists. Learning styles are like channels on television sets. We tend to stay with channels that come through clearly and avoid channels with static, interference, and unclear pictures.

Following the learning cycle, David Kolb has identified four basic modes:[9]

1. An orientation toward *concrete experience* focuses on being involved in experiences and dealing with immediate human situations in a personal way.
2. An orientation toward *reflective observation* focuses on understanding the meaning of ideas and situations by carefully observing and describing them.
3. An orientation toward *abstract conceptualization* focuses on using logic, ideas, and concepts.
4. An orientation toward *active experimentation* focuses on actively influencing people and changing situations.

Finding Balance

We would not want to say that biblical interpretation is not a challenging craft worthy of our best intellectual effort, but we cannot deny the simple, straightforward approach of seeking to connect with Scripture in order to handle the daily struggles of life. Bible study incorporates a considerable variety of patterns and a complex set of interactions. But learning for the sake of learning often comes in a distant second to learning for the sake of living. Stumbling along through these complex processes finds us most of the time out of balance.

We are out of balance because of the demands to live in two worlds. When we immerse ourselves in the world of Scripture, we find our most intimate companions to be prophets, psalmists, and disciples. They become our first family, often taking precedence over father, mother, spouse, and children. This strange world of the Bible captures us in such a way that we forget where and when we actually live. So we take the step back into our own world, facing situations and dilemmas different from any that have even existed before. If we walk in these two worlds long enough, we become more aware that they are not two worlds but one and the same world. The Bible becomes a mirror through which we see our world and ourselves. This transparency is missing in much Bible study. We walk too long on one side of the road.

C. S. Lewis in *Pilgrim's Regress* described the equal and opposite dangers of failing to find balance in our thinking-feeling processes.[10] Finding an enchanted island that awakened in him an intense longing, he explored the island from north to south. Only the trail through the center could safely be walked. To the north were the purists and doctrinaires, suspicious of everything that smacked of spontaneity and imaginative effort. An arrogant and hasty selectiveness cuts these types of people off from the sources of life. We find them among those with "high noses, compressed lips, and pale complexions," people of rigid systems and ruses. We experience them as cerebral, lacking affect, curt, terse, reserved, and aloof. They are the untouchables, "Aristocrats, Stoics, Pharisees, Rigorists, signed and sealed members of highly organized parties."

The people to the south are less definable, indulgent, and undisciplined, "Boneless souls whose doors stand open day and night to almost any visitant." Like the prodigal, they give themselves up to permissiveness and unrestrained enthusiasms. All barriers are broken down, all resistance relaxed. Every feeling is justified simply because it is felt. We experience them as visceral, excessive in the belief that "anything goes."

The extremes do not balance. Instead, they aggravate, creating mistrust, frightening people with charges and counter charges. Our concern, then, is to avoid the extremes and hold to the main road, honoring careful exegesis and practical application as well as personal experience and reflection.

So let us continue the journey into all the fascinating ways people learn. Biblical interpretation is not a uniform experience that is separated from all other areas of life. It is found in a wide variety of learning processes wherever the living, acting God works through all our diverse capacities. Taking many of these dimensions into account, we still are limited in our ability to understand the mystery of learning. The mysteries outside us are similar to the mysteries inside us, but the complexity can also lead us to curiosity, appreciation, wonder, and, finally, to gratitude and giving thanks for the endless number of ways we learn.

Perhaps the mystery is best told in the parables of the hidden treasure and the pearl (Matt 13:44-46). A poor day laborer discovers a treasure in the field. How did all the others who had passed that way miss it? The treasure was hidden and would only be discovered by accident. Something of tremendous worth can be present, waiting to be discovered, yet unknown to others who have been over the same area many times. The treasure is there, present but not perceived, because it is hidden and its presence does not overwhelm us. Were others close at hand? We do not know. We do know that the treasure can be possessed without the knowledge of others. It is hidden a second time so the finder can sell all to buy the spot where the treasure is and everything else around it. This is not "seek and you shall find." This is "find, even when you are not seeking." We find the truth even when we are not looking for it. We stumble across it amid daily living. It may be hidden away from the wise and the learned and revealed to little children (Matt 11:25).

The discovery of the pearl is another matter. This searcher is a vocational connoisseur of pearls. He is out searching for pearls every day and goes about it in an organized, systematic fashion. Chances are that pearls are the obsession of his life, and he has spanned the globe in search of the pearl that will make him the envy of all pearl merchants. He is on the hunt, an expert in pearl discerning. For the pearl merchant, the treasure is an expected surprise, found by the skilled eye and the practiced touch, using all the resources, navigational charts, and graphs available for searching and finding.

The searchers are so different but so much alike. Both findings elicit great joy. For both, the normalcy of life is shattered and all future plans invalidated. Neither searcher gets something for nothing. But the approaches are quite different. Both are captured by hiddenness and smallness, similar to the leaven and mustard seed seen earlier in Matthew 13. The pearl is small but visible. Through systematic searching it will be found. The treasure is perhaps large but hidden. Even when we are not looking, we may stumble across it.

NOTES

[1] Peter Elbow, *Embracing Contraries: Explorations in Learning and Teaching* (New York: Oxford University Press, 1986), 233.

[2] Although they say it differently, the "fathers" of experiential learning (John Dewey, Kurt Lewin, David Kolb) agree on these movements. See John Dewey, *Experience and Education* (New York: Scribner Reprint, 1997); Kurt Lewin, *Field Theory in Social Science* (New York: HarperCollins, 1951); David Kolb, *Experiential Learning: Experience as the Source of Learning and Development* (Englewood Cliffs NJ: Prentice-Hall, 1984).

[3] John E. Jones and J. Williams Pfeiffer, *The 1975 Annual Handbook for Group Facilitators* (San Diego: University Associates, 1975), 3-5.

[4] David A. Kolb, Irwin W. Ruben, and James M. McIntyre, *Organizational Psychology: An Experiential Approach* (Englewood Cliffs NJ: Prentice Hall, Inc., 1971), 24-29.

[5] James E. Loder, *The Transforming Moment* (San Francisco: Harper & Row, 1981), 31-35.

[6] A. T. Robertson, *Word Pictures in the New Testament*, vol. 2 (Nashville: Broadman Press, 1930), 292.

[7] Paul Ricoeur, *Freud and Philosophy* (New Haven and London: Yale University Press, 1970), 27. According to Ricoeur, biblical interpretation is the task of both the adult critic and the naive child. See Mark Wallace, *The Second Naivete* (Macon GA: Mercer University Press, 1990).

[8] Paulo Friere, *Pedagogy of the Oppressed* (New York: Continuum, 1981), 62.

[9] David Kolb, *Experiential Learning: Experience as the Source of Learning and Development* (Englewood Cliffs NJ: Prentice Hall, Inc., 1984), 68-69.

[10] C. S. Lewis, *The Pilgrim's Regress* (Grand Rapids: William B. Eerdmans, 1992), 206.

Taste and See: Metaphors

CHAPTER TWO

*He said to me, "Mortal, eat this scroll that I give you
and fill your stomach with it."*—Ezekial 3:3

Metaphors are often the tools of experiential learning. We confront what we do not know by making associations with what we do know. Many concepts, such as understanding, love, happiness, and health, are best understood through metaphor. Imagination and intuition are the triggers to understanding metaphors. We can imagine alternative ways of seeing and interpreting. Intuition gives an immediate meaning or significance to metaphoric analysis without going through intentional analysis. Metaphors are angles into the nature of the spiritual life. The personality of the metaphor colors and shapes the insights that are revealed.

However, metaphor is not merely a matter of language; it involves all the natural discussions of our experience, including our sense of experiences: color, shape, texture, sound, and taste. To reveal qualities, particularities, and essences, one must create a form that discloses and reveals. Without metaphor, understanding is digital and mechanistic, blind to all that is not directly in front of it. Metaphor gives us wonder and beauty, a way of expressing what is basically an inward or subjective process. Metaphor makes an outward image of this inward process for oneself and others to see. In a sense, each work of art is a metaphorical expression. When we draw a picture, write a poem, or act out a text of Scripture, we are saying, "The Scripture passage is like this . . . ."

I have chosen to use sensory metaphors as a way of explaining experiential Bible study. The place of sensory imagination in Scripture is prominent. When people have been awakened by God's word, their imaginations are aroused. Sensory imagination makes connections between what is sensed and what is believed. Scripture is read and heard and touched and smelled and tasted in order to be practiced. It does not come alive by putting it into a strong box and locking it in a bank. Scripture comes alive by keeping it active in everyday life—Sitting at

Table: Bible Study as Taste; Seeing the Horizon: Bible Study as Sight; Listening to a Friend: Bible Study as Hearing.

Sitting at Table: Bible Study as Taste

Taste is an ability to distinguish nuances, qualities, and small clarifying characteristics. Developing a taste is awakening people to certain aspects that lie dormant within them. If we don't have taste, then we must rely on some stated rule on the package that tells us the ingredients and why they are good for us. Taste moves from the labels on the package—the statements, promotions, and marketing—to an inner sense. Taste is education based on sensory experience and atmosphere.

The other senses may be enjoyed in all their beauty alone, but the sense of taste is largely social. Food is a social component of life. Business over meals, wedding feasts, friends uniting and reuniting, and birthdays are examples of the power of sharing food. Around tables there is love, friendship, power, ambition, and intrigue. If an event is emotionally significant, we can bet that food will be close at hand to sanctify and bind it. I have been to many funerals where the final event is a covered dish meal, primarily potato salad. At Passover, the Jewish people gathered at a Seder feast and ate horseradish to symbolize the tears shed by their ancestors as slaves in Egypt.

It should not surprise us that when the Bible talks about fully experiencing spiritual things, the word is *taste*. "O taste and see that the LORD is good" (Ps 34:8). To hunger after the things of the spirit is a need to be fed, much like an infant cries out to be held and nursed. Nothing in our spiritual growth is more primal or more important. To taste is to experience fully. Those with taste have experienced life in an intensely personal way, and those with "bad taste" are seen as vulgar and obscene.

The Christians of the Middle Ages took the experience of Ezekiel's eating the scroll as a model of their own task in reading Scripture. The oral reading of Scripture took place during the community's eating together. This was not a timesaving device. The practice grew out of the conviction that digesting food and reading texts were fraternal twins.[1] The digesting of food into the body and the reading of Scripture increased the digestion of wisdom in the mind. "While the body is fattened with food, the mind should be filled with reading."[2]

Tasting distinguishs between recognition and perception. Recognition is seeing enough to be able to classify. Classifications can be made without taking note of qualities and particularities. Recognition is able to make statements in the form of propositions and can be appraised by logical criteria. Logic is used to determine consistency between propositions to show what is reliable and quantitative and least likely to suffer from subjectivity. Recognition is perception aborted. Let us agree that the ability to make categories and propositions is not the same as understanding and perceiving. We may be able to describe and categorize hundreds of different food types without any sense of the qualities and richness of all that is on the table in front of us. Although we may know many characteristics of apples, the only way really to know an apple is to eat one.

Tasting is the art of connoisseurship. A connoisseur is one who appreciates, perceiving what is subtle and crucial. A connoisseur learns to attend to qualities and is able to recall from gustatory memory—smell, taste, touch, and sight all come into play. Perception, like taste, is a subjective act of focusing on unique characteristics. Taste is able to note the particular qualities of joy, grief, enchantment, irony, perseverance, and courage. To reveal these particulars, to capture these essences, one must create a form that discloses, reveals, and unveils. One must develop a taste for it.

To carry our metaphor further, we may say that a small group's Bible study takes on all the characteristics of a celebrative meal. We are invited to a table that holds zest, enthusiasm, and energy. "Come close. This is good and good for you. This is the way life is supposed to be lived." What the church has to offer to the world is extra—a proclamation of faith in a happier order of life. The table, where the bread of life is broken, refuses dullness and boring sameness and going through the motions. It is full of imagination, humor, and good stories. It revels in enthusiasm, a sense of adventure, and rich, full relationships. Sitting at table is a symbol of living for moments away from evil and disorder. We are like the Gadarene demoniac, finding ourselves sitting, clothed, and in our right minds.

I have been in the rooms of many churches where Bible study occurs. Many of those rooms are carefully arranged around tables. I'm not sure that denominational experts recommend tables for Bible study, and I question if tables make for the best group dynamics; however, there seems to be an intuitive sense that a table facilitates good Bible study. The people seem to be saying, "We're here to serve one another, to thank God for our life together, to engage in rich fellowship, and to be fed by the word of God. We can do that best around a table."

Sitting at table, we get a foretaste of the final consummation of all things when God's people sit down at an informal (I hope) dinner of 10,000 times 10,000. This is the way the Bible ends—not with corpses and tears, not with failures and disappointments, but with a party. We are there because we "have tasted the heavenly gift, and have shared in the Holy Spirit, and have tasted the goodness of the word of God" (Heb 6:4-5).

Bread

The hymn "Break Thou the Bread of Life" is often used to describe the process of Bible study and teaching. Bread has historically been the primary provision of food for people around the world. The primary nutrients of life are contained in golden loaves. It is little wonder that bread is called the staff of life. It should not surprise us that bread is the symbolic representation of the Body of Christ. Bread is good and good for us. Bread strengthens our ties to our origins and sidetracks us from pursuing some abstract and mechanical goal of technological bliss. We are reminded again of all that is artificial and synthetically created. We return to bread as we return to God's word—to nourish our bodies as well as please our palates. My Episcopalian and Lutheran pastor friends look down their noses at me and playfully say, "We serve real wine." I respond, "Well, duh, we serve real bread." We go away feeling like we have been fed and, in the process, satisfied. As Brother Juniper said, "Feeding bodies is an analogue of feeding souls, and bread is the perfect symbol of the meeting of the two worlds. It is certainly a better symbol than barbecue sauce."[3]

Bread is a path to self-discovery not because it is so unusual, but because it is so common and normal. It accurately reflects the unusual and an uncommon spiritual reality. The ingredients have disappeared in the process and become part of the whole. One piece is a cross section of the entire loaf. It is a microcosm of the whole. How bread works is how life works. Life is reflected in bread.

Like the Scripture, the standard for bread is that it is so good that it calls forth a response or a reaction when eaten. Neutrality and matter-of-factness are insufficient. Rather, there is a response of delight, of amazement that anything this close to us could carry such quality and goodness. And so we can say, not out of habit, but out of passion and conviction, "Here. Take this, break it, and eat it. It is good for you."

Cooking

Working with all the contrasting elements in Bible teaching feels like the daily task of cooking and baking. Peter Elbow described cooking as the interaction of contrasting, or conflicting, material. He said, "Cooking consists of the process of one piece of material (or one process) being transformed by interacting with another: one piece of material being seen through the lens of another, being dragged through the guts of another, being reoriented or reorganized in terms of the other, being mapped onto the other."[4]

Cooking is interaction between people, between words and ideas, between immersion and perspective, between you and elemental intrigues. Rebekah and

Jacob not only cook up food for Isaac, but they "cook up" a plot against him (Gen 27:5-17). Non-cooking results when there is plenty of contrasting material but no interaction.

What does it take to cook? Good ingredients, passion for mixing ingredients, heat, energy, and generally a big mess. When we put the proper ingredients together, combine, stir, massage, knead with energy, and place the results of our artistic endeavor in an oven, something wonderful occurs. We have fresh bread that warms up the whole house, pleasing to the eye, the nose, and the tongue. Here is something good for you: rich, golden brown loaves, warm to the touch; enticing aromas that awaken long-forgotten memories.

More than any other one thing, bread making has taught me essential principles of Bible study and teaching—the principles of patience and waiting, the method of "a slow rise." "The point of a slow rise is that, when you mix the right things, you do not want to fool around with them too much. You want nature to work, character to develop. You do not want to rush the process."[5] Some would call this "bothering the pot." With the right mix and enough patience, character develops in bread and in people. Slow rise is a way to live, a way to teach, a way to be, a way to see, a context in which things find their proper places.

Experiential Bible teaching is a test of our patience and faith in a process. First, we have to wait for a slow rise, then wait for a slow bake. Even when it's taken out of the oven there is more waiting. Most primal things cannot be fully explained. When one smells bread baking, it is soothing, reassuring, affirming, and it chases the blues away. There is the bread–in its out-of-the-oven-but-not-yet-ready-to-eat stage of life. Haste has serious consequences. The loaf, though out of the oven, is still cooking and tempering. The answers do not come easily. The outside looks ready, hiding the incomplete loaf on the inside. When you try to cut it, the loaf compresses. It's a "could have been," but it's lost, gone forever because you were too hasty to bring it to completion. When you cut into a loaf too quickly, you crush the spirit.

Bread making is the best metaphor I have ever found for Bible study, teaching, and preaching. You don't have to take my word for it. This is a book on experiential processes. Try it! Choose a simple recipe of your liking. You can measure out the ingredients exactly, but I would suggest using the recipe as a guide and "winging it." You may try to do all of this in orderly fashion, but it's more fun creating a mess. Note how the ingredients disappear and become a part of the whole. Note the interplay of contrasting elements. Knead with vigor and enthusiasm, believing that what you are doing takes much personal effort combined with unearned grace. Something is going to happen here that has nothing to do with our abilities or effort. Wait. Note how your spirits rise as the dough rises. Knock it down and wait again. Do some forming and shaping, and pop the loaves in the oven. Wait again. Remind yourself that such an act of self-giving can fill the whole house with the smell of loving. (See John 12:1-6.) When the loaves are rolled out on the table, wait for them to cool. While you wait, take a few quiet moments and look closely at what you have done. Reflect on the following questions: Where did the bread come from (the ingredients and their origins)? How were the loaves made? How must an act of grace accompany successful completion? Where will the loaves go? Qoheleth, the "preacher," said, "Send out your bread upon the waters, for after many days you will get it back" (Eccl 11:1). I say, learn from bread. It is like learning from Scripture. You will find healing for your soul.

Seeing the Horizons: Bible Study as Sight

I am writing at the Glorieta Conference Center in Glorieta, New Mexico. This is a beautiful, dry land where water is precious and sunshine is plentiful. It is springtime and the first signs of new plants and flowers are appearing, but the land is poor and much that will be planted will fall on rocky soil. Many of the people I will see today are limited financially, in poor health, and desperately hoping for signs that life will be better. But I have never lived, even for a short while, in a more hospitable community. No one goes by without a greeting. Everyone is neighborly. It's a community of open doors. Does this horizon sound familiar to you? It should. We find this horizon most often in the Bible.

There is another horizon. It is the horizon of a sixty-seven-year-old man sensing another transition coming. Life is turning again. The smell of change is in the air. He is blessed with a scintillating wife, two wonderful children who knew how to marry well, and five grandchildren who are beginning to "kick it up a few notches." He has worked for fifty years in church staff positions, denominational publishing, seminary teaching, and pastoring. People would describe him as semi-retired. He has never known a vocational life not beset by denominational political activism. He longs for simplicity but is swamped by addictions to power, the idolatry of materialism, political intrigue, and heavy taxes. Does this horizon sound familiar? Although it is a personal account, it, too, is a horizon found in the Bible.

I have used the word "horizon" several times. Every reader brings a horizon of expectations to the biblical text. Horizons refer to time and distance gaps. Gaps that are centuries long exist between the event, the recording of the event in the text, and the reading of the text. Although the text does not change, the language, culture, and people do change. What keeps us from imposing our world upon that of the text? "The most effective safeguard against a wholesale imposition of the interpreter's world upon the world of the text is the diligent study of the world that produced the text."[6]

Biblical Horizons

What is the world of the Bible? It is a world with different marriage practices, systems of taxation, architectural designs, home furnishings, weaponry for warfare, means of transportation, agricultural patterns, geographical concerns, and political systems. "Distance is the recognition that there is a gap between the sandal-wearing, demon-believing world of ancient Palestine and the mass-marketed, computerized world of contemporary America. Distance is the awareness that the context of healing which we take for granted today—intensive care units, drug therapy, and the latest electronic equipment—was unheard of when people brought the sick to Jesus. Distance is the realization that the problems of world peace in a nuclear age are far more complex than the problems of such a vision in an age when people literally hoped to 'beat their swords into plowshares' (Isa 2:4)."[7]

We can see these horizons looming behind the teachings of Jesus. The oral message of Jesus is embodied in his life and deeds. Jesus speaks through an embodied and acted-out word. His claim to be the bread of life emerges through the horizon of feeding the five thousand. His descriptions of himself as the light of the world operates out of the horizon of giving sight to the blind. His self-designation as the Resurrection and the Life comes in the context of the raising of Lazarus. His teaching about service is framed by the washing of the disciples' feet.

To understand biblical horizons is to reconstruct that world and seek to enter it by an imaginative sharing of its form. Jesus refused to let the disciples intellectualize his teaching. He constantly involved them in expanding the horizons. The first lessons of the kingdom are lessons of seeing. The disciples saw Jesus heal the sick, touch the untouchable, comfort the brokenhearted, befriend the lonely, and forgive the guilty. When he would teach lessons about prayer, he simply prayed. When he would teach about servanthood, he washed the disciples' feet. He constantly urged his followers to see things that normally went unnoticed.

Sometimes he did this by calling their attention to specific things on the horizon. "Do you see these great buildings?" (Mark 13:2). "Behold, a sower went forth to sow" (Matt. 13:3). "Lift up your eyes, and see how the fields are already white for harvest" (John 4:35). By example, he showed them how to see individuals among multitudes, focusing on a lame man at the pool of Bethesda, singling out a grief-stricken woman in a funeral procession on a busy road, spotting Zacchaeus crouching in a tree above crowds of parade watchers.

The early church placed a great premium upon "seeing" and "experiencing." John began his First Letter with the statement that he was an eyewitness and experienced firsthand the life of Jesus (I John 1:1-3). Luke wrote his Gospel account after listening to those who "from the beginning were eyewitnesses and ministers of the word" (Luke 1:2).

The teachings of Jesus abound in word pictures drawn from common life—what we can see and touch. The Sermon on the Mount and the parables abound in word pictures drawn from common life. These illustrations were verbal video messages—seeds and salt, vine and fig, bird and moth, dog and swine, sheep and wolf. Jesus used these familiar sights and sounds as a foundation for a larger and more fascinating spiritual truth. Jesus used the common, everyday events of people to make truth relevant, calling people to the present situation.

Personal Horizons

Take a look in a mirror. The eyes that look back at you are the eyes of a predator. We have eyes in the front of our heads for depth perception, but only for what comes at us "head on." We don't need binoculars to see this. Our eyes are binoculars. Those who are preyed upon have eyes at the sides of their heads. They have something we don't have—peripheral vision. For example, pick a spot on a wall and focus your attention on that spot. Without moving your eyes, what else do you see? That's called peripheral vision, and for most of us it's pretty limited, although basketball players with lots of assists are said to be blessed with it. The commentators claim they can see the whole floor.

Expanding our horizons is expanding our ability to see "the whole floor." Renate and Geoffrey Caine in *Making Connections: Teaching and the Human Brain* said that learning involves focused attention and peripheral perception.[8] The brain is constantly absorbing information and signals beyond our field of attention. Most of the peripheral enters the brain at unconscious levels and interacts at unconscious levels. But the brain responds to the entire sensory context in which teaching or communication occurs. The peripheral field can be purposefully organized to facilitate learning.

To taste something, you have to get close to it. Not so with vision. Our eyes can travel up the mountains, down the valleys, and across the open spaces. The psalmist could say, "When I behold the heavens. . . ." We see so much that we can get easily distracted. I suppose that's one reason we close our eyes when kissing.

William Abernathy and Philip Mayher built a model of Bible study based on the fusions of horizons.[9] A summary of discovering personal horizons is helpful.

1. Our immediate horizons are bounded by specific locations—walls, ceilings, and floors if inside a building and a broader horizon if outdoors.

2. Visible horizons change with location and time. Seasons of the year shape horizons in different ways. A beach, mountain, inner city, or hospital bed will provide vastly different perspectives.

3. When we move from immediate horizons to the feelings evoked from them, we begin to move from sensory experiences to imaginative ones.

4. Beyond the physically visible horizons are personal dynamics that affect what we see. Health, age, work environments, family dynamics, and interpersonal situations affect perceptions.

5. Historical elements are a part of the horizon. The economy, political situations, and the changing roles of men and women influence perceptions.

6. The changing world situation clouds the horizon. Donald Messer identified four world threats that will have a growing influence on our personal horizons: the threat of nuclear annihilation through the expanding of nuclear weapons to more nations and the potential for nuclear terrorists; the threat of global warming caused by worldwide industrial expansion and the altering of the chemical balance of the earth's atmosphere; the threat of a world crisis in food production, deforestation, disease, and population growth; the threat of genetic engineering that would potentially eliminate skin color, reduce our emotional tendency to cry, and make us all blond-haired, blue-eyed, and right-handed.[10] We could add the threat of international bioterrorism such as anthrax and smallpox and the explosion of worldwide infectious diseases such as AIDS and SARS (severe acute respiratory syndrome).

7. Personal horizons are affected by race, sex, age, life stages, class, and religion.

8. Horizons are shaped by all the senses—what we see, hear, taste, touch, and smell.

9. The meanings of life events change when personal horizons change. Horizons are broadened, refined, or reformed by education, travel, geographical moves, and interpersonal transitions.

10. Horizons change when brought face to face with the different horizons of others, particularly significant others.

Horizon thinking is not easy. In educational literature, we might call it horizontal or lateral thinking. Once a pattern of thinking has developed, it begins to dominate not only the thinking process but perceptual processes as well. Habits of thought become entrenched. Certain patterns are like beaten paths, binding us to a narrow range of options. The term "vertical thinking" describes logical analysis with one step or premise following another and building to a logical conclusion or solution.

By contrast, horizontal or lateral thinking describes a deliberate process of interrupting linear chains of thought, seeking to widen the range of patterns by exploring different ways of seeing. Brainstorming and free association are examples. The real value of horizon thinking is that it gives us new points of entry into the text and a wider range of alternatives available for consideration. Helen Keller was asked if there was anything worse than losing one's sight. She thought for a moment and replied, "Yes, losing your vision."

More to Seeing than Seeing

Seeing, really seeing, takes time, much like having a friend takes time. Through the fusion of horizons we see beauty and experience wonder. Whatever else is happening to the disciples in their first encounters with Jesus, seeing is at the heart of those initial relationships. Some form of "seeing," "looking," or "finding" is the dominant theme in John 1:29-51.

There is so much more to seeing than simply seeing. The visual image is the door that opens the emotions to Scripture. When we see the horizons of Scripture, the whole array of our senses wake up to behold them. Our other senses can trigger memories and emotions, but the eyes are especially good at symbolic perceiving.

It is Holy Week, and the image of the outstretched arms of Jesus on the cross have captured my attention. For a few moments I let my mind free associate with the images. As it is with all "horizontal" or lateral thinking, the images float in and out. Grandchildren running toward me with open, outstretched arms . . . Moses standing on the top of a mountain with arms outstretched . . . with arms outstretched, the Israelites were victorious, when his arms dropped they were slain . . . needing help in keeping the arms outstretched . . . Christ on a hilltop with arms outstretched . . . Christ nailed to a cross with arms outstretched . . . Are the outstretched arms a symbol of all the pain there ever was? . . . the arms outstretched showing us the breadth and depth of God's love . . . grandchildren running away from me toward Lela's outstretched arms because I scared them . . . the old song, "Deep and Wide" . . . the cross, a symbol of triumph . . . arms outstretched to ensure that the battle went God's way . . . banners, instruments of celebration and victory are strung on the crosses . . . Exodus 17:8-13 . . . It's still a mystery . . . How do we go about deepening and widening the discussion? . . . What does the body say? . . . standing, arms outstretched, leaning forward or sitting, arms folded, leaning backward . . . Let's practice it and listen to what the body has to say. . . .

All understanding and interpretation of Scripture proceeds from prior knowing. Every time we get into the biblical text, it moves into the stream and flow of our lives. We never step into the same stream twice. We are always affected by our present horizon of understanding. Without this world of pre-understanding, discovering meaning would be impossible. We would have to start over with learning every day, much like a newborn infant. We never engage a text without pre-understanding, specific questions about the text, or understanding of what the text is about.

There are ways we can describe the power of presuppositions. Thomas Green in *The Activities of Teaching* explained the dynamics of core beliefs.[11] Core beliefs are passionate convictions around which questions cannot be raised and doubts cannot be voiced because they touch us too deeply and too directly. They are held with intensity and ferocity. The more these psychologically central beliefs are multiplied, the less chance there is for success in teaching. G. K. Chesterton supposedly said, "There is a thought that stops thought. That is the only thought that ought to be stopped." These reflections are not attempts to belittle passionate convictions; rather, we are commending core convictions that permit the scope of teaching to be enlarged. Some core convictions are difficult to bring into the arena of open discussion. George Kelly discussed personal construct theory.[12] A personal construct is an anticipation based on experience that offers a prediction about the way things should be. Constructs are different from concepts. A concept has a kind of structure that can be discussed, debated, and analyzed. Constructs are not debatable.

Imagery

In recent years, some of the most exciting discoveries in learning have taken place in the study of imagery. Images are deep-seated, vivid, emotionally charged bundles of energy that have been called "eidetic images." Eidetic forms are marked by or involve extraordinarily accurate and vivid recall of visual images. These images are formative learning tools that have the power of bringing things together in such a way as to move us to action. They have a way of evoking or calling back experiences that are stored permanently within us. Some experiments have shown that strong images can change the heart pulse sometimes as much as thirty beats per minute.

The whole direction of a person's growth is profoundly influenced by powerful, inner, emotion-packed images. Significant changes in people come through transformation or healing of these images. To set in motion a course of action, we form an image and draw on previously recorded images. The power between these images is enough to bring any action to completion. In biblical language, the images were written on the heart, which was the storehouse of memory. Thus, we read the strong biblical imperative to remember.

These eidetic images (unique collection of significant life experiences) are powerful tools in bringing horizons together. Memory is the handle to our roots and individual uniqueness. The task is to make sense of experiences and how we see them (or understand these images). We cannot be memory-less. We unconsciously commit our lives to memory as we go. Our brains have an enormous capacity to store memories but also to be selective or filter experiences. What we remember from any given experience is eidetic—what we are open to or looking for in that moment. Those are the things that make "lasting impressions."

Horizons and Church Life

The fusion of horizons becomes evident in our visual participation in the life and work of the church. This becomes powerfully evident through the observance (the "seeing") of three historical symbols—baptism, the Lord's Supper, and the Lord's Day.

What does a church mean when its members say, "We are going to observe (see) baptism and the Lord's Supper"? What is the meaning of these two ordinances as symbols? What is the observance of a symbol? To observe a symbol is to see something that represents a concrete reality. A symbol stands for something because it stands on something. In this case, baptism and the Lord's Supper stand on the concrete acts of Jesus in behalf of our salvation. They are "visual aids" to help us dramatize our relationship with Jesus.

These two symbols become powerful because they represent experiences that we know not only with our minds, but with our bodies as well. In baptism we see, or observe, with our whole body the power of water, washing, immersing, and cleansing of death and rebirth. In the Lord's Supper we observe with our whole body the touch, smell, and taste of life-giving food and drink. Both ordinances are "pictorial sermons" that help us remember Christ's life, death, resurrection, and return.

Jesus asks us to do these ordinances both for him and with him. When we observe these ordinances by seeing with our whole beings, we remember Jesus, and he lives among us. These two ordinances provide the experiential, relational, and remembering events that provide the opportunities "to be with him."

The Lord's Day has come to mean a day reserved for worshiping God and for rest. For Christians the term describes a day that belongs to God. How Christians live the Lord's Day has to do with what we see (observe) and what we remember (commemorate, memorialize). The Lord's Day should be full of memorable experiences, events, and people seen and not easily forgotten. Boring and mundane experiences on the Lord's Day are faith defeating because what has been seen (observed) slips quickly from the memory and commemorating the resurrection of Christ becomes impossible.

Listening to a Friend: Bible Study as Hearing

When I lead Bible study workshops, I usually begin with a dyadic (one to one) experiential process. I ask the participants to share their experience as a Bible teacher. After ten to fifteen minutes, I intervene in the conversation and introduce a reflective process. "Who is that person next to you? What do you know about that person? If you were introducing that person to the group, what would you say?"

There are two mistaken assumptions we could make in the "knowing." The first mistake is in assuming we know that person. Much of that person is unknown to us. Who they are is hidden and a mystery. The chronological "facts" of the person's life, the significant events, the life world, and the way they use language are vaguely understood. Other factors complicate knowing a person. Distractions and failures to attend lessen our chances of getting into the person's life.

The other assumption we can make is that we *don't* know the person. When we reflect on what has happened to us in the conversation, we know much. The other person has come to us "whole" through voice, gesture, facial expressions, significant facts, feelings, and numerous other impressions. The impressions come through an immersion into the other's life in much the same way music immerses us when we hear it live or through some technological medium. In spite of all the limitations and distractions, we sometimes "catch" the person through intuition, identification, and empathy. The essence of the other person somehow gets through to us. No one really knows how that happens, but it does happen. So it is with Scripture.

Stepping on stage is Friedrich Schleiermacher (1768–1834). Schleiermacher was perhaps the first to emphasize the need for empathizing with the thoughts and feelings of the biblical writer. Understanding is not a "checking off" process of logical deduction. Rather, human understanding is closer to what is involved in the intuitive understanding between two friends. This intuitive feeling for Schleiermacher is an activity of grace described in the same manner as describing a conversion experience. Intuition and feeling are not activities of the human spirit in which reality is brought under control. They are primal acts of the Holy Spirit that work in the relationship. Through spirit we "breathe" on each other.

Technology

Let's establish a premise. Technology and intimacy are on a continuum between two poles. Telecommunications resembles an oxymoron, meaning "distant connections." In technology, speaking precedes listening. Speaking is the language of technology. Language is written, then spoken discourse. Discourse is determined by the Phoenician alphabetical code and relayed by the printing press, imposing strictness and abstractness on communication. The printing press led to the spread of our alphabet and the emphasis on writing, journalism, and books. Finally, computers give us enormous piles of informational bits and pieces without intimate knowledge of any people or subjects. Paul reminded us that, eventually, this kind of knowing will become obsolete and pass away. All knowing will be face to face and we will know as we are known (1 Cor 13:7).

The dominant organ in technology is the eye. The eye has the power to focus, reading words one after the other in a coordinated process. As a result, schools were built to organize classes to house the books to teach children (not adults) to read. There were specific times for a specific age to go to a specific place to carry on a specific activity. This problem is compounded with the Internet and email at our fingertips, completely detached from any breathing human being.

Johannes Gutenberg surely had no idea of the revolution he was starting when the first printing of the Latin Bible came out in the middle of the fifteenth century. Up to that time, the Bible served the people in much more dynamic ways. Now it became a printed book. Our friends who live in oral cultures can appreciate the difference. We can hardly imagine it in any other way. I became more convinced of the other way as I taught curriculum workshops in West Africa and then practiced my hunches in a year's teaching at the Liberian Baptist Seminary in Monrovia, West Africa. Communication was expressed through storytelling, proverbs, drawing and painting, drama and dramatic movement. An exciting world of biblical interpretation opened up. This new Bible was, in fact, the old Bible before Gutenberg. There was an exciting Bible before the buildings and books of the Renaissance of the fourteenth and fifteenth centuries. Hans-Ruedi Weber wrote:

> In literary cultures the sounds and gestures, the accents, and the music of oral transmission are gradually lost. The copying of Biblical manuscripts ceases, and in the course of time the incentive and faculty for memorizing disappear. The Bible becomes a collection of texts: texts to be read silently, analyzed, and interpreted. Uniformly printed pages create the illusion of a uniform and disincarnate message, burying the rich variety of biblical images, styles, and stories into a grey blur. Moreover, the Bible as a printed book appeals far more to the human intellect than to human emotion and imagination.[13]

Weber designed his book *Experiments in Bible Study* around the question, How did the Bible function before it became a printed book? His answer provides a basis for his methodology: through the hearing of an oral tradition, in the form of visual representations, and by participation in worship. In other words, the Bible functioned through stories, pictures, and dynamic enactment.

Printed Word and Personal Word

The printed Scriptures are a mixed blessing because the moment words are printed, they are in danger of losing the living resonance of spoken word and reducing the word to something that is looked at, studied, and interpreted, but not heard personally. It is separated from the voice that spoke it and, therefore, depersonalized. Yet, the essence of word is not print. Word is personal. It is the means by which what is within one person is shared with another person. Reduced to print and left there, words no longer do what they are designed to do—create and maintain personal relationships of affection and love. When a word is spoken and heard, it joins speaker and hearer in whole relationships; when the word is printed, it is separated into dramatic fragments and has to be reconstituted by the imagination in order to accomplish its original work.

Apart from the act of listening and responding, words cannot function according to the intent of the speaker. Language in its origin and at its best is the means by which one person draws another person into a participating relationship. Typed and printed memos and lists on paper or screen will eventually kill us. Even handwritten notes have more personal invitation and warmth.

The printed word has not done its work until we hear the words in a personal act of listening. The last word on Scripture is, therefore, primarily a work of the imagination—that act of mind and emotion by which letters on paper are converted to voices and visions in us.[14] We begin to think God's word is something wonderful in print, forgetting that print is a result of technological society and has the same tendency of all technology to dull our awareness that these words are spoken by a living God. How is it possible for people who give so much attention to the word of God to remain so unaffected by it? Not through unbelief, but through lack of imagination. The spoken word is converted into an ink word. Printers' ink becomes the embalming fluid that flows through our veins instead of blood. The moment that happens, the imagination atrophies and living words flatten into book words. It doesn't matter that the words are believed to be true, they are not voiced words—spirit-voiced and faith-heard—and so are not answered. They lose their three-dimensionality.

Intimacy

Intimacy and friendship are the counterbalances to all technological advances. Learning good group conversation is one of the best ways of doing battle with technology. Conversation awakens the soul, brings along the treasures of memory, and is rooted in stories. Thomas Moore, calling us back to long, slow intimate conversations, said, "Conversation hovers between people, takes its time to get in motion, finds its rhythm, and slows to an ending. . . . A conversation tends to grow at its own tempo and in its own direction."[15] These are not conversations of "politeness"—the exchange of pleasantries and pretenses. Finding the sore and painful places are sometimes the quickest routes to intimacy. Thus, the other end of the continuum—the development of intimacy. The word "intimacy is derived from the Latin *intima*, meaning "inner" or "innermost." We only know intimacy when we are "in" the relationship with someone or something. As an adjective it means personal, private, and deep. We can add those adjectives to Bible study and call it "in-depth" Bible study. As a verb, it means to make known, to intuit, or to hint at. This sense of touching our inner core is the essence of intimacy.

The outstanding quality of the intimate experience is this sense of being in touch with the self. To study the Bible intimately, then, is to have a fresh awareness of who, what, and how we are. It differs from introspection and meditation, which are ways of looking at ourselves. They are "between" us and ourselves, primarily "alone" experiences. Intimacy involves ourselves and an "other." In this intimate experience our "looking" happens in light of Scripture, the "other."

The term we have chosen to use in describing this relationship is friendship. Friendship calls for a deep appreciation for the "other" and depends on stimulation and depth of communication. In experiential Bible study, we are looking for a long-term depth relationship with the Bible. In friendship and intimacy, listening precedes speaking. We communicate through our blood, our bodies, our breath, and our traditions. Our first communication is an act of listening in the wombs of our mothers. In birth, our first form of communication is a nursing mother. An African proverb says, "The African child learns how to dance first in the mother's womb and then on her back." These first modes of expression and communication have permanent value and leave permanent impressions.

The dominant sense in intimacy is hearing. Faith comes by hearing. Hearing provides a sense of space and of the whole. Hearing puts us inside the reality. Understanding by seeing is from the outside looking in. Children hear and speak sophisticated language patterns by the age of three. Pierre Babin described this as modulation—communicating with the music of the language more than with words.[16] Modulation is the whole complex of vibrations varying in intensity and pitch with rhythms, tones, gestures, voice projections, and body language—a maximum appeal to the senses and imagination. Children "pick up" language through listening to the music of the language and expressing it with their bodies.

In intimacy we are not so much describing the other as we are providing a commentary on what happens to us. Instead of trying to explain who that person is, we try to verbalize what is happening in our hearts and heads. What is the main idea you are hearing? Which words or phrases stick in your mind? Describe the writer's voice. What do you want to hear more about?

Acceptance of the other underlies all intimate friendship. No personal openness is possible without this acceptance. You cannot be intimate if you do not listen. Making judgments too quickly is not listening. To say that we know all there is to know about this person or this text is to miss much of what is there. With paintings, deep forests, beautiful sunsets, biblical texts, and God's people, we respond before we reflect on experience. Too often we snap pictures and move on. To risk the insecurity of not knowing the other is what makes intimacy more likely. We all have the imprisoned preconceptions of what the other is, what our friend is "like." A willingness to give up our preconceptions makes intimacy possible. Our consciousness of our preconceptions helps us let go of them.

Relationships to people, including those of a more intimate nature, always remain a mystery. Already knowing people, as with Scripture, is a prejudgment and assumes a "taking for granted" relationship. Prejudging makes the intimate relationship with Scripture unlikely, maybe impossible. Many people experience the lack of intimacy in their lives. For them intimacy with Scripture will sound strange. Intimacy with Scripture means that Scripture knows us—not knows some part of us or knows us in certain ways, but knows us completely, every part of us. Intimacy with Scripture teaches us about ourselves. We experience ourselves in some different and more profound way. The essence of intimacy is feeling close to ourselves while in relationship to something other than ourselves. Even if this happens only for a few seconds, we know that we are different.

In intimacy, we take the Scripture inside ourselves and listen as we talk about what happens to us. Much of our commentary on Scripture is a commentary on ourselves. Let us acknowledge that dynamic and use it. In telling what happens to us, we are not simply giving subjective feelings. We are telling the truth, "empirical evidence," giving the facts of what actually occurs in the observer or reader. These are root interpretations, perceptions or reactions that underlie judgments and conclusions.

Many times we have no judgments and no accurate analysis of the text. All we have is the primal initial reaction—what happened to us when we heard it. But there is something powerful, appealing, and useful in telling what happened to us—the feelings, reactions, perceptions, and thoughts out of which analysis grows. From reading a text, I am encouraged, impressed, angry, confused, or annoyed. I feel that this text is inviting me in or keeping me at a distance.

How the Text Works

First Thessalonians 2:13 is an interesting text on how the Scripture works. The church in Thessalonica did not receive it as a word from man but as a word from God. "When you received from us the word of God's message you accepted it not as the word of men, but for what it really is, the word of God, which performs its work in you who believe." The word for "received" describes an objective, outward receiving. The ears hear the message. The second word, "accepted," describes a joyous welcome. They had not only heard it, but they had embraced it with their hearts. The word was heard, received, welcomed, and was "performing" in the inner lives of the believers. The word "accepting" is the same word as welcoming people into our lives. Are they received with caution and formality? Or are they received with open arms and hearts?

Paul at least implies that openness to the word is in some way related to our interpersonal openness. When we welcome others into our lives at an emotionally deep level, we "practice" the attitude that is necessary for God's word to touch us at a deep level.

For the word to become living and active in our lives, it must take on all the ambivalent qualities of friendship. The word finds us, singles us out, and takes us aside, speaking a personal message. It is "living and active, sharper than any two-edged sword, piercing until it divides soul from spirit, joints from marrow; it is able to judge the thoughts and intentions of the heart" (Heb 4:12). Some of the imagery of Hebrews 4:12 is taken from the competitive sport of wrestling. There is the circling of the mat, of stalking and being stalked, and of maneuvering and searching for advantage. Suddenly the movements become more frantic, the struggles more desperate, the grips more firm. There is no way to escape. We are "judged" (laid bare) by the transforming power of the word.

Perhaps "wrestling with the word" can be told best through the story of Jacob. The word is the attacker—God in another form—coming out of the darkness, somehow both strange and alien enemy and warm and compassionate friend. Like Jacob, we are confronted with our own inner conflicts. In spite of our many faults we want desperately to be in right relationships with God and others. But that reality must be a wrestling, an intense personal encounter, sometimes feeling like making love and at other times like waging war. Even amid a group, we find ourselves alone with the word with no help and no longer able to evade the truth about ourselves. Old memories and old fears haunt us. We are, like Jacob, the trickster, living with our own maneuvering. We are not what we pretend to be.

But in the darkness, the alien friend pounces on us. Friendship is much that way, a struggle of overcoming strangeness. In spite of the pain, we are not willing to let the other go until the blessing comes. Only through this intense personal encounter can we learn the truth about ourselves. Everything doesn't change with one encounter, but life is preserved even though we are hurt and humiliated and the marks of the encounter are left upon us.

Like Jacob, we are finally able to lift up our eyes (Gen 33:1) and see others around us. Knowing comes in the mutual recognition of faces and the realization that we live at the center of God's vision. We can imagine Jacob's taking the red-bearded face of Esau in his hands and saying, "For truly to see your face is like seeing the face of God" (Gen 33:10). Jacob, finally, was beginning to understand.

NOTES

[1] Milton J. Coalter Jr., "The Craft of Christ's Imperfect Tailors," *Theology Today*, L/3 (October 1993): 389.

[2] Mary Carruthers, *The Book of Memory: A Study of Memory in Medieval Culture* (Cambridge: Cambridge University Press, 1990), 166.

[3] Peter Reinhart, *Brother Juniper's Bread Book* (Cambridge: Perseus Publishing, 1991), xxi.

[4] Peter Elbow, *Embracing Contraries: Explorations in Learning and Teaching* (New York: Oxford University Press, 1986), 40-41.

[5] Reinhart, *Brother Juniper's Bread Book*, 2.

[6] W. Randolph Tate, *Biblical Interpretation: An Integrated Approach* (Peabody MA: Hendrickson Publishers, 1991), 27.

[7] William Beaven Abernathy and Philip Joseph Mayher, *Scripture and Imagination* (New York: Pilgrim Press, 1988), 43.

[8] Renate Caine and Geoffrey Caine, *Making Connections: Teaching and the Human Brain* (Alexandria VA: Association for Supervision and Curriculum Development, 1991), 83-84.

[9] Abernathy and Mayher, *Scripture and Imagination*, 20-21.

[10] Donald E. Messer, *A Conspiracy of Goodness: Contemporary Images of Christian Mission* (Nashville: Abingdon Press, 1992), 46-52.

[11] Thomas F. Green, *The Activities of Teaching* (New York: McGraw-Hill, 1971).

[12] George A. Kelly, *A Theory of Personality: The Psychology of Personal Constructs* (New York: W. W. Norton, 1963).

[13] Hans-Ruedi Weber, *Experiments in Bible Study* (Geneva: World Council of Churches, 1981), 10-11.

[14] No one has described the dilemma between personal word and print word better than Eugene Peterson. See *Reversed Thunder: The Revelation of John and the Praying Imagination* (San Francisco: Harper & Row, 1988), 11-25; and *Working the Angles: The Shape of Pastoral Integrity* (Grand Rapids: Eerdmans Publishing Co., 1987), 87-145. The other powerful development that personal word will have to confront is the expanding world of electronic communications. Changes in the dominant medium of communication create new situations for interpretation,

and electronics may be the most radical change since the printing press and possibly since the development of writing. See Thomas E. Boomershine, "Biblical Megatrends: Toward a Paradigm for the Interpretation of the Bible in Electronic Media," in *The Bible in the Twenty-First Century*, Howard Clark Kee, ed., (Philadelphia: Trinity Press International, 1993), 207-30.

[15] Thomas Moore, *Soul Mates* (New York: HarperCollins Publishers, 1994), 123.

[16] Pierre Babin, *The New Era in Religious Communication* (Minneapolis: Fortress Press, 1991), 86.

CHAPTER THREE

Nothing Never Happens: Experience

First, ministry has to accept experience as it is given and this process of collection cannot be censored. We must collect experience in its outrageousness, its wonderfulness, its meaninglessness, its meaning, its brokenness, and its wholeness. . . . This gathering includes the ungifted and disenfranchised, the poor and the hungry, as well as the best and the brightest. The first movement situates the work of ministry. This is a movement of primary recognition. It cannot be too polite. It must be uncompromised by doctrinal or ideological expectations or ministry will be an empty calling into a domain of exclusion and shallow privilege.[1]

When we speak of experience, we are grounding understanding on personal participation in the process of living rather than on categories of thought. Experience is direct, firsthand engagement with things or people. Our judgments and interpretations may be less than accurate if we have not had direct contact with the situations under analysis.

Experiential knowing has its roots in the biblical revelation. The biblical concept of experience runs the whole gamut of knowledge from knowing things to knowing people. In the Old Testament, knowledge is derived from the senses in personal encounter. To know other people is to know them "face to face," even as Moses knew the Lord. "Never has there arisen a prophet in Israel like Moses whom the LORD knew face to face" (Deut 34:10). While the Greeks were concerned with detached knowledge and speculative interests, the Old Testament regarded knowledge as something that continually arises from personal involvement. The New Testament concept of knowing is greatly influenced by the Old Testament understanding. This is seen in Mary's confusion of being with child, since she did not "know" a man (Luke 1:34). In Matthew 7:23, Jesus said of the false prophets, "I never knew you," or "I never had anything to do with you." The statement in 2 Corinthians 5:21 that Christ "knew no sin" does not mean that he had no intellectual knowledge of sin, but that he had no personal involvement with sin. This understanding of knowing brings out the irony of the statement "For our sake he made him to be sin who knew no sin."

The sensory aspect of experience in the Old Testament is seen in the word for taste in Psalm 34:8: "Taste and see that the LORD is good." This figurative sense is taken up in 1 Peter 2:2-3, "Like newborn infants, long for the pure, spiritual milk, so that by it you may grow into salvation—if indeed you have tasted that the Lord is good." The experiential quality is again described in the death of Christ where Christ is seen as tasting death for everyone or experiencing its bitter taste to the full. He did not simply sample and nibble at it. The statement of Hebrews 2:9 that Jesus tasted death for everyone shows his death as an act of salvation. This does not spare us from physical death but takes away the bitter taste of death, because death's power of eternal destruction is broken. Jesus promises in John 8:52, "Whoever keeps my word will never taste death."

Let us decide about "knowing," for the way we define knowing shapes the way we study and teach the Bible. In Scripture, "knowing" comes from the concrete experiences of daily life, intimate relationships, efforts to live in community, and seeking to follow God's purposes. The peak experience of knowing is to love and be loved. Both the Hebrew word *yada* and the Greek word *ginoskein*, translated "to know," are used for lovemaking.

Parker Palmer has reminded us of the fleeting and fragmentary aspects of all knowledge.[2] The time will come when all of it will fail. Our multiple sources of information create a technical arrogance that eventually damages and deforms. Personal, intimate knowledge finally creates a space where we can become obedient to truth. "For now we see in a mirror, dimly, but then we shall see face to face. Now I know only in part; then I will know fully, even as I am fully known" (1 Cor 13:12).

Thomas Groome saw the driving intent "to know" as the root of sin, or to know as God knows. Since we see "dimly," all of our knowing is to be taken with a grain of salt. There is no one privileged group or starting point for knowledge—anyone can know from anywhere. All knowledge comes from personal perspectives, and no view can explain everything; mystery remains and every perspective is partial. No perspective is innocent; all knowledge is intertwined with systems of power and serves some interests and neglects others.[3]

Beginning with Interest

Starting from experience addresses one of the major problems of Bible study—not lack of information but lack of interest. Beginning Bible study with interest (what people already know) attracts attention, overcomes indifference, apathy, and preoccupation, and brings the biblical focus from "then" to "now." You are reading this because of some measure of "interest." Our understanding and inter-pretation of Scripture proceeds from some prior understanding. Otherwise, we would have to begin all over again every time we pick up our Bibles. As a part of the structure of reality, we can never fully escape the present moment.

Experience is the interest-generating part of the Bible study, the "hook" on which the learning methodology hangs. Experiential activities provide meaning-fulness to people by addressing not only "Is it true?" but "Does it matter?" In beginning with experience, we begin with "what matters" in the present and go back to "what mattered" in the biblical text in order to move forward again to the present situation.

In coming to terms with interests and experiences, we face the issues of pre-understandings, preconceptions, and "prejudices" in biblical interpretation. Understanding involves prejudice, a biased approach to interpretation. The dom-inant bias is the one of belief. We come to Scripture as believers, wanting to believe more and with a prayer that God will help our unbelief. Believing pre-cedes understanding.

This was the main thrust of Hans Gadamer's idea that interpretation begins with "prejudice." Gadamer did not use "prejudice" in a negative sense, but as "a judgment that is given before all the elements of a situation have been finally exam-ined."[4] "A person who is trying to understand a text is always performing an act of projecting. He projects before himself a meaning for the text as a whole as soon as some initial meaning emerges in the text. Again, the latter emerges only because he is reading the text with particular expectations in regard to a certain meaning."[5]

These prejudices and projections can be helpful or hindering. Those "inter-ests" and "prejudices" that bring us to the text and motivate our reading, studying, and listening can be both clarifiers and blinders. They can focus the attention for informed learning, or they can fix the gaze so that only certain interpretations are allowed. The mind is a two-edged sword, sharp enough to cut through our veils of prejudice and preconceptions but also sharp enough to stand guard so that new understanding cannot invade and threaten us.

Experience tells us that little in life is predictable. Our tendency is to deny that and follow Scripture plans that are clear and well arranged. My life is not like that. Is yours? Experiential activities mess up the points and plots, play tricks on us, and lead us down a road of strange twists and turns. In other words, they lead us into an adventure. With these expectations in mind we begin with expe-riential activities, which must always be done from the standpoint of belief that something new is possible rather than from the sidelines of suspecting and suspi-cious doubt. In that light, we begin with excitement, expecting and hoping for a new reading. The processes of experiencing will focus on the present activities, the past stories, and the next week.

Present Activities

Event-oriented Activities

Event-oriented activities include almost any activity that involves self-assessment and interpersonal interaction. This can involve making or creating objects or products, writing, role-playing, and any number of activities associated with games, analysis of case materials, or guided meditations. These event-oriented activities can be carried out by individuals, dyads, triads, small groups, group-on-group arrangements, or large groups. Either explicitly or implicitly, they are related to the Scripture theme and text.

Event-oriented activities focus on direct, hands-on contact—activities that engage feeling and emotions and a high degree of personal involvement. Event-oriented activities assume that learning is by nature an active endeavor. Through activity, people spontaneously and unconsciously become themselves. Beginning the learning experience with activity awakens people to their own responsibility for learning, connects them with others in the learning environment, and symbolically suggests that they are bringing "all of themselves" to the learning experience. Event-oriented activities are transactional processes and can be divided into several categories:[6]

1. *Personal Activities:* Activities in self-disclosure, sensory experience, feelings awareness, and decision-making.
2. *Communication Activities:* Activities in communication awareness, developing trust, listening, and assertion.
3. *Group Characteristics:* Activities in process observation, power issues, leadership styles, and belief formation.
4. *Group Tasks:* Activities in problem solving, group feedback, competition/-cooperation, group resolution, and consensus.
5. *Group Building:* Activities in group problems, group building, and action planning.
6. *Facilitating Learning:* Activities in getting acquainted, forming new groups, group contracts, giving and receiving feedback, group energizers, and closure.

Structured Experiences

Structured experiences have been identified by many names—activity learning, programmed activities, exercises, and "fun and games." Educators who design and use them point to several advantages:

1. They enable learners to understand personalities and roles.
2. They equalize the participation of dominant and less expressive members.
3. They foster group exploration in learning.
4. They provide group members an opportunity to experiment with a wide repertoire of behavior patterns.
5. They help reduce the anxiety of an unstructured format.
6. They stress the emotional aspects of a person's experience.
7. They develop more cohesive groups.
8. They provide deeper, more intense, and longer-lasting learning experiences.

A structured experience is a group learning design based on the experiential learning cycle. Structured experiences begin with an activity designed to produce reactions, feelings, insights, experiences, and learning. Following the experiential learning cycle, the process moves through a planned sequence of events. Structured experiences provide immediacy and personal impact, creating quick awareness and personal relevance. Learners have the immediate impression that this is about me and my life. Many activities and methods are available for facilitating learning through structured experiences. These are listed in Pfeiffer's *Using Structured Experiences in Human Resource Development.*[7]

1. *Constructions:* making or building something, assembling or taking apart puzzles.
2. *Data Collection:* counting, measuring, interviewing, checking resources.
3. *Discussions:* conversations, question-and-answer sessions, dialogue.
4. *Games:* adaptations of standard games or the creation of variations.
5. *Graphics:* collages, drawings, finger painting, clay sculpture, charts and graphs, posters.
6. *Guided imagery:* tapping into internal feedback systems, stories, open-ended meditations.
7. *Instruments:* inventories, checklists, rating scales, questionnaires.
8. *Media:* charts, audiovisual aids, projective techniques, audiotapes, videotapes, films.
9. *Models:* conceptual schemes and diagrams.
10. *Movement and Nonverbal Communication:* milling around, interpersonal sculpting, symbolic communication.
11. *Role-plays:* play reading, acting, impromptu theater, role reversals.
12. *Simulations:* Structured role-plays, microcosms, simplification of complex phenomena.

Individuals, dyads, triads, small groups, or large groups can carry out these activities. The learning purposes and biblical texts will inform both the activity and the appropriate groupings.

It is important to note that the purposes of structured experiences are necessarily general. They are stated in terms such as "to explore," "to discover," and "to probe." Experiential learning is learning through discovery, and specific learning cannot be predicted; experience sets the stage for all that is to follow and provides a common base for the ensuing cycles and polarities. Whatever happens in the activity becomes the basis for learning because it is a reflection and perhaps a parable of life.

The Action Parable: Experiential Learning in a Biblical Setting

Robert Dow first introduced me to the concept of the action parable in 1971 in his book, *Learning through Encounter*. Dow introduced the action parable as one of the three ways Jesus used parables in teaching: "Of all Jesus' teaching tools (preaching, healing, parables, demonstrations, discussion, ritual, drama, encounter, and interpretation), the parable, whether it was in an art form, an action form, or in his own modeling of behavior was the most effective."[8] The parable is a dynamic process that can lend itself to every teaching occasion. When the direct spoken word seemed to have little effect, Jesus refrained from directness and used the indirect form of the parable. Three major categories of the parables are found in Jesus' life and ministry: (1) the spoken parable, or art parable; (2) the action parable; and (3) the fuller, more complete parable of Jesus' life and modeled ministry.

The action parable is real, concrete, and observable. The word becomes flesh and dwells among us. The word becomes an actual event, happening to someone at some time in some place. Its implications go far beyond the event, time, and place. It affects everything that follows. It goes beyond but includes the conceptual. But the action parable is a stumbling block to that which is only rational and conceptual. For those who believe, the action parable is the "evidence of things not seen" and provides new insight into faith.

What are some ways Jesus used the action parable? He sat the crowd down in groups of hundreds and of fifties and fed them (Mark 6:35-44). He ran the moneychangers out of the temple (Mark 11:15-16). He cursed the fig tree (Matt 21:18-22). He bent over the earth and wrote characters in the sand, the only example of a written parable (John 8:1-11). He took bread, broke it, and shared it, saying, "This is my body . . ." (Luke 22:19). He took a basin of water and a towel and washed the disciples' feet (John 13:5). There is no way of counting the number of volumes written seeking to interpret the meaning of these events.

The action parable is a multidimensional encounter—a confrontation involving all the senses: seeing, hearing, smelling, touching, and tasting. It is a direct and somewhat primitive contact to life through concrete elements—water, bread, food, nature, wind, and fire. It reveals a truth, descriptively and dynamically.

The action parable is a teaching method using present experience. It combines word with an intensity of activity that seeks to awaken memory and meaning. Most of the action parables in the Bible are hinges on doors that swing back to the Old Testament and forward into the future age of God's rule in kingdom life. They awaken us to mystery and wonder, always pointing us toward something we do not presently understand. Every gesture, element, and object takes on significance.

The action parable expresses the common life in an uncommon framework. The natural patterns and practices of group life receive an intentional focus through critiquing and debriefing. Greeting, departing, handshaking, standing, sitting, giving, receiving, eating and drinking, serving, offering, knowing names, and telling stories are group actions that take on life as action parables if they are examined for underlying memories and meanings. They are most helpful as useful learning experiences when we stay close to the essentials of the experience, the personal expressions of meaning (what happens to you), the quality of relationships that develop (what happens with others), and the debriefing of meanings (asking questions of the experience). Remember this: "Nothing never happens."

At times an action parable takes the form of a worship experience. An action parable helps us remember and rehearse God's actions. God breaks through our everyday lives with living presence. We are reminded of the God who acts, using people, objects, and activity to reveal God's nature. In those moments, education and worship flow together, overcoming the split that often characterizes church life. Worship as education and education as worship are combined in the action parable.

Action parables contain both blessings and obligations. Some of the best clues are found in watching hands—the gestures of taking, breaking, blessing, giving, receiving, and offering. The hands reveal the vulnerable humanity of it all, seeking and evoking God's presence. Sometimes, without warning, the kingdom life breaks through and transforms life. The action parable becomes kingdom enactment, giving us a picture of a different way of living, a vision of the way God intended life to be lived. Here is a foretaste of another existence, where God's will is done, here, right now, at this moment, in this place, in the same way God's will is done in heaven.

But there is also obligation. Following action parables are challenges: "go," "do this," "do as I have done unto you." There is an urgency requiring commitment. In action parables we can't stand on the sidelines and watch. Are we participants or observers? The supper is prepared and the guests are invited (Matt 22:1-14; Luke 14:16-24). Are we coming to dinner? Let us decide right now!

The Cone of Experience

Edgar Dale's Cone of Experience is an audiovisual representation of the methods of learning.[9] The cone of experience includes a comprehensive range of learning experiences. These experiences are not separated entities because each is enhanced with exposure to methods from other areas. The position on the cone determines the depth and breadth of the method in terms of direct experience. The higher levels of the cone are more dependent on the experience of others and therefore more restricted in terms of personal experience. Direct, purposeful experiences involve the senses and embodied experience. The further up the cone one gets, the more direct experience is edited out and the method becomes more dependent on the imaginative involvement of the learner. An action parable seeks to connect the bottom of the cone (direct, contrived, dramatized, and demonstrated experiences) with the top of the cone (visual and verbal symbols).

Diagram 2: Cone of Experience

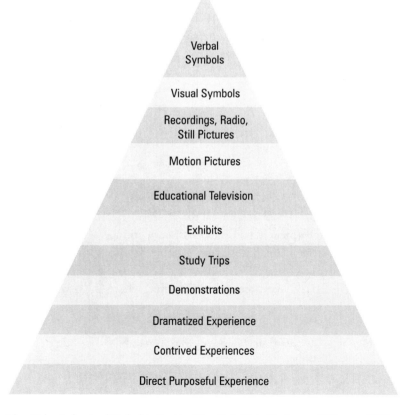

Source: Edgar Dale, *Audio-visual Methods in Teaching* (New York: Holt: Rinehart and Winston, 1954).

An action parable seeks to bring together word, action, symbols, sights, sounds, and gestures. The experience may be contrived, dramatized, or demonstrated. An avalanche of words is not needed, but *the* Word is essential. Gestures, actions, and symbols are important; they come together in words. The one common characteristic of all levels in the cone of experience is the use of words. The word takes on a visible form. By implication, take away the word, and what is the action parable? It is nothing but a human gesture. Words in action parables may be misused and abused, but they are essential to the action parable's meaning.

Who knows what action parables will emerge as communal events in the lives of Christians. Any time Christians put together an action that celebrates our life together, symbolizes God's love for us, and brings us close to one another, an action parable is in the making. Games, simulations, bibliodramas, and various aspects of active learning take on a transcendent element. Something happens that we neither prepare for nor plan. God moves into our fragile forms and gifts us with God's presence. We are left with a sense of mystery and awe.

Games and Bibliodrama

Let me describe a Bible study "game" I have seen played out in the smallest rural church to the mega-church in a metropolitan area. The group sits in a circle. Each member reads a couple of verses and comments on the meaning of the verses. The process moves to the next person, who follows the same procedure.

This simple activity provides insight into the nature of play and games. In all games, the tasks and problems provide insight into real-life situations. Their purpose is to develop awareness, to stimulate discussion, and to aid in the application of learning. Participants tend to feel responsible for the outcome of the group's work. As they move into the process, they tend to act naturally, as they would in situations outside the group. Participants are able to use what they know and to gain confidence in verbalizing what they know and in communicating effectively with others.

This simple Bible activity provides the basis for more sophisticated Bible experiences. In "going around the circle," each person develops the basic rudiments of performance. Performing is an act of presenting oneself, of making an outward display of what one knows. Performance eventually goes beyond acting to a level in which something is risked and accomplished—a truth-telling and a proclamation.

This simple Bible study method also reveals another important aspect of learning. Learning requires expression. The group is not simply an audience "absorbing" a presentation. Learners express themselves, and this creates an instant stage and audience. "At the same time, the individual learner is aware of himself as both performer and spectator, trying to notice what he himself is experiencing, what he is saying, where his difficulty lies, where the pleasure of excitement is, and thus to anticipate where his present path of discovery will take him."[10]

Learning is a performance—a way we extend ourselves through memory, imagination, and communication; a process of "playing" to ourselves and others. In this simple process of "presenting" ourselves, we begin the practice of experiential Bible study.

In most games, players have roles played out by individuals or teams. Games begin with a scenario that describes the roles and tasks or problems that must be achieved or solved in a definite period of time. Participants generally work in teams where they gather information, examine relationships, and explore options.

Role-playing is similar in nature. Role-playing is a technique in which people are presented roles in the form of cases or scenarios, then act out the roles in order to experience them. Role-playing is a spontaneous interaction that involves realistic behavior under simulated or imagined conditions. The method of role-playing came from the ancient practice of rehearsing and theater. Role-playing in its modern form was first used by J. L. Moreno, a Viennese psychiatrist, in working with mentally disturbed patients. He called it "psychodrama," and he sought to give patients insight into their relationships with others through taking on the others' roles. Moreno saw role-playing as an opportunity for people to shed inhibitions in order to use the creativity and spontaneity needed for learning and change to occur. Moreno gathered his first impressions of the healing power of play while telling stories to children in a public park. In the 1920s he shifted his practice to spontaneous role-playing, which he called the "Theater of Spontaneity," a forerunner of the work of improvisational theater developed by Viola Spolin.[11]

Since 1980, a movement has developed in which adults reenact Bible stories and involve themselves in biblical personalities in order to learn about themselves and the text. This playful and dramatic approach to biblical narratives is called bibliodrama, a method that involves both psychodramatic and exegetical principles.

Imagine four chairs in the center of the room for four roles in the Genesis account of Adam, Eve, God, and the serpent. From the first role-playing scene, the biblical models and the modern scene are intertwined. We listen to them speak on two levels: as role figures in the biblical account and as modern individuals. Both players and observers constantly switch from past to present and from present to past; from the events then to the events now.

The energy that develops in this spontaneous interpretation of Scripture is enormous. People stand up, move around, argue, sit quietly, withdraw, and reflect. Humor often eases tension and creates new insights. Samuel Laeuchli called this the "somatization of the text."

"We allow the body to participate. We do not merely think; we experience and express. We feel. We respond with shoulders, the lips, and the knees. We look at one another. We lean forward or backward; we crouch, laugh or stare. Our hearts pound; and our faces flush. The stomach churns. We have difficulties breathing deeply."[12]

The Past Story

Once upon a time a small-framed, twenty-seven-year-old woman lived with her parents on the outskirts of Orrick, a small town east of Kansas City, Missouri. The year was 1934. The young woman spent two years at the Teacher's College in Warrensburg, Missouri, and came home, teacher's certificate in hand, prepared to settle in and be what her mother always wanted her to be—a teacher in her hometown.

But in early summer 1934, her life changed. A cousin invited her to make the long trek to California for a vacation. The two women drove across the country looking for new adventures. A week later they arrived in San Diego, marveling at the discovery that there was life outside of the protective boundaries of the home state. While in San Diego, the little twenty-seven-year-old woman met a white-haired, fifty-nine-year-old man. No one seems to know how they met and what kind of relationship developed, but after five days the two women returned to Missouri and the young woman began preparation for her fall teaching assignment.

Two weeks later the fifty-nine-year-old man showed up in town. He knocked on the screened-in porch door of the twenty-seven-year-old woman's home. When the mother answered the door, he simply announced that he had come to marry her daughter.

For the next three days, there was war in the peaceful Missouri town. It was by far the biggest event of the season. Every morning the same scene occurred with growing crowds gathering to watch the match between the man and the mother. The mother seemed to be winning, but every morning the man was back for more. On the fourth morning, the twenty-seven-year-old woman pushed her way past the screaming mother and got into the car with the fifty-nine-year-old man that she had known casually (I guess) for five days. They went to Kansas City and got married. That was May 28, 1934. On July 26, 1935, my mother's birthday, I was born.

I have heard this story from many people, always with a twinkle in their eyes and laughter on their lips. I've told it in the same way. It must have been quite a sight—two people a little less and a little more than five feet tall. I wake up in the middle of the night laughing. Two of the "little people," a young woman and an old man, starting a family.

God at Work in Our Past

Stories seem essential to our development. They may be essential for two unspectacular reasons and perhaps one spectacular reason. First, they are interesting. We get into stories. We participate in them; in some way they invade us. I have often been captured by a personal story told with intensity and meaning. Secondly, they are accessible. They are always there, a part of us. Our stories are like many rooms locked in a large house. The rooms can be unlocked and rediscovered as accessible resources available to us any time we want to use them. No bags, notebooks, or PowerPoints are needed.

But perhaps our stories have more spectacular purposes. God is seen as present and active. We can investigate our stories: psychologically, theologically, and sociologically. Our stories are formative of our religious identity, who we are, and maybe what is eternal and essential within us. As taking that first step is fundamental to our physical development, perhaps putting our lives in narrative form is essential to our spiritual development. Without stories, our lives never quite make sense.

While not attempting to define everything personal stories do for us, I suggest seven ways that stories provide a "situational base" for experiential Bible study.[13]

1. We tell and retell the significant events in our lives in story form. In other words, we tell our stories again and again until their depth and density become clear. We understand our stories only as they capture us in the retelling. All of our experiences are there somewhere in the memory attic, but they cease to be influential unless they are shared. That which is not told loses its vitality. We keep telling our stories until we get them right, until we get the inner impact of their meaning. This makes it hard on our friends. "I've already heard that," they say. Our children roll their eyes as they hear the same tale once again. But the truth is, we tell it again and again because we have not heard it. Only as we tell and retell our stories do we capture their true meanings.

2. A story comes from the way a past event appears to us now told in narrative form. In some ways we see the events on the screen behind our eyes—the turning points, the marker events, the significant peak experiences, or the major headlines. Those stories may come from geographical moves, changes in primary relationships, losses of significant other people, and times of breakthrough or growth as well as opportunities and crises. We tell them as we see them. They are "eidetic images"—deep-seated, emotionally charged, powerful bundles of energy channeled into mental pictures.

Close your eyes and recall an event in your life about which you have a strong feeling. Instead of merely thinking about that time, try to reenter the past experience and be the person you were then. Remember what was important to you, how you looked, where you lived, important people in your life, and what you enjoyed doing. In what ways are you the same now, and how have you changed? What was the nature of your faith in God's presence, power, and judgment? Note the nature of your faith. Reenter that experience and live through it again. If you were to put that event into narrative form, how would you tell it? "Once upon a time, I . . . ."

For our stories to be effective, they must have strong visual character. By that I mean they can be pictured vividly and concretely in the imagination. Every good story is a picture story. It has visual dimensions that serve as an attention base. It rivets interest so listeners are prepared to invest themselves emotionally and hear the full import of the message.

Along with one's capacity or incapacity for remembering, there are varying levels or depths of recall. "Level" and "depth" suggest that one has to dig deeper in memory to describe what is retained. The first degree or level of recall is the identification of some experiences as meaningful. People recall events or brief periods in their lives as important but do not remember exactly what happened. They may sketch the bare bones of an event without being able to recover it fully. At deeper levels of recall, people's descriptions are more fully fleshed out. They remember times and places and can describe events in great detail. Other characters are introduced not so much as individuals but as roles within the story. Subthemes are woven in as the plot develops. At deeper levels of recall, verb tenses frequently change from past to present. "Thereness" takes on "hereness." Pronouns shift from "I" to "you." It is as though the storyteller is trying to draw you, the listener, inside the event. Because the teller gets into the subjectively vivid present of the original experience, there is more of an investment in pulling the listener inside.

Each level of depth uncovers more detail. The deeper the dwelling, the fuller the recovery of meaning. When we are in the immediate flow of an experience, it commands our attention fully. When we reflect on the experience, we assign it meaning in the overall scope of things. Previously constituted meanings may be recovered or even constructed for the first time.

3. The acknowledgment of God and the use of God-language seems naturally to slip into the narrative. If you listen closely to people's stories in their more primitive and unsophisticated narratives, God is seen as present and active. An immediate theological interpretation of the events becomes evident as people

describe births, illnesses, deaths, falling in love, and other significant events by simply intervening in the narrative, saying, "And God . . . ."

Our personal biographies give clues to God's presence and power. A "story theologian" like John Shea said that whenever our biographies are deeply probed, a root metaphor appears—a narrative that gives meaning to our lives.[14] The God-language in stories comes when we sense the presence of God. We notice God and God notices us by calling our name. The relational flow goes both ways. These experiences become life-changing when the relational flow is perceived as a loving relationship. I notice God and God notices me. But that is not all. This is One who notices me, chooses me, and loves me. And the One who loves me has something for me to do. In simplest terms, that is the meaning of being called by God. Either immediately in the experience or upon later reflection, God is discerned to be present, active, and loving. Psychology and sociology can illuminate what happened, but they cannot determine what happened. A transcendent otherness characterizes the experience where divine reality has been felt and known.

4. The story is existential rather than chronological. In other words, the story is told in terms of personal impact and not in terms of days, months, and years. A year, or even five years, can be told in a single phrase. That is why it is often difficult to get the sequential events of a person's life in perspective. The narrative is described in this way: "One day I . . ." and "then I . . . ." Between those two phrases might be days, months, or even years. The significance of the event is the essential thing and comes in our ability to distinguish between quantity time and quality time, in terms of *chronos* and *kairos*. Quantity time (*chronos*) is time in sequence. It is from this word that we get our word chronology. It is calendar time and clock time, one event following another. It can be measured through moments, days, periods, and hours. "How long have you lived?" is a question about *chronos* time. Most people eventually learn to tell *chronos* time.

Quality time (*kairos*) is different because it calls for interpretation. It is time tied to a specific event and locked in a definite time period. *Kairos* time is diffused with meaning, calling for reflection and interpretation. "What happened to you?" is a question about *kairos* time. Tell me about one day in your life, or one month, or one person. Many people never learn to tell *kairos* time.

5. We remember past significant stories when something in our current lives resonates with them. Storytelling has a contagious emotional effect on listeners. As we listen to stories, the cameras in our mind flash on and begin to run on the screen in the back of our eyes. Most of the time feelings trigger stories. The things we experience and learn while feeling sad, joyful, angry, or fearful are most

easily recalled when we are again in that same mood. Moods have a way of persisting in triggering the events of our lives. An experience, long forgotten, suddenly reappears with an immediacy and intensity that startles us. Anyone in mid-life or another transitional life stage is dealing with the question of what is important and what is not. Where should I spend my energies? A story focuses the questions of time and energy for the teller.

6. Storytelling depends on the revelation going on inside the storyteller. If the story were told for historical purposes, there would perhaps be some misrepresentation. We recollect the story and, in the recollection, facts are told in the light of inner revelation. This has often happened when my children respond to stories with this comment, "Daddy, that story just gets better and better." The point is that it should.

7. Stories engender a particular sensitivity and precipitate certain life directions. Stories create our sensitivity to certain issues in life. When sensitivity springs from experience, it has unmatched power and perseverance. The sensitive response to present situations is at least partially determined by the past situations we have undergone. Who we are is prior to any situation in which we find ourselves. Our past history functions as a stethoscope to hear the heart of the present.

My Story

I will begin and end with my own story, hopefully illustrating my last point of sensitivity to particular issues. The environment of being born into a family with a sixty-year-old father and a twenty-eight-year-old mother suggests distinctive themes. When I was ten years old, my father had a massive stroke that paralyzed him and left him bedridden for the next eighteen years. There were two other children—a sister, Carrah, age seven, and a six-month-old brother, Fred. Mother made the hard decision of sticking close to the family rather than venturing out into the work world. We were destitute, with little income and little hope for more.

At this time, the local Baptist church discovered us and shaped the emotional vow I would make with the denomination. This church was the safety net that kept us from falling into the despair of the poor and homeless. In this Baptist church, I first heard the story of Jesus. I never saw him. I never heard him. I never touched him. But there were those who did and they told others, who told others, who told me. It is people, always people, who carry on the memory of Jesus. We have access to the Jesus story through a long line of personal telling and retelling. The story thrives because people re-express it out of their own flawed experiences and in their own halting voices.

I remember those days of dependence—gratefulness for the church's care and yet owing something in return. We were a part of the church, yet not quite. The members were not condescending, but in a way we were marked off as a family who needed care. We were adopted sons and daughters of the church, not quite legitimate, but there nevertheless, and all needing special attention and care. I came out of that experience with a vow to pay back. This was not a conscious decision but was energized by an emotional contract—a willingness to meet the expectations of the church with my life.

I have always felt a deep indebtedness to the people called Baptists. I am a denominational child, raised and educated through the gifts of Baptist people. My life of employment and recent retirement has been and will continue to be funded by Baptist institutional support. I live in debt. Without the support of church and denomination, I would have been lost in a vacuum of the meaning-less work of the poor without hope of getting out and with no means of escape.

In 1962, we loaded my invalid father in the back of a station wagon and drove him to "Baptist Home" in Ironton, Missouri, where he had wanted to be since the early years of his illness. He died there a month later, a ward of Baptist life and cared for by the funds and concerns of Baptist people. In May, I graduated from Midwestern Baptist Theological Seminary amid denominational controversy that has continued throughout my vocational life.

In a period of ten weeks, the themes of my vocation and calling became the chapter headings in the story of my life. These themes continue to this day—the ambivalence of being the adopted child of a denomination, belonging, yet not quite belonging; a sadness that comes from not finding one's true home.

Are you interested in this story? We may be surprised to discover the number of people who think their lives are uninteresting. Many people have never articulated their life narratives to themselves or to others. The tendency to restrict our sharing often results in a sense of inferiority about the significance of our lives. People tend not to tell the story of their lives unless certain occasions prompt the telling. These experiences provide the "hook," the slice of life that initiates the first movement in experiential Bible study. The "story" shapes consciously and unconsciously the way we see and interpret Scripture.

The Next Week

I will begin with an opinionated statement. Most biblical interpreters are professionals who have little contact with the daily lives of ordinary people. They have been trained in the skills of biblical interpretation and publish the results of their discipline. They know the texts without knowing the people. One of the purposes of experiential Bible study is to discover biblical interpretation outside the profession of biblical interpreters. This is not to say that the professionals in biblical interpretation do not provide an essential and crucial service in the study of the Bible. But professional interpreters are plagued with the same problems of all the professions—distance from the common lives of ordinary people.

I have often wondered what would change in biblical interpretation if the writers of commentaries spent time in secular employment. The purpose would be to learn what people do in daily work, the problems they confront, the competition they face, and the grinding routines they encounter. I have often compared modern biblical scholars with Paul, the writer and interpreter of Scripture, who "worked night and day, so that we might not burden any of you while we proclaimed to you the gospel of God" (1 Thess 2:9). What do we think tent making was, anyway? Tent making meant rising early, toiling late with leather, knives, and awls, accepting the social stigmas and humiliations of the artisan experience. Without daily work, our notions of God become too mental, not actual enough to inform our daily lives, and too "personal" to share the depth of it with others.

Because of the years invested in professional training, there is often an excessive claim to position and authority. One's opinions are due more consideration and attention. There is an inclination to exaggerate the importance of one's own views and a willingness to speak for more and more people.

This need to "have the answers" results in a "trained incapacity" to see the enormous complexity of the human situation. It also leads to a hierarchical pecking order in many Bible study settings. People seem to have an intuitive sense concerning where they will fit in a group's pecking order of biblical facts and information. There is no fear like the fear of making a mistake in biblical facts. Therefore, there is a continual assessing, looking down at those perceived to know less and looking up to those perceived to know more. At the top of this "know more" ladder is the religious professional. Students know this dynamic well. One semester at the seminary moves them to the top of the hierarchical rung in any Bible study class they enter back home. Once this pattern has developed, there seems to be no end to it. The only way to get out of it is to stop this hierarchical thinking completely. One way of stopping it is through the appreciation and processing of personal experience.

Traditional Bible study settings are characterized by the "invisible week." We don't know what the week was like for the people around us. "How was your week?" we ask. "Fine!" is the usual response. Behind this "fine" are a multitude of experiences. Occupational dilemmas, long work hours, dual working patterns in families, conflicting work and family responsibilities, and self-imposed pressures are a few examples from the work world. Changing family patterns, role definitions, leisure activities, time pressures, economic struggles, sickness, boredom, and fatigue characterize many families. For the most part, these issues remain invisible. The curriculum planners of Bible studies know this problem in their bones. "We don't bring our personal lives to these tables," they say. So the personal experiences of people never mix with the Bible study design.

What Happened to Monday through Saturday?

We study the Bible as if God speaks only on Sundays and ignores the rest of the week. But in this world that begins for many on Monday morning, God addresses us.

> And yet many days slip by without being noticed. Some vanish in what seems a moment because they are so wonderful. While living such a day, I know beyond saying that it is a day that is large, a day when work or love is flourishing. Only later do I realize that I lost track of time because I was lost myself, in something or someone utterly captivating. Most often, however, a day is lost to smallness. Patched together with obligations, then shredded by interruptions, it disintegrates into fragments that blow away in the wind, I am left empty-handed and exposed, unable to answer a simple question.[15]

In 1970, the major publishing house of Southern Baptists produced a quarterly curriculum product titled *Now*, which was designed in a *Newsweek* or *Time* format with the expressed purpose of providing a biblical interpretation to daily life. We were committed to addressing the problems that life experience brought before us—economic, environmental, biological, international, educational, medical, sociological—the entire spectrum of life issues. The energy and excitement the design brought to designers and writers was phenomenal. It was difficult work, but there was a strong commitment, both internally and externally, to throw the light of biblical revelation on the issues of daily life—the Bible in one hand and the daily newspaper in the other.

The response to the curriculum was strong and predictable. There was a small but devoted following to the curriculum offering. It was countered by passionate letters of appeal to cancel the publication. Protesters did not want to study the material and did not want anyone else to study it either. Some things in daily life simply should not be discussed in church. *Now* became "not *Now*" in three years.

Robert Banks wrote a thoughtful book on the theology of everyday life in *Redeeming the Routines*. By everyday life he means "the regular situations we find

NOTHING NEVER HAPPENS: EXPERIENCE

ourselves in throughout the day or week, the ongoing responsibilities we have or activities we engage in, the issues that regularly claim our attention, the most insistent pressures that we feel, the things that we commonly think and talk about, the desires, values and beliefs that most shape our lives."[16]

Imagine taking a time log of all activities in thirty-minute segments each day for a week. This would be much like the time studies businesses do with employees. When we have done this, we will have an example of the "slices of life" where experiential Bible study can begin—travel and commuting, cooking and eating, buying and selling, sleeping and awaking, dressing and daily hygiene, work and leisure, communicating and relating, joining and separating, engaging and waiting, reading, writing, listening, and watching.

The resistance to interpreting this hard but rewarding work is puzzling. People see the church as an enclave, a fortress and retreat from the foils of the week, rather than drawing meaning from daily events. William Diehl in *Christianity and Real Life* made this claim: "In almost thirty years of my professional career, my church has never once suggested that there may be some type of accounting of my on-the-job ministry to others . . . . In short, I must conclude that my church really doesn't have the least interest whether or how I minister in my daily work.[17] Banks supported this insight: "Even work-based Bible studies and study groups rarely address the specific questions, dilemmas, pressures, and aspirations that arise in the employment situation. In fact, the concentration on pure Bible study in some of these groups is often an escape from grappling with the real issues of life.[18]

Martin Luther made a valiant attempt to remove these distinctions in two significant ways. One was in the doctrine of the priesthood of the believer, whereby all Christians become priests and hierarchy and rank are eliminated. The other contribution Luther made was to teach all worthwhile work as a calling from God. Luther saw the Scriptures written on the tools of the worker: "Look at your tools, your needle, your thimble . . . your articles of trade, your measures, and you will find this saying written on them . . . use me toward your neighbor as you would want him to act toward you with that which is his."[19]

But the distinctions persisted. As soon as all Christians were identified as "priests," there was still someone who was called "pastor," a title no one else in the congregation had. The location and time of ministry on Sunday seemed quite different from the location and time of ministry on Monday. "The concept of everyone's work being a calling had the unintended effect of locking everyone in place, both the privileged and unprivileged. When someone's work is regarded as a calling from God, it is set in holy cement. Thus, one can see how the separation between workers with brains and those specializing in brawn could come to be seen as divinely inspired."[20]

Robert Banks wove a texture of daily life experiences where experiential Bible study can begin. He identified these themes as major external pressures that surround and affect us.

1. *Busyness*–the "new poverty" of disposable time
2. *Mobility*–the compulsion of continual migration
3. *Debt*–the "life sentence" of permanent debt
4. *Conformity*–the preferences and patterns of the majority
5. *Security*–the temptation to place security above freedom
6. *Regulation*–the growing professionalizing and bureaucratizing of life[21]

The language of this world is significantly different from the language of a church world. There is one vocabulary and set of ears for Sunday and another language spoken and heard on Monday. Grace, compassion, truth, acceptance, and justice are heard on Sunday. Efficiency, performance, acquiring, production, and achievement are heard on Monday. For many people, work is drudgery, and they look forward to the day they can retire. Work is a necessary evil for achieving other personal goals. When there is no spiritual meaning in work, people are condemned to living a dual life where Sunday has nothing to do with the rest of the week. Daily work comprises such a large slice of life that if it isn't related to the biblical message, Scripture is diverted, incompatible, or not heard at all. But when the word of God is connected to daily work, the dilemma is clarified. The gospel is the source of awareness of the incompatibility between Sunday and Monday and the need to bridge the gap. When Scripture is read and interpreted in its true context, all of life becomes one.

NOTES

[1] Charles E. Winquist, "Revisioning Ministry," in *Formation and Reflection*, ed. Lewis Mudge and James N. Poling (Philadelphia: Fortress Press, 1987), 32-33.

[2] Parker Palmer, *To Know As We Are Known* (San Francisco: Harper & Row, 1983), 14-16.

[3] Thomas Groome, *Educating for Life* (New York: Crossroad, 2001), 277.

[4] Hans Georg Gadamer, *Truth and Method* (New York: Crossroad, 1975), 240.

[5] Ibid., 236.

[6] J. William Pfeiffer and Arlette C. Ballew, *Using Structured Experiences in Human Resource Development* (San Diego: University Associates, Inc., 1988), 21-24. Structured experiences are produced in two annual handbooks currently imprinted under Jossey-Bass/Pfeiffer, 350 Sansome St., San Francisco CA 94104.

[7] Pfeiffer and Ballew, *Using Structured Experiences*, 53-54.

[8] Robert Dow, *Learning Through Encounter* (Valley Forge: Judson Press, 1971), 39.

⁹ Edgar Dale, *Audio-visual Methods in Teaching* (New York: Holt, Rinehart and Winston, 1954).

¹⁰ Tom F. Driver, "Performance and Biblical Readings," in *Body and Bible*, ed. Bjorn Krondorfer (Philadelphia: Trinity Press International, 1992), 165.

¹¹ The most comprehensive book on improvisation in experiential learning is Viola Spolin, *Improvisation for the Theater* (Evanston: Northwestern University Press, 1963). Also, see her book *Theater Games for the Classroom: A Teacher's Handbook* (Evanston: Northwestern University Press, 1986).

¹² Samuel Laeuchli, "The Expulsion from the Garden and the Hermeneutics of Play," in *Body and Bible*, ed. Krondorfer, 46.

¹³ For an expanded treatment of storytelling using an experiential model, see Susan Shaw, *Storytelling in Religious Education* (Birmingham: Religious Education Press, 1999).

¹⁴ John Shea, *Stories of God* (Chicago: Thomas Moore Press, 1978), 62. Also see *An Experience Named Spirit* (Chicago: Thomas Moore Press, 1983).

¹⁵ Dorothy C. Bass, *Receiving the Day: Christian Practices for Opening the Gift of Time* (San Francisco: Jossey-Bass Publishers, 2000), 16.

¹⁶ Robert Banks, *Redeeming the Routines: Bringing Theology to Life* (Wheaton IL: Victor Books, 1993), 46.

¹⁷ William Diehl, *Christianity and Real Life* (Philadelphia: Fortress Press, 1976).

¹⁸ Banks, *Redeeming the Routines*, 60.

¹⁹ William E. Diehl, *The Monday Connection* (New York: HarperCollins Publishers, 1993), 29.

²⁰ Paul G. Johnson, *Grace: God's Work Ethic* (Valley Forge: Fortress Press, 1985), 24.

²¹ Banks, *Redeeming the Routines*, 72-76.

CHAPTER FOUR

Word Weaving: Exegesis

The words themselves must show the internal marks of long use;
they must contain their own inner conversation.[1]

Stop reading for a moment and look at the clothing you are wearing. Our first impression is of total pieces—shirt, blouse, sweater, skirt, and slacks. But take a closer look. Every piece of clothing is made of sections woven together to form one piece. When we begin a process of unraveling a small section of clothing, we discover tiny threads intricately woven into one fabric with slightly visible seams. After examining more closely, we find that the cloth itself is composed of interwoven threads that join to give strength, good fit, and long-lasting wear to the garment.

Scriptural themes are interlaced and joined in kaleidoscope patterns in much the same way. Like a craftsperson, we lovingly examine the fabric of the Bible until it begins to yield its finer points to our understanding. This process is called an *exegesis*, an intimidating concept for most people. Like weaving, it has the appearance of complexity, but it can be broken down into a process all of us can use.

What Is a Biblical Text?

Text is a Latin word coming from *textus*, the past participle of *texere*, meaning "to weave." From the same word we get textile, a woven cloth, and texture, something composed of closely woven elements. In Bible study, a text is a section of writing with words. We talk about biblical "material" as if describing a fabric of some sort that has texture and a particular weave. Like a woven piece of material or fabric, the text has complex threads interwoven into patterns. It would be a big job trying to unravel all these threads and put them back together again, but that is the task of biblical exegesis.

The writers and translators of the Bible communicated to us through a combination of words, phrases, sentences, paragraphs, sections, and entire texts.

The authors and translators combined words and phrases to express certain ideas. This explanation of words, phrases, and sentences that make up the messages of paragraphs, sections, and books is an exegetical study of the Bible. Exegesis is the study of the text of Scripture. When we exegete Scripture, we recount, declare, and explain what comes out of Scripture.

Exegesis means "to explain, expound, interpret, or tell."[2] In the Old Testament, the word translates the Hebrew *sapar*, meaning "to recount, tell, or declare." It is used to tell a dream (Judg 7:13), to describe a miracle (2 Kgs 8:5), and to declare the Lord's glory among the nations (1 Chr 16:24). Another form of the word means "to talk, or to sing," as in telling God's wonderful works (1 Chr 16:9; Ps 105:2).

In Luke and Acts, the word means "to relate or tell." Cleopas and his companion explain what happened on the road to Emmaus (Luke 24:35), and Cornelius relates his vision to his servants (Acts 10:8). In the remaining passages in Acts, people relate what God has done (15:12, 14; 21:19). In the last passage, Paul relates God's "acts" in detail or "one by one." Exegesis, then, is a process providing the orderly, systematic, step-by-step procedure in interpreting the texts of Scripture one by one.

A form of the word "exegete" is found in John 1:18. In this verse, John declares that Jesus "exegeted" the Father to us. In other words, Jesus explained and made clear the meaning of the Father. Jesus was a unique explanation of the Father, a visible commentary of God. He was the one who "interpreted" and clarified the one we know as Father-God.

For many of us who are bent toward action-reflection as a learning style, it might sound strange to say that ultimately the exegesis of the text gets the juices flowing. We have said many times that the learning process is an extremely inaccurate hit-and-miss operation. What happens when imagination dries up and reflection gives out? The exegesis of the text in an orderly form gives shape to an otherwise chaotic learning process. When all else fails, read the text! Let the text say what it wants to say. We can learn a lesson from German theologian Karl Barth. When the Nazis no longer permitted him to lecture at the University of Bonn, he left the lecture room shouting, "Exegesis, exegesis, exegesis!" What he meant was that the German nation was being bewitched by a special brew of Nazi ideology and Christian theology. Many times in his earlier years, Hitler would stand before an audience with a Bible open in his hands, claiming that he was saying nothing more than what was in the Bible, which the people had learned at their mothers' knees. If German Christians were to unmask the bewitching Nazi religion, it could only be done by a continuing accurate study of Scripture. This was the meaning of Barth's crying, "Exegesis, exegesis, exegesis!"

Exegesis stands between the text and a commentary. Our tendency is to go directly from the text to the interpretation of the text, letting others do the exegesis for us. The possibility of encountering the biblical text without the help of an interpretive commentary is threatening. In *Church Bible Study Handbook*, Robin Maas addressed the issue: "The worst fallacy the church has perpetuated in respect to biblical education is the notion that the laity can learn to understand the Bible only by reading books about the Bible instead of wrestling with the actual biblical texts themselves."[3] Maas stated that engaging the text before we engage commentary is like working on an archeological dig. The exegete sifts through the material, even the smallest fragments, in a slow and methodical way. This sifting process requires patience and curiosity, but there is also a sense of fascination, as if in an entirely new world of learning with a new language and a new intellectual terrain. Fascination comes with the lived "rootedness" of many abstract theological words, with the location of particular biblical events, with the way people lived, what they wore, how they traveled, what they felt, and how they related to one another and to God.

The themes of the Bible are simple and primary. Life was involved with a few basic activities—fighting, farming, family, intrigue, leaving home, and finding home. We confront basic virtues and primitive vices. The world these people journey through is elemental—fire, earth, water, wilderness, mountains, stories, sun, moon, stars, clouds, seasons, seedtime, and harvest. Amid all of this is worship. Suddenly, we discover that these were real people, living in specific locations, facing the same kinds of problems you and I face. Rather than this effort being laborious and exhausting, many people find it to be exhilarating because it requires a dramatic change in our relationship to the text. Instead of buying lessons and commentaries, we participate in the development of our own commentary.

Learning a new language is often tedious and frustrating. By language, we mean talking in new ways, using new words, and, in a sense, a new vocabulary. The new language does not mean learning Greek and Hebrew, although a brief study of the biblical language will give you on appreciation for the limitations of all English translations. Walking into the world of biblical exegesis is like walking into a strange new country, exciting and fascinating, and at the same time bewildering and a bit overwhelming. At first, the learning process is slow and the possibility of carrying on a coherent conversation seems impossible. "The willingness to continue learning after the initial burst of enthusiasm is basically an act of faith—faith that the value of the exchange with the alien other will justify the investment of time and strenuous effort."[4] Learning is a discerning art—the ability to lovingly stay with each phrase, sentence, or paragraph until we discern the finer points of style, structure, beauty, and special nuances of meaning.

Although the language of biblical exegesis is strange, it is still human language. This might seem odd to say, but it is important to remember. The Bible was written with human language using human conversation. The Greek and Hebrew language in the Bible is to be understood in the same way as Greek and Hebrew outside the Bible. Most words had long histories of secular usage but were modified (transformed) within the context of Christian faith. In the same way we understand ordinary language in conversation, we also understand the more technical aspects of the biblical language since it, too, was written in normal language used in normal ways. God chose to be revealed through human language. The writers did not develop or communicate a new religious language.

What is the language of biblical exegesis? What do we do in exegesis? We do several things. We read and compare translations, formulate the main points of the passage and compare them, identify key words, prepare an outline in keeping with the paragraph development, refer to related passages or words, and share our findings with others. In simple terms, we work with reading, the context, connections, words, and meanings.

Reading from Different Translations

We have all had the experience of finding a book we were unable to read a few years earlier but now read with great interest. It is not that, in the interim, we have become smarter, but that our language, thought forms, and experiences have been enlarged to share the thought world of the author. Without such sharing, words are not vehicles of communication but formidable barriers. All of us read Scripture in that interpretative context. The meaning that seems to us to come directly from the words upon the page is actually an interpretation, the result of an instantaneous process by which the words on the page receive specific meanings in our minds. Every understanding of the text and every statement of its meaning is an interpretation. There remains always a significant distance between the interpretation and the text, a distance that causes humility in the interpreter and excludes the absolutizing of any interpretation as though it were the final truth.

To avoid these assumptions from our readings, it is best to read from several translations that tend to differ. These comparative readings will highlight many of the exegetical issues and turn us to a more precise examination of the text. Let us remember that the Bible is an odd language written for an odd and peculiar people. We are not only looking for more information. We hunger for beauty, mystery, and the sounds of music in our reading. Do you really want a translation that sounds like everything else you hear today? What about reading a translation that sounds a little strange, almost like we were hearing God talking?

How many of our modern versions went under the scrutiny of oral reading in the final revision as did the King James Version?

The Context

Context comes from two words—con, meaning "together," and text, meaning "woven." Context is how the Bible is woven together. When we work with context, we state what the section of the text is about and how each paragraph contributes. We seek to identify the connections of thought that run through the text and weave it into one piece. The context is the flow of the river that moves like one stream from smaller tributaries and streams. Context may be seen as a unity of complete meaning with an introduction, a middle section of development, and a conclusion.

Context means looking at the whole and the parts. What is the subject of the text? Does it relate to another section of the book? What theme runs through the passage that weaves it into one piece? When have we heard that theme coming from that author or another author before? The simplest way of examining context is to refer to cross-references of related and parallel passages mentioned in the marginal notes of your Bible. Is the author relying on earlier or later events or traditions? How is the author using this material? Are there grammar clues, questions, or changes in settings that divide or bring together sentences and paragraphs? For example, Paul used the phrase "now concerning" to introduce new subjects in 1 Corinthians 7:1, 25; 12:1; and 16:1. Sometimes there are repeated terms, phrases, or clauses. Genesis 1–11 can be divided with the phrase "These are the generations of . . ." or "These are the descendants of . . . " (Gen 2:4; 5:1; 6:9; 10:1; 11:27). Sections in Matthew close with "Now when Jesus had finished . . ." (Matt 7:28; 11:1; 13:53; 19:1; 26:1).

Sometimes these slightly exposed seams in the text will be noted with a change in time, location, or setting. How does the text fit into the total plan and purpose of the book? Does the writer bring forth the purpose of the book or must the purpose be formulated? What does the writer ask the reader to do? Answering these text questions will give a hint to the writer's purpose. Sometimes the writer will tell us the purpose in writing. John tells us the purpose for writing his Gospel in John 20:21: "But these are written, so that you might come to believe that Jesus is the Messiah, the Son of God, and that through believing you might have life in his name."

McCartney and Clayton suggested an unraveling of the text followed by a "reweaving" that brings the fabric of the text back to a whole piece.

The context specifies this particular meaning of the word which is intended. So word studies must be carried out with their sentences in mind. Likewise sentences should be understood within their paragraphs, and paragraphs within the basic complete unit of meaning, the "nuclear discourse," of all the material around a particular subject or topic. Therefore we recommend starting with a look at the discourse, working down to the words, and then back up to the discourse.[5]

Connections

How the text is connected and woven together is a study of syntax. "Syntax is one of the most important avenues for the interpreter to use in reconstructing the thread of the writer's meaning. The ways in which words are put together as to form phrases, clauses, and sentences still aid us in discovering the author's pattern of meaning."[6] Syntax study is depth work on the paragraph, a discovery of the author's weaving together of meaning. A paragraph is a group of sentences woven together around related meanings. The original text of the Bible was not marked by paragraphs. Translators added paragraphs and verses. One helpful exercise is in developing one's own paragraphing of the text, identifying how the seams of meaning fit together, and developing units of thought.

In looking at paragraphs, there are several things to note:

1. The type of literature composition: prose, poetry, narrative, wisdom, and apocalypse.
2. Sudden changes in the text.
3. The identification of themes and the relationship of sentences, clauses, and phrases to that theme.
4. The connection of one paragraph with other paragraphs.

In syntax, it is important to locate performative and emotive language. Note the texts that perform an act. This "performative" language describes what actually happens. Performative language commits the speaker to stand by his or her words. It says what the actor is actually in the process of doing. In addition to performative language, it is important to recognize the place of emotive or expressive language. The emotional feeling found in a passage is an important aspect of its total meaning. The true meaning of the text can be lost without the portrayal of the emotions to guide the interpretation. Depth is found in this identification with the underlying tone. When we are able to feel into the underlying tone, we grasp the intensity of the text. To be able to grasp the intensity level gives us another depth of interpretation. The feeling words of the text are often as difficult to identify as our own feelings. A study of the emotive language of the Scriptures brings us to a new dimension of depth. Jeremiah and Paul, for instance, are emotional writers who wear their feelings on their sleeves. One can expect highly charged terms from them. They tend to choose words that run the gamut of human feelings.

The basic unit of communication in the paragraph is the sentence. Words have meaning when they are contained in sentences. Sentences have meaning in relation to other sentences that precede and follow. The most basic question to be asked about the sentence is what does this sentence offer to the overall contribution of the text?

Words

The next level of exegetical development is a single word. While there might be a danger in overemphasizing single words, we cannot ignore them. It is important to determine the key words in the text—words that call out to us for more focused attention. Probably the most important words are those that give us the most trouble. We would do well to examine more deeply the concepts we least understand.

Word study opens a treasure chest of rich findings for those willing to search. But the words cannot be detached from their context. Most often the meaning of words is determined by the way they were normally used when the author wrote them. A good rule of thumb is to note the words that are theologically loaded, that are crucial to the meaning of the passage, and that are repeated so often that they become themes. Words are like people. They are known by the company they keep. These words are "trigger" words, calling to our minds other images and concepts.

Some words will receive an extraordinary amount of attention. When words inform a whole body of material, they become biblical themes or doctrines. In the overall canon of Scripture, a theological center exists, and the texts that unfold this center are attached to certain words. The Bible has many of these "seed words," which take root and grow in many directions. There are theological centers around which words, phrases, sentences, and paragraphs revolve. A center is found in 2 Corinthians 5:18-19: "So if anyone is in Christ, there is a new creation: everything old has passed away; see, everything has become new! All this is from God, who reconciled us to himself through Christ, and has given us the ministry of reconciliation." Such words as God, Christ, reconciliation, new creation, and ministry are like barnacles on a ship. They refuse to let go no matter which way we turn. Such words are always with us in exegesis.

I cannot tell you when I first began comparing exegeting with running. I suppose it began with being "stuck" in sermon or lecture preparation until I got my feet moving. Over the years this imagery has stayed with me, and maybe it will make sense to you. We say the biblical words are living and active, meaning they have a long life with legs that have carried them on an enduring journey. While traveling, they talk to themselves, carrying on conversations with their own root meanings. But they do not run alone and soon engage other words in social events where they all seem to run in the same direction with an internal sense of destination. Sometimes in packs and other times in twos and threes, they carry on conversations, enhancing and energizing those around them. They are all "originals" with a certain style and pace of running and will surprise you at times by moving ahead or dropping behind and connecting with a new and unlikely group. Once in a while you get a lone runner, "weaving" in, out, and among, but still knowing a sense of the same social entity and fabric. What do you get? You get an enormous sense of support and encouragement, maybe friendly competitive disagreement at times, but never an act of turning on each other.

You don't have to take my "word" for this. Pick any word that you find early in the biblical text and "run" with it, seeing where it takes you. Notice what other words it picks up along the way, some of its favorite partners, and take special note of its final destination. Some of my favorite words are water, breath, garden, hand, face, bread, and fire. You will find your own.

Meanings

The final test of exegetical study is our ability to communicate it. Studying the text is not enough. The Bible is a public book that should be used in the context of God's people through the ministry of the Holy Spirit. Meaning comes when we are able to identify the true message of the text and express it in a way that personally touches others. An outline provides the best means for such communication.

Some practical steps in developing outlines are communicable. Focus on the major concerns of the writer and identify not more than two to three paragraphs or six to eight verses. Identify the theme sentences and the instructive features of the passage. The tendency may be to transfer from the text all names, places, and incidents. This recording may miss the main points and subpoints of the text. Anything that focuses attention on the "themes" of the text rather than the "now-ness" should be avoided. Focus on the abiding permanent teaching of the text. If possible, express the outline of main points and subpoints in parallel fashion. If one point is a phrase, then all should be. If the first point begins with a preposition, others will follow. Some texts lend themselves to this type of outlining more easily than others. If, however, one is committed to following the development and sequence of the text, an orderly and easily remembered pattern and design can usually be found. You don't like outlining? Then try mind mapping in the chapter "Rearranging the Furniture of the Mind: Preaching."

Paraphrase

Once the wording of the text has been examined as thoroughly as possible, a brief paraphrase is the most helpful step. Far from being mere busy work, the construction of an accurate, unvarnished paraphrase is probably the single most effective means for arriving at an understanding of what the text really does or does not say. Restating something in a few, well-chosen words is not easy. The tendency is always to expand the original meaning by elaborating on it instead of restating. We generally interpret or explain, but an expanded or interpreted paraphrase simply clouds the issue. The point of a biblical exegesis is to discover meaning and not to impose it.

Examining the Threads Verse by Verse

The best way to exegete a passage of Scripture is to follow the original weaving pattern verse by verse. The process can become slower when each verse is taken word for word in analysis. Weaving and reweaving is done the same way; you can't start on the next thread until the last thread is completed. A Bible dictionary, or wordbook, and a complete concordance will help in this process.

Not every word will be examined in every situation. Your own intuitive curiosity will lead you in the direction that provides the most meaning. You must decide if this particular excursion is creating energy and meaning for you and others. But verse-by-verse creates a discipline in following the integrity of the text and avoids the temptation to work only with the familiar, the assumed, and the known.

Consider these suggestions. When all else fails, read the text. Grab paper and pencil. Begin making notes, and if your notes are not all slicked up coming out of a computer and printer, you won't fake yourself out by thinking you're finished. Write down words and phrases, especially words that seem different, strange, light, hot, cold, sweet, or sour. Argue or complain about what you are reading and writing.

Take a good look at what comes before and after the text. Why is this here and not somewhere else? Where has this text been and where is it going? If it were placed somewhere else, what difference would it make?

Compare a couple of translations. Don't forget that the Bible was not written in English. Take a stab at the Greek and Hebrew. I hate to admit it, but a good computer program will run the English version parallel with the original language. You can do the same thing with an interlinear New Testament or a good concordance. If your curiosity has taken hold by now, you can find all the ways those words have been used and marvel at the shades of meaning different authors are offering you. Best of all, you will be building a concordance of sorts in your head.

You are not finished. By now you should have a couple of pages of notes with all kinds of images and word pictures. Your notes are warm and personal because they are your own handwriting. Take your notes and walk the neighborhood, letting your imagination and intuition play over the images and maybe, through some happy hunches and lucky guesses, you will get a fresh take. Walking the neighborhood will help you get grounded. Now that your hands and feet have gotten involved, you may be ready for a little sensory exegesis.

Sensory Exegesis

The purpose of working through the text with the senses is to examine how the text is full of living details. When we examine the living details in the text, they bring the hearer on board or into an experiential encounter with the text. The details bring living color to the text and draw the readers into a living encounter. We may call the senses the vehicles that make the Scriptures come alive. This is not merely a chance happening, but a skill in verbal concreteness and picture painting. We know now how to reach people in depth. There has been enough study of the intuitive and the emotive that we can develop skills in reaching people in depth. An abstract idea comes to life in concreteness. People can see it, hear it, touch it, taste it, and smell it. They are able to associate it with truth. Abstractions become meaningful when they are grounded in this sensory experience and the concreteness of daily life.

Nothing has familiarity as do the senses. Clarence Jordan's *Cotton Patch* translations of the New Testament are effective because he pulled the senses into his translations. The senses provide a bridge for communication in a way of expressing ourselves in particulars rather than generalities. Words do not merely point, but they stand for something, and to stand for something they must stand on something. Words stand on particular concrete events in history. The Old Testament writers saw this concreteness in the word of God. The word took shape through the senses. The dynamic, urgently pressing force of the word of God emerges in the Old Testament text. This was particularly true in the prophets. The revelation of the word to the prophet was not a word given in a mechanical sort of way, but an event that overpowered the prophet, sometimes physically. Isaiah 21:3 provides a powerful sensory illustration of how the word impacted Isaiah: "Therefore my loins are filled with anguish; pangs have seized me, like the pangs of a woman in labor; I am bowed down so that I cannot hear, I am dismayed so I cannot see." The word of God appeared as a powerful force that left a dynamic impact on the hearer. It was not merely a word but "the word of God" coming through an effective event. Jeremiah 4:19 describes how the word impacted Jeremiah in a physical way: "My anguish, my anguish! I writhe in pain; . . . my heart is beating wildly; I cannot keep silent; for I hear the sound of the trumpet, the alarm of war."

The sensory images of the word become more graphic in Jeremiah and Ezekiel. Jeremiah greedily takes in the word as if it were his favorite dish: "Your words were found and I ate them and your words became to me a joy and a delight of my heart" (Jer 15:16). The prophet's decision not to proclaim the word of God any longer (Jer 20:9) encountered the irresistible force of the word, which pressed in on him like an objective force from within and without. The word of God that Jeremiah tried to deny burned like a fire inside him, threatening his total disintegration so that it seemed preferable to endure ridicule from others rather than to be consumed by the burning fire of the word. "Then within me there is something like a burning fire shut up in my bones; I am weary with holding it in, and I cannot." Jeremiah saw the crushing power of the word. "Is not my word like fire, says the Lord, and like a hammer which breaks the rocks in pieces?" (Jer 23:29).

Ezekiel's sensory imagery is even more graphic: "He said to me, O mortal, eat what is offered to you; eat this scroll and go, speak to the house of Israel. So I opened my mouth, and he gave me the scroll to eat. He said to me, Mortal, eat this scroll that I give you and fill your stomach with it. Then I ate it; and in my mouth it was as sweet as honey" (Ezek 3:1-3). The scroll is offered to Ezekiel and he is commanded to eat it. Jeremiah's picture of devouring God's word as it comes to him (Jer 15:16) is turned into dramatic reality in the experience of Ezekiel. The eating of the scroll and the absorbing of what is eaten into the inner self clarifies the call to become one with the word of God.

The word of God is also creative in Ezekiel. Ezekiel is taken to a field of completely dried out bones, and the prophet is given the charge of speaking God's words to this field of the dead (Ezek 37:4-6). At the spoken word of God, the bones come together and the sinews, flesh, and skin grow over them. In the word from God the breath of life comes into that which is lying dead on the ground, so that they rise and stand up live (Ezek 37:9-10). This vision is God's reply to the declaration of the people (Ezek 37:11) that "our bones are dried up." Through the word of God the bones come to life.

The power of the word comes to life in the spoken words of Jesus. In Mark 2:11, he commands the dead, "I say to you stand up," and through his word of command the dead come to life (Mark 9:25). The connection between Jesus' word of forgiveness (Mark 2:5) and his word of healing (Mark 2:11) is to be noted. The word of healing is the physical expression of Jesus' word of forgiveness. Jesus' deeds are connected to his word where the healing takes place by means of Jesus' word. "But only speak the word and my servant will be healed" (Matt 8:8) was something without parallel in Jesus' world and, thus, striking for the eyewitness (Matt 8:16): "he cast out the spirits with a word." Paul commends his congregation to the word of God (Acts 20:32), and the word is proved to be powerful (Acts 19:20) in that it grows and multiplies (Acts 6:7; 12:24) and spreads throughout the whole land.

Our words do not merely express our thoughts, which are already present and fully formed. Words stimulate thought and influence people around us. At the same time, they do not operate at an intellectual level only. They do not merely convey information from one mind to another. They also stimulate our senses, arouse passions, and open our senses to imagination and emotions. The words may provoke a whole range of actions, and the speaking of the words may affectively perform certain actions. To say "I do" in the marriage ceremony is to actually gain a spouse. To say "I appoint you" may actually send someone to another country. The words not only say, but they also do. In making a will, the words "I give" and "bequeath" bring about a specific settlement of possessions. The gospel comes not in words only, but the words carry power (1 Cor 2:4; 4:19-20). Words do have physical properties and are influenced by the actual settings in human life. Language is relative to its surroundings. It has been said that Eskimo people see the world in a distinctive way because of the enormous range of words they have for the degrees or kinds of whiteness.

Words are tools. They are much like tools in a toolbox—hammer, pliers, saw, screwdriver, etc. They are used for particular purposes. Words are to be used in particular ways and do not work in other ways. The language of faith is not necessarily a special kind of language but, rather, is ordinary language put to a special kind of use. When we talk about hearing the voice of God, we do not use a special word for hearing, but we do use the word *hearing* in a special way. So it is with the other senses. We do not use different words for hear, see, touch, taste, and smell, but we do see them used in a special way. Hearing does not mean the specific sound waves striking the ear. If that is the case, one might need a hearing aid, but a different course of action is needed for someone who has difficulty hearing God.

Nicodemus is told that birth in the kingdom has a different logical grammar from birth in the world. The living water offered by Jesus to the woman of

Samaria is different from the running water as she images it (John 4:10). The disciples misunderstand the grammar of food of which Jesus speaks (John 4:31-34). The Jews misunderstand the meaning of bread in John 6:31-35. There are special surroundings wrapped around these teachings. Jesus gives otherwise ordinary language a distinctive meaning or grammar. The Bible does not merely inform us about the love of God and the love of Jesus; it conveys the reality of this love. We are drawn into it, as it were, to see these realities in the same way Jesus does. Our horizons are enlarged and our senses sharpened. These words have meaning in the stream of life.

The warning against "careless words" (Matt 12:36) points to words that are ineffective because they have no backing in actual experience and in practical conduct. Empty promises and vain intentions fall into this category. Words that merely chase other words have no anchor in reality. This is illustrated in one of Kierkegaard's writings about a shop sign that promises "Pressing Done Here." "If a person were to bring his clothes to be pressed, he would be duped, for the sign is merely for sale."[7] Jesus embodied and lived out God's word made flesh. He did not merely talk humility—he took a towel and washed the disciples' feet. He did not merely talk about sacrifice—he was actually crucified. He did not merely speak words about forgiveness and new life—he actually brought it about in people's lives. Words carried the power of action.

In *The Son of Laughter*, Frederick Buechner dramatizes the story of Jacob, whom he calls Heels. Rebekah speaks to Heels before he steals the blessing: "If you speak a word with the strength of your heart in it, you can never get that word out of the ears of the one you speak it to and back into your mouth again. Once a word goes forth, it makes things happen for better or worse. Nothing you do will ever make those things unhappen even though you live for a thousand years. Do you understand me?"[8]

Reweaving the Text

The exegetical task falls into two stages—unraveling the text and weaving it back together. Unraveling the text breaks it down into component parts. All these separate tasks interlock and inform the others. Gradually, the weaving back together takes place as understanding increases. The surprises come in doing both. Totally new meanings may be discovered and old meanings may be affirmed or discarded.

How is the text to be woven back together into whole units? Many would put it back together book by book. Some have attempted a chronological weaving with graphs and charts. Walter Brueggemann in *The Bible Makes Sense* suggested the following:

I suggest that the place to begin in determining the shape of the tradition is with the primal narrative, that most simple elemental and nonnegotiable story line which lies at the heart of biblical faith. Such a narrative is presented with the passion of fresh believers and with the simplicity of a community which had screened out all uncertainties and felt no reason to explain. It is an affirmation in story form which asserts this is the most important story we know and we have come to believe that it is decisively about us.[9]

The primal story can be told around two texts—Joshua 24:1-28 and 1 Corinthians 15:3-8. Joshua 24 begins with a speech and the people's response. This is a national assembly where Israel sees itself as a covenant community, perhaps for the first time. The story is told and they identify it as their story. They know these events to be experientially true. Joshua assembles all the people, rehearses the mighty acts of God, and challenges them to choose whom they will worship. "I took your father Abraham . . . I sent Moses also . . . I have brought your fathers out of Egypt . . . I have given you a land . . . we [the people] also will serve the LORD for he is our God."

In 1 Corinthians 15:3-8, Paul outlines the saving message of the New Testament in a clear economy of words. Paul directs attention to the primal elements of the gospel, which he insists have been strongly laid in history and in personal experience: "Christ died for sins in accordance with Scriptures . . . he was buried . . . he was raised on the third day . . . he appeared to the disciples . . . he appeared also to me."

Around the Old Testament primal narratives were woven expanded narratives, which were more elaborate and complete presentations than those found in the original fabric. In the same way, the primal narrative has been expanded to become the whole gospel. Likewise, the primal narratives are found in the birth, life, ministry, death, resurrection, and ascension of Jesus the Christ.

Empathy, Identification, and Imagination in Exegesis

We return to a basic principle of this book. Understanding Scripture is like understanding people, even in the hard work of exegesis. In understanding people, as with Scripture, we seek a basis in what is said, in who the author-speaker is, and in the world of the author-speaker.

In listening to people, we are always searching for an exchanging of clues. In our study of the Bible, we devote our time to the discovery of clues from which we can reconstruct our interpretation. Again, this is a natural process of everyday life. We constantly do this whenever we read texts or listen to people. Our daily life is experienced in a woven web of relationships.

Understanding Scripture, like understanding people, is giving up "gamesmanship" in order to preserve integrity of both biblical text and people. We must understand how language works, what happens when people express themselves. In normal language, the writer uses language to say something. We understand when we realize what the speaker wants us to comprehend. The speaker seeks to communicate, and the listener, as the receiver, tries to understand. However, what happens in studying the Bible is something like what we do in understanding people. We short-circuit the process by engaging in a predetermined game. Honest understanding is based on taking author and language seriously. We understand another's words as he or she wants them to be understood, not as we want to understand them. As in conversation, we try to discover what a speaker means by the words that are used. Unless there is some powerful reason for disregarding what and how a person says something, we should take it seriously.

If we reflect a bit about our everyday experiences with language, we realize that we can and do understand specific meanings intended by others, in spite of our presuppositions. We are often aware that we misunderstand and that we make incorrect judgments about what people say. Likewise, we know that others understand us as well as misunderstand us. From our experience, we believe we are capable of discerning incorrect understandings from correct ones, although we often "miss" both objectively and intuitively.

Not only are we able to discern understanding and misunderstanding, but we can also transcend our presuppositions and enter into another's thought processes. In other words, we have the capacity for identification and empathy. We understand others even though we do not act as they do nor believe as they do. Empathy and identification lead to understanding another, both from intuition and inductive analysis. This simple process of seeing things from another point of view plays a major role in biblical interpretation. Without this empathy, we will be ethnocentric, interpreting things according to our own viewpoints instead of the authors' perspective.

Part of understanding an author or speaker is trying to understand motivation. If they are "inspired" (spirit moved), then what moves them? To understand motivation is perhaps the single most useful key in understanding what a person is trying to tell us, but it is perhaps the most difficult. This is because what "moved" an author long ago is not readily available for us to examine. It must often be determined by reconstructing the circumstances surrounding the life of the author, especially those events surrounding the time of writing. Misunderstanding does not usually arise from not knowing the meaning of words, but rather from not understanding words in a correct way. To understand a passage is to determine the actual meaning its author intended. Since this dimension is never open to direct observation, it must be gotten at indirectly through the clues in the lines and in between the lines of the text. From these clues and by exercising the powers of empathy, we make practical inferences as to what the author intended.

Part of the difficulty in understanding is the impoverished state of the average adult's imagination. Exegetical study provides an effective corrective for this type of problem. One of the first things a new exegete learns is that what is most familiar becomes a hindrance rather than a help. This is true of both Scripture and people. The riches to be mined in a single verse of Scripture became a matter of much astonishment. A little additional reading about one key word can yield a host of new insights or suggest many other questions to pursue. The practical exegete has learned that an essential part of the discipline of study is recognizing and avoiding the trap of overconfidence when dealing with an especially familiar material or relationship. To assume that we already know what it means is to assume that God has nothing new to say to us. The wealth of new detail we uncover through exegesis provides a powerful stimulus to our imaginations, making it possible for us to participate in what we read at deeper emotional levels. The strength of exegesis is that, while it nurtures the imagination, it also disciplines it by establishing basic parameters beyond which the stimulated imagination may not go. Through practice we become increasingly sensitive to the problems encountered and to what can and cannot be done in staying honest with the text. Too little imagination is a bigger problem than too much!

Put on the New Clothes

Practice in exegetical method will do more than help us understand Scripture. It will reorient us in relation to the Bible; as we work at this task in community, it will also reorient us in our relationships with one another. Exegesis is a discipline, using the skills and tools of a craftsperson. It teaches us to defer judgment until we collect sufficient data. It teaches us to treat texts (and eventually people) with great care and respect. We learn to listen more attentively to what the text (and our neighbor) has to say before leaping in with a response. We learn to share the responsibilities of research and where discussions are leading. We learn the intricate processes of unraveling and reweaving, while continually building our own story into the pattern. We learn to look at questions contextually to probe for, collect, sort, and weigh evidence. We learn to measure what we have learned from our faith or tradition against the realities of our experience. We learn to subject ourselves to the authority of the text before we attempt the mastery of it either as a sermon, teaching, or discussion material. We learn that a direct and immediate relationship with Scripture is a source of empowerment and that we are responsible for exercising this power in changing our lives.

Doing our own weaving of Scripture is like trying on a new set of clothes. They give us a new feeling about ourselves and sometimes carry us into new areas of experience. Clothing wraps directly over our skin, so it shouldn't surprise us that Scripture wraps around a whole range of biblical processes that we "put on" in becoming a new person. (See Isa 61:10; Ps 30:11; Job 30:18; Col 3:9-10, 12; Eph 4:24; 6:13-15.)

Try on the new patterns you have woven with the biblical text and see how they fit. When you put on the new text you may discover that "you have stripped off the old self with its practices and have clothed yourselves with the new self, which is being renewed in knowledge according to the image of its creator" (Col 3:9-10). In the process of exegesis, you may have awakened to the old behaviors of deceit, anger, envy, and greed. No longer will you be dressed in these. Now you "clothe yourselves with compassion, kindness, humility, meekness, and patience" (Col 3:12).

NOTES

[1] Lewis Thomas, *The Lives of a Cell* (New York: Bantam Books, Inc., 1974), 154.

[2] See Colin Brown, ed., *The New International Dictionary of New Testament Theology*, vol. 1 (Grand Rapids: Zondervan Publishing House, 1979), 574-75.

[3] Robin Maas, *Church Bible Study Handbook* (Nashville: Abingdon Press, 1982), 17.

[4] Ibid., 58.

[5] Dan McCartney and Charles Clayton, *Let the Reader Understand* (Wheaton IL: Victor Books, 1994), 170-71. According to McCartney and Clayton, "discourse" is a coherence that involves the connection of paragraphs to form an entire argument, development, explanation or story (171). "Unraveling" and "reweaving" are my terms and an interpretation of their process.

[6] Walter C. Kaiser, Jr., *Toward an Exegetical Theology* (Grand Rapids: Baker Book House, 1981), 89.

[7] Søren Kierkegaard, *Either/Or (Part 1)* (Princeton: Princeton University Press, 1987), 32.

[8] Frederick Buechner, *The Son of Laughter* (New York: HarperCollins Publishers, 1993), 74.

[9] Walter Brueggemann, *The Bible Makes Sense* (Winona MN: Saint Mary's Press, 1997), 45-46.

CHAPTER FIVE

The Heart Has Its Reasons: Reflection

The heart has its reasons that reason does not know.
—Blaise Pascal

*In order to understand what another person is saying, you must
assume it is true and try to imagine what it might be true of.*[1]

Reflection is the interplay between experience and exegesis, holding both in solution. In reflection, we talk back to Scripture in the light of the significant events of life. Hidden beneath the abstract concepts people verbalize are the experiential processes for which we listen in reflection. In seeking to capture what is hidden, we hold Scripture and experience together loosely, letting them speak to each other in informal ways. Reflection is a pause, turning all that is outside in. "All reflection involves at some point, stopping external observations and reactions so that an idea may mature."[2]

The Pondering Heart

The reflective turn can be seen most clearly in Scripture through the heart, the seat of feelings, emotions, affection, and love. The heart is the embodied sense, the center of our innermost longings and desires. Reflection is the act of pondering something in one's heart as Mary "treasured" all the words of the shepherds and "pondered them in her heart" (Luke 2:19). Through Jesus' early years, Mary continued to "treasure all these things in her heart" (Luke 2:51). To reflect is to mull over, to consider a thought carefully, turning it over and over continually and constantly.

The heart is closely connected to the feelings and affections of a person. Joy originates in the heart. The psalmist declared, "You have put joy in my heart" (Ps 4:7). Isaiah said that the heart contained both the gladness of singing and the pain of crying (Isa 65:15). God promised Israel that he would take away their stony heart and give them a heart of flesh (Ezek 11:19). The Gospel writers would see the heart as the field where the word of God is sewn (Matt 13:19; Luke 8:15), and Satan attempts to take away the word from the heart (Luke 8:12). When the Scriptures were opened to the disciples on the Emmaus road, their hearts "burned" within them (Luke 24:32). The heart expresses the totality of the interior life, and that which comes out of the heart is a reflection of the total person. Reflection is wholehearted involvement with Scripture, or throwing ourselves into it "heartedly."

The Bible warns us that the workings of the heart are difficult to perceive. Without the work of God's spirit, no one can understand the heart, let alone change it. God alone can reveal the hidden person of the heart. When the Lord comes, he "will bring to light the things now hidden in darkness and will disclose the purposes of the heart" (1 Cor 4:5).

There is always something in us that wants to move on to the next step, the next point, the next stage, the next place. The heart, for its own reasons, lingers, hangs on to complications, stays attached to what is actually happening, not to what could be or might be. Our plans move us on, but the heart, in memory, imagination, and dreams, clings to the former attachments, waiting for reflection.

Mary Mullino Moore told the story of an active four-year-old who was still going full steam at ten o'clock in the evening.[3] Someone asked him if he still had energy and his response was, "Yes." His mother, now curious, asked him if he knew what energy was. He responded, "It is something that runs through you and makes you go run, run, run, then it slowly runs out of you and you fall down and close your eyes." Then he added, "It goes through your heart." His mother asked, "What is your heart?" The little boy answered, "It is a muscle—a great *big* muscle; it has to hold all your blood and energy and brain."

That's pretty much the way it is, as far as the Bible is concerned. The heart is the energy center that holds life together, the source of our physical, mental, emotional, and volitional being. We have many ways of saying it. We listen with the heart, speak from the heart, cut to the heart, and lose heart. To remember is to call to heart, learn by heart, have an open or hard heart. The disciples on the Emmaus road were sluggish of heart, and the breaking of bread reminded them of burning hearts. The heart goes on pumping away, no matter what the rest of the body is doing—whether it be emergencies or routines, crises or ordinary times. As far as the Old Testament is concerned, everything gets stored in the heart.

But, alas, sorrow of sorrows and horror of horrors, the Greek word for heart does not have the same power as the Hebrew word, and New Testament interpretation offers confusing groundwork for the separation of heart and mind, feeling and thinking. Loving God with all your heart and loving God with all your mind were two different things. Nothing plagues education more than this split, dividing into two branches or two domains the cognitive and the affective. Shame on us for buying into that heresy. They cannot be divided organically or any other way. The heart pumps blood to the brain to keep it alive, and the brain sends messages to the heart. Every part of the body participates in mental activity. To love God with all our heart, soul, mind, and strength is to love God in the way we put things together.

The heart keeps pumping away, every second taking a beat, creating the totally unpredictable reasons for everything. Why are relationships given birth and then die? Why do friendships endure long absences and more immediate ones fail? Why do good marriages fall apart and bad ones survive? Why do our hearts move in different directions from our intentions? Why are we totally involved in work and family while the heart is somewhere else? Why do we say it's time to move on and the heart does not move one bit, hanging on tenaciously with recurring thoughts and dreams? Why did someone say the primary task of marriage is to protect and nurture the solitude of the other's heart? Do you have the answers to these questions? No, you don't, and neither do I. The heart refuses easy answers and comes up with its own reasons. We chase after swifter and more efficient bits and pieces of information without intimate knowledge of any of it. But the lingering heart remains "stuck" and rooted, telling us that it is organic and systemic, having to do with emotion, passion, and intensity, moving slowly, simply, bodily, and intimately when everything around us is quick and slick.

The heart is our best metaphor for reflection. The heart has its own reasons, seeing what it wants to see, what is actually present, but also what it wants to be present, always looking beyond what is assumed or taken for granted. How else can we explain our fascination with emotion, imagination, and fantasy, the exquisite pain of loss, and the ecstatic pleasure of finding and being found? The heart loves complexities, the "twistedness" of entanglements that can sometimes be named but not explained. One of the hardest things in life is having words in your heart that cannot be uttered, and so we have the endless ruminating, turning things over and over, following fleeting intuitions and nuances. Some would call this obsessing, and maybe it is, but the heart craves and hungers for a depth of reflection and food for ruminating, the faint epiphanies where mystery finally reveals itself.

I must warn you that this lively, coursing "red" heart full of vitality and energy sometimes turns dark gray, cloudy, and even "blue," rummaging around in deep shadows. It leads us into the emotional underworld of the dark night where we might find the scary shadow self. If this is depression, then I would say let it be and quit denying it. There's an old story told from many traditions about a man crouched under a lamp stand looking for something.

A passerby asks, "Have you lost something?"

"Yes, my key."

"Did you lose it here?"

"No, over there, but there's light here."

Depression seems to be an ongoing experience of life, with its dark clouds hovering not far off and ready to move in. I cannot say that depression is either good or bad; it's simply what the heart does in its own time and for its own reasons. Granted, it does make us more obsessive and compulsive, more anxious and insecure, with the depletion of energy and enthusiasm and vague feelings of hopelessness. But it also deepens the possibilities for reflection. The heart refuses to keep our lives bright and warm at all costs and is probably disappointed when we try to cure it mechanically and chemically.

What do I do with this seemingly endless pattern of turning things over, ruminating and oscillating over things past and present? I keep thinking of John Dewey, who said that all experiences are educational if they can be reconstructed. Would I exchange these twisted entanglements for sentimentality, optimism, and denial—the religion of contemporary culture? Never!

The Reflective Turn

In the experiential learning cycle, reflection is the publishing and processing of what we "know" from working with experience and exegesis "in solution." What do we see and how do we feel about what we see? The intent here is to make available to the group the experience of each person. This movement involves what happens to the learner at both cognitive and affective levels when experience and Scripture meet. It is the systematic examination of shared experiences around the biblical text. This "talking through learning" part of the cycle is critical and cannot be ignored or designed spontaneously if useful learning is to occur. Publishing and processing may be carried out through free discussion, but leadership must be firm in avoiding random anecdotal activity. A number of methods help facilitate the publishing/processing movement:

1. Adjectives describing feelings at various points
2. Quick free-association on personal reflection
3. Subgroup sharing—generating lists of "what we saw and how we felt"
4. Systematic interviewing of people concerning what has happened to them when experience and Scripture come together
5. Thematic discussions—looking for recurring topics coming from personal reflections
6. Interviewing pairs—asking the what, when, where, why, and how questions of the biblical text

Insights are fragile. They flicker and are gone quickly. Some type of reflective activity clears the space. Reflection must bring in activity that evokes more than intellectual responses. True reflective activity seeks to weave feeling and thinking together into one piece. Walter Wink has suggested many activities that may evoke feeling responses to the exegetical work on the text.[4] Activities should serve the intention of the text, but there must be some intersection between the text and our own lives. Activity should serve to get the reflective process in motion, not simply to engage in activity.

1. *Paint pictures.* Artistic skill is not the issue. Group members can choose to paint or draw any aspect of the text.
2. *Write dialogue.* What problem or issue is the biblical author addressing? People in Scripture can ask the questions and group members provide answers or vice versa.
3. *Mime.* Mime each character in the biblical story.
4. *Role-play.* Act out the situational aspects of the biblical drama.
5. *Work with clay.* With eyes shut, the hands have a wisdom that the mind does not know. What is this text saying that I can express with my hands? Is there a common experience with the biblical knowledge that only my hands will know?
6. *Gestalt characters.* Enter imaginatively into the skin of a biblical character or concept. Carry on a conversation with the character or concept.
7. *Paraphrase the text.* Rewrite the text using no theological or "religious" language.
8. *Work with two sets of texts.* Match the biblical text with a current text, newspaper, or magazine.

What follows are expanded treatments of reflective methodology: the method of belief, the interpretation of the bodily felt sense, the use of imagination and intuition, the art of asking questions, and a summary of feelings and subjectivity in biblical interpretation.

The Method of Belief

How do we get serious about the activity of reflection in the believer? The method is a game of sorts (as all methods are) and a covenant of group life. Covenants are promises. Each group member promises to try to believe what others see in return for others trying to believe what we see. We promise not to be dependent on anyone else's "looking" or our immediate sense of correct interpretation. We promise to attend to our own experience and honor the experience of others. At this point, we are not constructing or defending an argument or a position. We are simply communicating to others our way of seeing.

Peter Elbow described the believing game: "The believing game seems, and indeed is, extremely permissive. But a paradoxical principle of extreme rigor emerges: you may not reject a reading until you have succeeded in believing it. If you have merely listened politely, even entertained it intelligently, or restated it to the satisfaction of the proposer (a la Carl Rogers), and decided it is wrong, it might be right and you are simply too blind to understand how."[5]

Let us contrast methodological doubt and methodological belief. Methodological doubt is the systematic, disciplined attempt to criticize everything. Doubt is the rhetoric of propositions.

Doubt invites analyses, critiquing, and evaluation. It is said that Socrates had a voice that spoke to him and it only said one word—"No." Everything sounds a little "fishy." Doubt implies distancing, a disengagement, or holding back. When we doubt, there is a tendency to pause and detach ourselves from action. Experiential activities are difficult for many intellectuals who engage in methodological doubt. Experiential activities engage understanding by doing and require an inner act of asserting or entertaining an idea. We doubt better by standing on the sidelines or observing from the stands. The engaged "doer" is perceived to be less thoughtful. Experiential education is an act of chewing and swallowing, not merely discussing what is on the plate. Few Bible study groups are able to survive consistent, insistent methodological doubt.

Methodological belief is a systematic, disciplined attempt to believe everything, no matter how unlikely or repellant. Belief is the rhetoric of experience. It is not only listening, but a disciplined procedure of actually trying to believe the participant's point of view. Belief implies action and activity. When we believe, we tend to act, and by acting, we discover beliefs we didn't know we had. The method of belief invites intimacy, empathy, and identification. Belief invites experiential activity such as role-playing and simulation. What is it like seeing things this way? What do you see or notice now? There is something crucial in the imaginative act of taking another role that frees people from habitual ways of thinking. Methodological belief invites images, word pictures, metaphors, and narratives.

Elbow described principles of methodological belief that are crucial to a reflective process in groups:[6]

1. A high degree of trust. Without trust it is hard for people to try in good faith to enter into views they experience as disagreeable.

2. A five-minute rule. For five minutes, no criticism of the interpretation is permitted and there is a concerted effort to believe it.
   a. What is interesting or helpful about the view? What are intriguing features that others might not have noticed?
   b. What would you see if you accepted the interpretation?
   c. In what sense or under what conditions might this interpretation be true?

    d. What would a narrative be like if the idea or interpretation were true? Tell all the things that would follow from this interpretation.

    e. If you cannot ask or answer these questions, be quiet and listen to those who can.

3. The speaker must feel that others want to believe. Ask help from others who have had success in believing. Some of the most interesting and telling support may come from someone who initially disagreed.

4. A relaxation of preciseness. Think of what happens when we are trying to engage someone in conversation using a different language.

5. If we carefully attend to each word, we lose all sense of understanding. We succeed by "loosening the construing" (by playing the game) and letting the conversation "wash" over us.

6. We commit to listen with a spirit of trust and a sense of identification with the speaker. "This is something worthwhile that will enrich my understanding. How can I see the truth in it? The speaker is seeing something I can't see. What am I missing? What can I get from this insight? In what sense and under what conditions would this interpretation be true?"

7. Finally, there may be, surprisingly, a grasping, an understanding, an enriching of the interpretation that can be held "in solution," without making ultimate belief commitments.

The clearest example of methodological belief may be found in Quaker meetings of consensus. These are not meetings of all sweetness and light. Assent can come without conviction or the felt force of the belief. Quakers are fierce doubters, which comes out of a refusal to submit to easy answers. Methodological belief leads to strong affirmations and firm convictions, not to insipid statements that are least objectionable.

The Felt Sense

Expressions like "I feel it in my bones" and "I have a gut feeling" seek to describe physical sensations in knowing. Often, they are feelings that seem to radiate all over. People describe them as a "glory," a "burning sensation," or "electricity running through me." Knowing includes an ability to recognize and decipher the body's messages. Understanding incorporates verbal, visual, and kinesthetic forms that are subtle and can be grasped clearly only where they are vivid.

Reflection brings us to a process saturated with feeling. Feelings are embodied, affective responses to the biblical text. Our capacity to feel is the response of our entire beings to knowing God and God's word intimately.

> Feelings, then are an important component of the movement toward insight. They are clues to the meaning of our experience. We cannot have transformative insights without them. In the movement toward insight we consider them to be gifts . . . . When we encounter a particular feeling in our experience, we want to think of it as neither inevitable, nor fleeting, nor eternal; we do not want to cling to it or control it, but simply to experience the feeling, to notice it, and reflect on it. True feelings are intimately connected to the sensations of our bodies. Unless we can locate an identified feeling in our body, and our whole body is involved, we have not named a feeling.[7]

Eugene Gendlin in *Focusing* described this bodily knowing as a "felt sense," deriving meaning from a body sensation concerning a particular situation or problem.[8] Reflective activity is attending to these feelings to see what they are saying.

For some people, Bible study takes on an intensity and meaning that seems to be lacking in others. What is the crucial difference? It does not lie in the teacher's technique or in the group members' information about the Bible. The crucial difference seems to be in what happens to people on the inside. It is a process in which a person makes contact with a special kind of bodily awareness.

When we read Scripture, we open ourselves to how the words grasp our entire beings. Words vibrate with our past experiences and our present anxieties. They create pictures in our minds. They call up smells and tastes and sounds. They make the heart beat faster. They fill the head with lightness. Words have a kinesthetic and emotional impact on listeners. If we ignore the emotional effect of language, we miss some of God's addresses to us.

Reflective activity seeks to retrieve some of the creative powers of the biblical text. There is a shift of attention from what lies behind the text to what occurs in front of the text. One important aspect of interpretation is how texts touch the reader, what processes they set in motion, and how these processes influence the reader. The reader asks the question, "What does this text do?" Something happens to those who read. Part of experiential Bible study is a proclamation—"This is the effect of the text on me and my group."

This act of group focusing has simple movements. They seem to flow together, much like an athlete is able to put separate body movements into one fluid motion. Many people who experience meaningful Bible study do this without a conscious awareness of what they are doing. We are trying to describe what happens and the environment that makes it possible.

The first movement is the act of pushing aside the most current immediate concerns. Somehow we must get past this baggage of preoccupation to do serious Bible study. Whatever is preoccupying the mind and body at the moment is temporarily put on hold. This is something like coming into a room so cluttered with stuff that there is no place to sit down. You push things around in order to clear space for yourself. It's like you have walked miles with a heavy backpack. You find a place to stop, set the backpack aside, and sit for a while to enjoy the scenery. Hopefully, prayer does this for you. But we all know how mechanical prayer can be, and often the "busyness" continues. Silent prayer is better—a time to turn in to oneself and to God. For one group, a small candle is lit in the center of the group as a signal to "focus in."

The second movement focuses attention on the biblical text—the words, phrases, sentences, paragraphs that make up the body of Scripture. We set our heavy burdens down and enjoy the scenery of the text. At first we see the whole landscape, the territory of Scripture that can be viewed at one time from our particular vantage point. Our attention then focuses on something in that landscape that draws our attention. This is an awkward moment. We must deliberately avoid trying to decide anything about it. Our first impressions of a landscape are large, vague, formless feelings that defy analysis. We do not have words to describe what we see, lacking labels, identifications, or categories. This is a time of patient waiting, letting the landscape of the text be in its own way.

The next movement is the most difficult. The background, landscape, and scenery of the text are first experienced in our bodies. Let's get it right. The first impression of a biblical text is not a mental experience but a physical one. In other words, it is a feeling. This feeling encompasses everything you "know" about the subject at a given moment. This "sense" wraps around the text and communicates it whole, all at once, rather than word by word or detail by detail. The closest sensory experience is taste; an explosion of total experience; a big, round feeling. This feeling doesn't come in the form of words or separate units of thought but is a single (though often puzzling, surprising, and complex) bodily feeling.

This is like our first sense of a person. Our introduction is not broken down in terms of height, weight, color of hair, complexion, and clothes. Given enough time, we could come up with hundreds of descriptions; but what we see covers all, at once—a single total body sense that is felt, with a sense that I "know" this person or this person is a puzzle to me. This feeling encompasses dozens of different component parts but no specific words.

The feeling contains many details, just as a piece of music contains many notes. A big music production carries hundreds of musical tones and timbres through many different instruments in expanding progressions, but you don't need to know all that to feel it!

There's more. This feeling often has the sense of tying all these component parts into a knot or weaving them into a tight piece of clothing that becomes a wrapping around our bodies. It also wants to be locked up or hidden from us. Our initial reaction is to avoid it and do nothing that would cause us to confront it. Trying not to experience feeling has a way of keeping us from seeing anything too clearly. We are like the people Jesus described as seeing but not seeing, hearing but not hearing.

The next movement seeks to bring this personal bodily knowledge into conscious awareness. The word or words have a way of floating up from the feeling itself rather than from the confused busyness of the mind. The issue here is in finding the right words to describe what God's word is causing to happen in us. Often, this identification may best be described through metaphors, similes, pictures, or stories. What does this feeling bring to memory? What would this feeling do, how would it act, what would it say? Does it have a name? Where would it take a stand?

When the biblical text touches our experience, something shifts on the inside. There is the sense that something lost is found, something hidden is discovered, something tied up is loosed, something cramped finds open space. Someone might say, "I just remembered something I had forgotten." There is that inner confirmation: "Yes, it is something like this . . . ." In fact, the whole body feels better. The felt sense is experienced as a bodily shift. Something falls into place, the heart does its work, and the mind and body connect.

There is a knowing that feels good, a kind of Bible study that we would call "a satisfying experience." This satisfaction might have a sustaining effect over a period of time, continuing far past the actual experience of knowing. In *The Courage to Create*, Rollo May discussed the sustaining quality of such knowing: "I experience a strange lightness in my step as though a great load were taken off my shoulders, a sense of joy on a deeper level that continues without any relation whatever to the mundane tasks that I may be performing at the time."[9]

The final movement is a test. Check the pictures, metaphors, and stories again with the feeling. Perhaps the words will change. If there are other ideas and interpretations that are not a part of the feeling, drop them for another day and another time. Work with the feeling to see if it will lead you to something more.

Surprisingly, these movements work well in a group setting, but it must be a disciplined group setting that understands the rules of focusing. In ordinary group conversation we often stop others from getting far on their inward journey into Scripture. Our additions, reactions, encouragements, and well-intended comments actually prevent people from feeling understood. The skill is simple. Focus on the person without saying anything. If you must speak, ask them to say it again another way. If you must say something else, voice back their points as you understand them.

Each person's experience at any moment is woven into a specific and unique pattern and shape. The way the biblical message touches that unique human pattern cannot be explained and labeled. It has to be discovered, encountered, touched, attended to, and allowed to show itself. The only way to do that is through focused listening.

The purpose of this reflective process is change—something shifts on the inside. We are all people in process, capable of continual change. If we touch people at all, we will touch them "in motion." This reflective or "focusing" process is a way of surfacing felt needs that have been delayed or blocked or knotted up. The biblical text has a chance of becoming a living word, sharper than a two-edged sword that loosens the wrappings, opens the blocked paths, and gets us moving again.

What do we get from this mind of reflective process? Surprisingly, what we get is commentary. "Living commentary" is not so different from the best exegetical commentaries on the shelves of the scholars but unavailable to millions of people outside of academics. Even if these commentaries were available, the "living documents" have the distinct advantage of being "owned," coming out of the believers' reflective wisdom and confirmed through both the believers' experience and the accurate exegesis of the biblical text.

Lectio Divina

Without this interior "felt sense," the ancient practice of *Lectio Divina* (holy reading) is difficult and unrewarding. I have seen some people simply close down with this exercise because they have no idea what is going on while others are touched deeply and profoundly. *Lectio Divina* is a slow, contemplative praying of the Scriptures initiated in Benedictine monasteries nearly fifteen hundred years ago. If practiced over a period of time, one may discover the "seasons of soul" as a daily, underlying spiritual rhythm. In listening to the "ear of the heart," we attend to our memories and word pictures and listen for God's presence in daily life. The process is simple but powerful, with a vast amount of literature to help us become more practiced in the discipline.

Choose a text and a quiet place.

Focus on breathing, a prayer word, or a "centering" exercise.

Read and reread the text slowly until a sentence, passage, phrase, or word "touches" or "rests" on the heart. The rereading is as important as the reading. The second reading may be spoken so you hear it through the sound of your voice.

Take the word, phrase, or passage into yourself slowly, repeating it until it interacts with the inner world of memories, images, and recollections. Allow this ruminating and pondering to invite you into a prayerful conversation with God. Speak to God through any of these impressions you have found in your heart.

Rest and relax in God's presence with words of thanksgiving and silence.

You can follow the same process as a group exercise. The same text is read three times, followed each time by a period of silence and "circling the group" in sharing words or phrases without commentary. Each reading is heard from a different voice, preferably changing genders. The first reading calls forth a word or phrase that touches the heart. The second reading suggests how the word or phrase has meaning for that day. The third reading asks what Christ is calling us to be or do. There are many variations to this exercise, but all have some involvement in the suggestions of this chapter–the method of belief, the felt sense, and the "lingering heart."

Letting the Imagination Be

Letting our imagination "be" is not as simple as it sounds but much simpler than we might expect. There are no prescribed thoughts or images that must appear. We sit quietly waiting to see what will come through the doors of our minds. We allow whatever will to come to us and open ourselves to it with whatever sense evokes it, whether it be sight, sound, touch, taste, or smell.

In reflecting, we want to see what is there rather than imposing what we want to be there. We simply behold it. Such a letting be concentrates on the ways things are. The way things are is usually concrete—no large abstractions, no great conceptualizations. We take in and concentrate on this moment, this picture, this image, this feeling.

Letting be is not passive. We do not ever simply pass by or let anything come past us. We remain alert to what is happening in the immediate present, in the now. When images and reflections arise spontaneously from within us, they may be all the more startling. They often come from our unconscious, but they may also fix our attention. They are usually oddly mixed combinations of personal peculiarities and familiar human themes. To see what arises in this reflection is the next step. We must look hard, using our mind, our memory, our sense of the past, and our feelings. Reflection acts as a sort of picture frame, marking off the reality it points to from ordinary daily things and making it easier to understand. The framing image makes the work of our imagination safe. Imagination is both hard and soft. It is naturally open. It wants to see everything. That is a large part of its healing power. It includes both the negative and the positive. It naturally renounces denial. It includes everything outside of our normal thought patterns, as well as the grounded, centered ones. Imagination instructs us that seeing what is there means looking directly at what is off-center, at the gaps. When we consent to let be and look at what is there and what is not, we see crowding onto us and into us all the things we usually deny, all that we screen out of our lives. We acknowledge our greed for money, food, things, status, power, and sex. We see our fear, envy, and anger. We see our inertia, our apathy, and our lack of caring.

When I try to describe this in easily understood metaphors, I speak of a film running in the back of our eyes. It is this hop-skip-and-jump presentation of the human experience in film that provides the closest picture of what happens in our images. We do not know how long or how far the gaps are between events in film. The gaps may not ever be perfectly bridged, but at least they are acknowledged. We must acknowledge the gaps between the meaning Scripture discloses and those that the learners harbor in their hearts.

The danger is in being too enamored with our own images. Our own images are important, but they need much more nourishment than what they bring with them. Our images are small. The biblical images are large and rich. The Bible is crammed with broad ranges of pictures about God, of dinner party hosts, of wind, fire, rock, and water. If we do not hear the biblical images, we tend to identify with our own images and push them into the public arena. A tutored and practiced imagination removes us from that trap.

The next movement is a systematic reflection on what we have let be and what comes to us as a result. Imagination helps us sort out what comes to us. Understanding comes from this sorting, finding, and connecting the fragmented parts of our experience. Reflective learning is a collecting and recollecting, allowing our memories to gather all the bits of past, present, and future into a connected necklace of the personal.

The Intuitive Leap

Intuitive learning usually refers to a relatively loose, unstructured, and informal approach to learning that contrasts with a more deliberate, systematic style. The sense of the word implies spontaneity and immediacy, a knowing that is not mediated through a conscious or deliberate, rational process. We know something but we don't know how we know it.

Let us establish the premise that the relationship between intuition and rationality is much richer and more complex than we would generally acknowledge. Rational thought is the result of intentional thinking, drawn out over time, taking place in sequential steps. Intuition is experienced as nonsequential. It just seems to happen when least expected, without the application of specific rules. When you arrive at a conclusion through rational thought, you can trace the processes backward and identify the journey. Intuition is not that easy to explain, and one would be hard pressed to explain the process.

Rationality is often said to precede and follow intuition. We reason, analyze, and gather facts, then comes the breakthrough. Then we go back to reasoning and analyzing again to get some verification of intuition. This seems to be the way minds work, both in individual and group processes. Sometimes, though, it works the other way. Intuition feeds and stimulates rational thought and evaluates the work of rationality.

Both reason and intuition have systematic qualities. They feed each other and work together. This seems to be readily apparent in the informal knowing of everyday life. If Bible study follows this informal knowing pattern, then it seems that we hop back and forth between consciously applied analysis and intuition. The intuitive connections aid the reasoning process. We begin an orderly process of the systematic exegesis of the biblical text, and then something happens. We have a spontaneous hunch and leap to another mind track altogether, and something suddenly "pops" to mind, taking us in a different direction but eventually bringing us back to our original work on the text. At any one point, it would be difficult to say, "I am being intuitive with the text" or "I am being rational with the text."

Although we have a tendency to think differently, reason alone leads to shallow understanding and conviction. It is the difference between reading a travel brochure and making the actual journey. The actual experience draws us to a level of feeling as well as thinking. The systematic relationship between intuition and rationality lets us "enter into" the knowing. Intuition brings us to the knowing implied by the biblical use of "know"—intimate, embodied, unifying, and fertile.

There must be checks on intuition. Frequently, an intuition concerning Scripture is vague and hazy, providing little more than an inkling of direction. Intuitions may only be partly correct, with numerous blind spots. Circumstances have a way of shaping intuition, and circumstances usually boil down to the amount of information a person has to draw on and the precision of that knowledge. Intuition does not come from anywhere. The preparatory work of exegesis supplies the intuitive mind with the "raw" material it needs.

We refuse to believe our minds work like computers. Our thought processes are doing many things at once. When we are doing "work" on a biblical text, that work is being done while we are sleeping, eating, jogging, walking in the woods, or taking care of babies. The work of the mind is still going on while the "thinking" boss is out, putting things together that the boss knows not of. This is what William James meant when he said we learn to swim in winter and ice skate in summer.[10] Gutenberg's mind merged three unlikely elements—the wine press, the process of minting coins, and the stamping of playing cards—to come up with the concept of moveable type. If the church had known that, the printing of the Bible may have been left to someone else.

In summary, we might say intuition is both experiential and conceptual. We may say intuition takes in the experiential cycle completely and all at once. That instant "flash" may contain an extraordinary amount of information.

It is like a train speeding past your field of vision: you don't see any details, just a blur accompanied by sounds—and yet in that instant you know, at the very least, that it was a train . . . . We normally experience and conceive of meaning in a linear fashion, as a sequence of symbols and concepts strung together. An intuitive experience, however, may contain no clear boundaries, no obvious demarcations, and no sequential arrangement. It might contain the essence of the knowledge, the way a seed contains the essence of a tree, or it might contain some details; it might be a fragment of the whole, or almost complete. It will usually contain a richness of meaning that will take an eon to articulate compared to the time it took to apprehend.[11]

Questions Are the Answer

At the heart of reflective activity is the art of asking questions. Reflection comes in making connections, pondering what we already know, experientially and conceptually, with the immediate curiosity about the text. A well-known quote from Rainer Maria Rilke says it best:

I want to beg you as much as I can . . . to be patient toward all that is unsolved in your heart and try to love the questions themselves. . . . Do not seek answers which cannot be given you because you would not be able to live them. And the point is to live everything. Live the questions now. Perhaps you will then gradually, without noticing it, live along some distant day into the answer. . . . Take whatever comes with great trust, and if only it comes out of your own will, out of some need of your innermost being, take it upon yourself and hate nothing.[12]

The questioning method is often called the Socratic method, taken from the ancient philosopher Socrates, who responded to questions by asking more questions. What kinds of questions were the biblical writers seeking to answer when the text was written? In forming our own questions we approach the text with a childlike mind of curiosity and imagination, seeking to give up all of our assumptions and presuppositions about the text. When we see something being done that we have not seen before, we ask all kinds of questions. Curiosity creates this inquisitiveness concerning what the biblical writers were thinking and feeling. There are many questions in the text, waiting for someone to ask them.

Robert McAfee Brown described a scroll that should be placed on a wall for all those to see during experiential Bible study.

BE IT HEREBY ENACTED:
that every three years all people
shall forget whatever they have learned
about Jesus, and begin the study all over again.[13]

When we give up our presuppositions about the text, questions will come faster than we can handle. Before looking at any other sources (commentaries, dictionaries, etc.), we should discover our own questions.

1. Read through the biblical text several times and then ask of it everything that pops into mind. Do this before consulting reference works or other people's questions.

2. Ask questions for which we have no right to expect an answer. Although some questions are left in mystery, we can still ask them. We can now turn to authoritative works. Some of our hunches may be wrong. New questions or the refining of questions may develop. "We can begin by consciously suspending our assurance that we know the answer. We can deliberately bring ourselves to look at the text from unaccustomed angles. We can try with all our powers to come to the text as supplicants with our hands outstretched, entreating it to speak to us in its own right."[14]

3. Some questions will be exegetical in nature. What is the context? What weaves the passage into one piece? What are the important themes or words in the passage? How do several versions of the text differ and why?

4. Remember that the goal in asking good questions is not gathering more information but evoking life-changing insights.

5. Make your questions as simple and clear as possible. Never ask several things in one question. Avoid asking questions that can be answered with yes or no.

6. Ask questions that bring thought and feeling to the text.

7. Ask questions that explore the meanings of symbols, metaphors, and similes. Push toward visual, sensory responses rather than abstractions.

8. Try out the questions on yourself. When it stimulates your thinking/feeling processes, it is likely to have the same effect with a group.

9. Avoid the invasion of group members' privacy. Personal expressions can be made without overexposure or violating privacy.

Questions should be posed in an atmosphere of "invitations to participate," with the suggestions that contributions are not only welcomed but essential to the group's understanding. Frequently, good reflective questions will create an atmosphere of comfortable or uncomfortable silence. The leader must take a deep breath and wait. The reflective turn often takes time for the biblical text to do its inner work in the heart of the believer. Often, people are accustomed to not having their word valued. The discovery of voice for many people is a long, tenuous journey, and much time is needed for those questions to be "loved" into verbal expression.

Ask all the who, what, when, where, why, and how questions that come to your mind. Who are these people in the text? How are they related to each other? What are they doing there? When did this event happen? What were the events before and after this event? What is the location of this event? Why are they responding in this way? How is this situation going to resolve itself? If I were in this situation, how would I be responding? Where am I standing or sitting? What would be the consequences of my response?

Feelings and Subjectivity

An emotional response to Scripture brings us to subjectivity in biblical interpretation. The reflective turn introduces, without apology, the subjective self-involvement of the reader. Subjectivity is tied to emotion and brings another dimension to the stable objectivity of Christian revelation.

Bible study groups pay a heavy price for the denial of feelings. The fear that feelings will "contaminate" the interpretation and bring total subjectivity to interpretation does not happen. What does happen is a return to the text with even more interest and intensity. A return to more exegetical activity provides a needed balance to the emotional response. The reflective turn in experiential Bible study affirms the importance of the accommodation of feelings in the interpretation of biblical texts. Thoughts and feelings are not separable entities in reflection but are interconnected aspects of people's responses. The reflective turn causes us to be aware of various emotional responses in an experiential Bible study group.

People may capitulate to their emotions, believing themselves to be helpless victims of feelings over which they have no control. Group responses may be snap reactions, overreactions, feelings of helplessness, low self-esteem, and extreme susceptibility to attitudes and opinions of others. However, gradually, a group can grow into the accommodation of feelings. Learners recognize and accept emotions that are evoked from the biblical text and seek to integrate those feelings with thinking processes. Their reactions are appropriate to the situation and result in deeper understandings and acceptance of emotional responses of others. There is also a willingness to take other emotional risks with the group. Group leaders must realize that an emotional response to Scripture is an event to which the group members respond with strong feelings of their own. Group members are faced with the problem of coping with their feelings and returning to some psychological balance. Remember: "Everything is debriefable."

Debriefing allows a group to deal with the emotional aspects of the group's life through an expanded range of options. Emotional experiences in group life should be positive in the sense that deeper involvement with the text and with one another is possible. Experiential Bible study will bring intense times in a group's life together, and the accommodation of feelings provides a group with more options and an aid to reentry into a more normal group environment.

Killen and de Beer saw the reflective turn as a circular spiral of experience, feelings, images, insight, and action. "When we enter our experience, we encounter our feelings. When we pay attention to those feelings, images arise. Considering and questioning those images may spark insight. Insight leads, if we are willing and ready, to action."[15] It is to this active behavioral response that we now turn.

NOTES

[1] George Miller, "Thirteen Maxims of the Mind," in *Embracing Contraries: Explorations in Learning and Teaching,* ed., Peter Elbow (New York: Oxford University Press, 1986), 254.

[2] John Dewey, *How We Think: A Restatement of the Relation of Reflective Thinking to the Educative Process* (New York: D. C. Heater and Co., 1933), 210.

[3] Mary Mullino Moore, *Teaching from the Heart: Theology and Educational Method* (Minneapolis: Fortress Press, 1991), 197-98.

[4] Walter Wink, *Transforming Bible Study*, 2d ed. (Nashville: Abingdon Press, 1989), 109-19.

[5] Elbow, *Embracing Contraries*, 261.

[6] Ibid., 273-81.

[7] Patricia O'Connell Killen and John de Beer, *The Art of Theological Reflection* (New York: Crossroad, 1994), 27-28.

[8] Eugene Gendlin, *Focusing* (New York: Everest House, 1978).

[9] Rollo May, *The Courage to Create* (New York: W. W. Norton and Co., 1975), 45.

[10] William James, *Principles of Psychology,* vol. 1 (New York: Dover Publications, 1890), 110.

[11] Philip Goldberg, *The Intuitive Edge: Understanding and Developing Intuition* (Los Angeles: Jeremy P. Tarcher, Inc., 1983), 72.

[12] Rainer Maria Rilke, *Letters to a Young Poet* (New York: Norton Publishing Co. 1954), 34-35.

[13] Robert McAfee Brown, *The Bible Speaks to You* (Philadelphia: Westminster Press, 1965), 87.

[14] Wink, *Transforming Bible Study*, 88.

[15] Killen and de Beer, *Art of Theological Reflection*, 21.

The Reflective Practitioner: Application

Should an honest man wish to become a thief, the necessary action is obvious: he must steal—not just once or just occasionally, but frequently, consistently, taking pains that the business of planning and executing thefts replace other activities which in implication might oppose the predatory life. If he keeps at it long enough, his being will conform to his behavior; he will have become a thief. Conversely, should a thief undertake to become an honest man, he must stop stealing and must undertake actions which replace stealing, not only in time and energy, and perhaps also excitement, but which carries implications contrary to the predatory life, that is, productive or contributive activities.[1]

I continue to struggle in how to name this movement in the experiential cycle. I like the word "practice," but my favorite expression is "active experimentation." I will use these words along with application, knowing there is a subtle difference but choosing to say that they all point to action and behavior.

Action describes a person's character. We are not the first to believe that. Aristotle saw that virtue and wise character are formed by the repeated choosing and doing of right actions. "Only an utterly senseless person can fail to know that our characters are the result of our conduct."[2] Behavior is a result of actions that have been repeated over and over in such a way as to become coherent and independent responses. Insight is not enough. Effort and will are crucial. One of the most common illusions in learning is that insight produces change, and the most common disappointment in learning is that it does not. Insight is instrumental to change, often an essential part of the process, but does not directly achieve it.

For the Bible to be understood at any level involves both choosing and willing. Here we have a problem. Most of us know more than we choose and will to do. A problem in understanding may not be lack of knowledge, but lack of will. In this case, additional knowledge does become irrelevant, because no complete understanding is possible. This does not mean that the knowledge itself is

irrelevant, only that, for us, it cannot become useful knowledge until we are
ready to act on it.

Sometimes profound change occurs spontaneously, without effort or intention. Other changes are often slight, subtle, unnoticed in one's ways of dealing
with oneself and others. Over a long period of time these changed actions may
achieve a change of being. One feels oneself to be profoundly different without
knowing how or why. And what if one is asked, "Well, what did you learn?" or
"What was the main insight?" One may stumble about without being able to
name what exactly has changed, yet may know certainly that there has been a
transition, a shifting of life patterns. This sort of change is rare. We can't count
on it or make it happen, and when it occurs it is a bonus. Usually change, when
it occurs at all, follows long and arduous wanting and willing.

Change in being usually follows change in behavior. Since what we are is
expressed in what we do, if we want to change what we are, we must undertake a
new mode of action. Entrenched forces in us will protest and resist. New learning
is often experienced as difficult, unpleasant, forced, unnatural, and anxiety-pro-
voking. We discover strong winds of resistance that oppose the behavior we
expect of ourselves. Some emerging obstacles will seem insurmountable.
Changed behavior can be sustained only by considerable effort. Change will
occur only if such action is maintained over a long period of time.

Learning that is moving toward change involves taking action to implement
insights derived from reflection. The movement toward change often begins with
the recognition of discontent with the way one is living. This begins the exploration of new roles, relationships and actions, and planning a new course of
action. The problem is that the new course of action is so threatening or demanding that we are too paralyzed or immobilized to undertake it. Thus, the actions of
compromise, stalling, self-deception, and the old churchy term of "backsliding."
The new insight brings an overwhelming response but an inability to act.

Application and Behavior

Behavior is the outward evidence and manifestation of belief coming from the
momentum and energy of experience, exegesis, and reflection—congruence
between belief and action. Application is the strengthening of intentional behavior to reflect conviction. What is known can be identified by changes in behavior
and must never be equated with verbal responses only.

The parable of the two sons in Matthew 21:28-32 focuses the issue of application on change and obedience. The call to both is the same: "Go and work."
The first son said, "I will not go." But something happened to him. He had been
curt and rebellious, choosing his own way. But he changed (repented) and went.

We don't know the quality of his work or his long-term staying power. But he acted in obedience and went. The second son said he would go, but he did not go. The second son was not insincere, enthusiastically said he would work, and probably intended to obey, but the acid test of application does not happen, and what he verbalizes dies through inaction.

The application of the word will result in right action and right conduct. Human activity is never neutral. It is either in obedience or disobedience to God's claim on us. Paul tells us in 1 Corinthians 10:31, "So, whether you eat or drink, or whatever you do, do everything for the glory of God." All activity is subject to Jesus' claim of lordship. "Why do you call me 'Lord, Lord' and do not do what I tell you?" (Luke 6:46). Doing, or leaving undone, is related to actions toward one's neighbor, either positively or negatively. Jesus censors the Pharisees for doing their work in order to be seen by others (Matt 23:5). But the deed of the woman who anointed him is seen as a lovely act (Matt 26:10).

Right action is grounded in Christ and made possible by the power of his spirit. Christ is the model for the application of the word. In contrast to much application that is inactive, the believer is seen as the doer of the word. "But be doers of the word, and not merely hearers who deceive themselves. For if any are hearers of the word and not doers, they are like those who look at themselves in the mirror; for they look at themselves and, on going away, immediately forget what they were like" (Jas 1:22-24).

The biblical language of application is seen concretely in the work of our hands and feet. Hands and feet are expressions of the total person: "If your hand or your foot causes you to stumble" (Matt 18:8); "Look at my hands and my feet; see that it is I myself" (Luke 24:39). The hands show a person's total activity, a symbol of human power, competence, and dexterity. Washing the hands purifies but also affirms innocence and a clear conscience (Ps 26:6; Job 17:9). Something made by human hands clarifies the distinction between God's actions and our actions (Mark 14:58; Heb 9:11, 24). The feet are a concrete way of expressing the walk of a person, translating knowing into practice. Walking is the way one conducts life (Gen 5:24; Rom 8:4). 1 John 1:6-7 tells us to walk in light rather than darkness. This walking came to be known as "the way," and Jesus can be followed en route, "on the way" with the disciples (Matt 5:25; 15:32; Mark 8:3; 10:52).

The Application of Scripture: Proclamation

Ultimately, the application of Scripture takes place through preaching, teaching, and learning. The actual purpose of Scripture is not merely explanation, but proclamation. Although people may go away with new understandings and impressions, their lives will still remain untouched. The "horizon" of the listeners must be fused with the horizon of the text in true preaching and teaching.

It is true that there are depths of meaning in the text of Scripture that remain hidden until the text is preached and taught. Any application of the text is somewhat limited until it faces the crucial question of how it is heard in the church.[3] The ultimate content of Scripture is a word in which God comes in judgment and in mercy. This content has to be taught and heard and have its fruits in life before anyone can rightly understand its nature. In other words, it is understood only in the dynamic of teaching and learning. If the word of Scripture had its full reality in its original situation only when it was proclaimed and heard, it recovers that reality today when it is proclaimed and heard. Frequently the assumption is made that, without further research or assistance, one can move from the original meaning to the modern meaning as though there were no serious problems in making that transition.

In active experimentation with the text, there is both a forward and backward movement in the learning cycle. Active experimentation promotes lived Christian faith but also leads into deeper reflection and exegesis of the biblical text. The "doing" of God's will is a source of revelation, as expressed so precisely in John's Gospel: "If you continue in my word, you are truly my disciples; and you will know the truth and the truth will make you free" (John 8:31-32). By "doing the truth," learners come to the truth that sets them free.

Dramatic Change

A new perspective that transcends an old one may come from a sudden insight, but it also comes as a gradual awareness. The transformative experience is often described as a leap of faith, a creative leap, a contextual shift, or a reframing of experience. But action brings a "grounding" of that experience in a commitment to the new perspective. This is a sense of transcendence, a process of change that originates in one's heart and expands outward into the hands and feet, with a vision of freedom and a sense of the potentiality to become what one is not.

Sometimes change may proceed with increasing momentum and finally to solid completion. Such a change is experienced as an absolute turnaround, a conversion, and may even call for a change of name. Jacob's name is changed to Israel, Simon's to Peter, and Saul's to Paul. Even then, change is often partial and provisional:

> The homosexual man gets married, has children, but never feels
> entirely safe with women . . . the depressive character can work, may
> occasionally feel glad to be alive but is not likely ever to be described

as of sunny disposition. He who undertakes to transform himself, therefore, should think not of all or none, sick or well, miserable or happy, but of more or less, better or worse. He should undertake only to do what he can, to handle something better, to suffer less.[4]

Following the lead of James Loder, Ross Keane studied the transformational change in himself and five others committed to a faith lifestyle.[5] A transformative learning experience begins with disorientation, an inner disequilibrium in which the harmony of the self is disturbed, yet the problem is neither understood nor satisfactorily named. Old perspectives are perceived to be inadequate in the light of this new awareness. A process of movement follows. It is important to identify some of these possible movements toward action. As people move into application, some of the following behaviors may become evident.

1. A move from reliance on a limited number of sources of knowledge and assistance to multiple sources.
2. A move from uncritical acceptance of advice to a more critical stance.
3. A move from viewing "helpers" as a source of instant answers to viewing them as resources in finding one's own answers.
4. A move from rigid boundaries of thinking and feeling to a testing of boundaries.
5. A move from reliance on others' sense of truth to one's own inner sense.
6. A move from disregarding physical and emotional changes to trusting the messages they contain.
7. A move from insensitivity to feeling to interpretation of the rich contrasts and variations in feelings.
8. A move from "stumbling around" in change to identifying and naming changes in behavior.
9. A move from fearfully clinging to the known to risking and experimenting with new behavior.
10. A move from resistance, avoidance, and denial behaviors to seeing them as challenges and invitations to change.
11. A move from silence to a satisfactory voicing and describing of experience.
12. A move from an acknowledged truth about the self at a rational level to recognition and acceptance of a personal truth.

Thomas Groome describes the possibilities of the transcendent, or revelatory, potential as a process of reasoning, remembering, and imagining: "The deeper our levels of reasoning, remembering and imagining, the more likely we are to uncover the transcendent that is immanent in our lives, the 'beyond' present in the every day."[6]

Dramatic change often brings people to marginality with everyday life and can be terrifying but also liberating and transforming. Both in practice and reflection, our life gains the greatest part of its richness from experiences of stepping outside the taken-for-granted reality of everyday life into the mystery that surrounds us on all sides. Dramatic changes, those that deliberately and intentionally turn to a new life, not only are seeking to change themselves but to change the mainstream of society as well.

Experiential learning says people often work out changes in behavior verbally before actually attempting them. Application encourages the development of new behavior at a verbal level before trying to live it out. If Scripture evokes a desire for change, learners should have opportunities to explore alternatives. The challenge of application is to harness that "want" and "will" energy from the other movements. A "learning leap" must be made at this point. Bible study moves from the reality inside the group experience (experience, exegesis, reflection) to the reality of everyday life outside the group experience. Group members are led to focus and verbalize their awareness on situations in their personal lives. This process begins with the attempts to verbalize a different way of living. What people see in Scripture becomes the single most important factor in how they practice their faith.

Application activities often lose their steam because they do not come from "want" energy. Application processes suggesting "oughts" and "shoulds" do not carry that energy. "Oughts and shoulds are simply not a strong enough energy source to enable us to take the risk of moving out into the territory of actually changing our behavior."[7] Wants and wills, our heart's deep desire, coming out of conviction and commitment carry that energy. "Now that I know this about the text and this about myself I want to . . . , I will to . . . , I choose to . . . ."

Several group processes can facilitate this process:

1. Imaginative activities–guiding learners to imagine realistic situations "back home" and determining what they have learned that could be applicable.

2. Truth with a little "t"–tentative statements coming out of "hunches" and "lucky guesses" concerning what is "true" about the real world.

3. Identifying learnings–exploring what we have learned about ourselves during the other movements. Much of this can be done through sentence completion statements:

>   I am beginning to learn . . .
>   I was surprised that I . . .
>   I was disappointed that I . . .

I expect to . . .
I'm afraid that I . . .
I hope . . .

4. When people grasp a biblical truth, the application turn can be made by asking questions: "Do I?" "Would I?" "How would I?" "What would happen if?" This is an accountability step—working through what is emerging in us and beginning to act upon it.

Goal-setting and Covenants

One of the best ways to begin verbalizing "wants" is through a goal-setting process. Goals should be short-term (a week or less) and behavioral in nature. A short-term goal is not intended to include everything in the want statements, but it does "ground" the want energy in concrete behavior. Robinson in *The Transforming Power of the Bible* established criteria for short-term goals:[8]

1. *Measurable*–possible to do within a given time frame
2. *Desirable*–flowing from want energy, not "shoulds" and "oughts"
3. *Conceivable*–possible to write in a few sentences that make sense to others
4. *Believable*–a conviction that I can really do it
5. *Doable*–a concrete behavior that I can see myself doing
6. *Achievable*–within my power to achieve
7. *Controllable*–within my control to do and not dependent on the responses of others
8. *Valuable*–within my overall value system and growth producing

Another important aspect of movement toward right action is in the establishing of covenants. Covenants are a way of expressing commitments and another way of grounding the want and will energy. For application of Scripture to be effective, these silent expectations must be articulated and understood. Commitments come out of deeply personal expectations, hopes, and dreams. Covenants are made with people but also with Scripture. Our encounter with biblical texts is a personal, covenantal relationship. A covenant simply spells out in concrete ways our expectations and what our intentions toward these expectations. Consider the following values of covenants:

1. A covenant makes possible a relationship between people that can be known, understood, and depended on.

2. Through a covenant, an appeal can be made by means of the relationship. Covenants sustain commitments and relationships. They help us get through the inevitable resistance and obstructions.

3. Covenants provide a way of testing priorities. They prevent us from spending time on trivialities.

4. Covenants ensure repeatable experiences. People who develop lasting relationships have deeper experiences because of recurring cycles of life together. Covenants provide a structure for repeatable experiences.

5. Covenants set limits on the future. We bind some things about the future in order to preserve, in both the present and the future, those things we consider of value. A covenant is a responsible way of dealing with the future in the present.

The Token

I am indebted to Avery Brooke's *Learning and Teaching Christian Meditation* for insight into the "token." The token is exactly what it sounds like—some small thing that betokens the insight you have received. It should be as simple as writing a letter, making a phone call, or saying a prayer. It should also be something you can do within the next twenty-four hours.[9]

Thinking of a token is difficult for several reasons. The new insight into Scripture may have opened our eyes to larger horizons, and we want to pick something of significance and importance, something more than a "token." A token is an action "trimmed to size." Secondly, we may have difficulty finding the right metaphor or symbol related to our insight. This is not important. What is important is that it be your token. If you think it betokens the insight, then it does.

If tokens are so simple and difficult, why bother? We need to bother because insights are fleeting and can be gone in a moment or become so unreachable that we soon lose interest in the lofty ideal. The token brings you back to earth and brings something of your message with you.

Most of our insights leave when we leave a study group. We shake them off or leave them parked in the parking lot. They soon fade away into dim memory, not because they were too vivid but because they were too much. The change demands too much from us. It is less painful if we put the insight aside. It was an ideal we could not reach, a change we could not risk. "The token acts as a bridge between the insight and where you are. It offers a chance for a small and possible step in the direction of the insight, so that you don't give up before you begin."[10]

A token is something we carry away with us that will bring us back to the insight within the next twenty-four hours—something we will run into again amid the ongoing events of life, something that connects us to the larger frame of our biblical insight.

I discovered, almost by accident, that focusing on a lectionary text for all ages and continuing that theme in worship and preaching was a powerful impetus for learning in following the twenty-four-hour rule. Much more is retained if the text comes by us again, even within the next hour, giving us sometimes startling insight that "we have been this way before" and "we learn what we already know."

Change in Behavior and the Study Group

For learning to be complete, the formulations of change must be produced in actual behavior. Here is where the words "apply" or "execute the understanding" or "practice" or "active experimentation" come into play—to denote the acting out of discovery and insight. The most difficult part of applying new learning is in making the transitions from the study group into the outside world. A learner may have valuable new insights, even transforming ones, but not enough competence to change the "living environment" in a significant way. Many new insights are lost because they never become integrated into the environment.

The dynamics of the learning group become critical factors in the trying out of new behaviors. New behaviors may be tried out under moderate stress in a study group. The group stimulates and encourages the new. An atmosphere of acceptance in risk-taking is critical during the process. Providing feedback on how new behavior is perceived is necessary for growth and change. No part of the learning process is more loaded with dynamics than a person's movement toward change. Exploring these dynamics can often lead a group into a totally different direction, with a return to Scripture for direction, illumination, and guidance. The small group provides the most safe and secure place for this search, which often seems like a groping in the darkness with no map or compass.

Feedback

The educational world wobbled and shifted a little on its axis in 1946 in an unlikely place called Bethel, Maine. Kurt Lewin and staff designed a two-week program encouraging skills in group discussion and decision-making. During each session, researchers made detailed observations and recordings of what was happening in the group. Some of the participants asked to be a part of the observer sessions, and Lewin agreed to this unusual request. As the observers reported to the group, one of the participants, a woman, disagreed with the

observer's perception of her behavior; other participants agreed with her assertion. A lively and energetic discussion followed. Near the end of the conference,
all the participants were invited to bring perceptions of what had happened
during the day's sessions. A significant innovation in training and group dynamics was established. Learning is best facilitated in an environment where there is
tension between immediate, concrete experience and analytic detachment. By
bringing the two together in an open atmosphere, a learning environment is created that is characterized by remarkable vitality, energy, and creativity.

This experience led to the National Training Lab in Group Development in
Bethel and the birth of T-groups, encounter groups, and field theory (helping-
hindering forces). Terms such as "feedback," "nothing never happens," and
"everything is debriefable" began to emerge. You might hear something like this
at the end of a session: "If you have anything to say about the session say it now,
so that we may all hear and learn."

The ability and willingness to communicate effectively are the keys to experiential Bible study. Communication effectiveness is based on the ability to
maintain effective contact, regardless of the situation. One specific area of communication may require additional thought. That is the area of giving and
receiving feedback.

One of the most important skills for enhancing the growth possibilities of
people is through the proper use of feedback. Feedback may be viewed as
supportive feedback (reinforcing an ongoing behavior) and change-oriented feedback (indicating that a change in behavior is possible and appropriate). In this
sense, all feedback is positive and potentially growth enhancing. "The purpose of
all feedback should be to assist an individual in maintaining or enhancing his or
her present level of effectiveness or appropriateness."[11]

Clarence Jordan's experience with feedback at Koinonia Farm in Americus,
Georgia, gives testimony to the power of feedback. Only in practicing the principles of feedback (speaking truth in love) did the group break the logjam that was
keeping them away from the biblical concepts of Christian community.

Feedback is not easy, often bringing with it a sense of drama, anticipation,
and sometimes fear. Surprisingly, responses often involve the five stages that
Elisabeth Kubler-Ross described for people confronting death and dying: shock
and denial, anger, bargaining, depression, and, finally, acceptance.[12]

Two major principles govern the use of feedback. The first principle relates
to how feedback is conducted. This principle can be paraphrased, "I can't tell you
how you are, and you can't tell me what I see." The person giving feedback is
responsible for relating the situation as he or she observes it. The person receiving
feedback is responsible for relating what he or she meant, felt, or thought. Only
the person giving feedback can tell what is observed in behavior.

The second principle is that feedback supports growth. We cannot see ourselves as others see us. An experiential Bible study group will give us many insights into the behavior of ourselves and others. Although people may be aware of their own insights, they may be able to stretch themselves and grow by paying attention to feedback from others. This principle can be paraphrased, "I can't tell you what you see and you can't tell me how I am." Although feedback may be uncomfortable at times, we may look back later and realize that feedback was the spark that inspired a significant, transforming change in behavior.

Learning Our Way Out:
Completing the Learning Cycle

We must say again that all processes of learning cycle theory are associated with changes in behavior. Learning has occurred when individuals adjust or modify behavior. The movement and momentum of the learning cycle are toward change. Although insight and understanding are a part of learning, the learning process is completed only when individuals actually produce new behavior, either in an unfamiliar situation or in a situation that was previously experienced as unsatisfying or lacking in growth-producing actions.

Skill in all phases of the cycle is required for effective learning. Many people do not know how to learn effectively, and our predispositions toward certain learning styles shape our learning effectiveness. Although our primary objective in experiential Bible study is the transforming experience with Scripture, we may also be teaching "learning how to learn" at the same time. Learning to learn may be as fundamental as anything else that is done.

It should be clear by now that the interaction between movements is complex. No one goes through the process step by step. It is always possible that we become fixed at some level prior to application because changing the way we live and act is sometimes frightening and always emotionally demanding.

People leave study groups with new insights into Scripture and with "wanting" and "willing" to live in a different way. Hopefully, they have tried out some of these new behaviors with an understanding and accepting group. Now they must face life and living in environments that are the same and with people who are wondering: "What's wrong with . . . ? What's happened to . . . ?" It is important to note that, on the diagram of the experiential cycle, there is an arrow from "applying" to "experiencing." This is meant to indicate that the actual application of the learning is a new experience that is to be explored inductively, also. People need to be able to return to their groups with examples and stories coming from their new actions. These experiences have become the bases for new experiences and a new learning cycle. But again, there is a warning. There is value in verbalizing change, how others will respond to these changes, and how they will respond to responses. However, such discussions are not substitutes for new living.

Integration: The Call to Courage

Different combinations of relating experience, exegesis, reflection, and application will create symbolic, behavioral, affective, and perceptual complexities. Integration can be described as a centering experience, providing a holistic perspective that carries on in a flow of experience.

The pinnacle of development in experiential learning is integrity. For David Kolb, integrity is the master virtue that integrates value and fact, meaning and relevance, and the specialized virtues of courage, love, wisdom, and justice.[13] In moving from practice back to experience, exegesis, and reflection, we seek to place experiential Bible study in the field of practical theology. When we act, think about, and reflect on our actions, we have become "reflective practitioners."[14] In other words, we express what we know by what we do and by the way in which we do it. We know more than we can say, and we can say "thanks be to God" for that! By reflection in action, we turn thought back on itself, thinking about what we are doing as we do it. We see ourselves conducting an "action experiment" on the spot, in our tracks—an experiment of testing our new way of seeing a situation and, at the same time, trying to change the situation for the better.

In Bible study, we have called those four movements experience, exegesis, reflection, and application. Let's say it in language we all understand—throw out the hook, move to the book, take a good look, and see if it took. This reminds me of my childhood fear of polio. I can remember the day when the Salk vaccine was announced in the daily newspaper. I also remember the terminology used for all inoculations and vaccinations. It has to take!

The prime function of integrity and integrative knowledge is to stand between what is known and the ever-novel predicaments and dilemmas in which we find ourselves. The goal is to guide us through these straits in such a way that we not only survive, but perhaps make a new contribution to knowledge for generations to come.[15] In integrative learning, knowledge comes from viewing predicaments through the four basic knowledge structures (concrete experience, reflective observation, abstract conceptualization, and active experimentation) and then acting sensibly and purposively.

The primary integrated virtue of experiential Bible study is courage—pushing forward when circumstances signal danger and retreat. There is no fear in church life like the fear of getting Scripture wrong. One questionable interpretation ripples through church life quickly, pushing the creative interpreter toward marginality. We could not count the number of people who have been marginal-ized in church life because of some interpretation that brings the response, "I never heard that before." For that fear we pay a heavy price. The result is "the strange silence of the Bible in the church" that James Smart so prophetically described in 1970.

> But let the deeds be done unobtrusively, not by any concerted plan of any faction but as the result of factors that are at work unconsciously in all of us, and let the surface appearance be maintained so that what is happening below the surface escapes the notice of most people, and we could awaken one day to find ourselves a church almost totally alienated from the Scriptures.[16]

Better to say nothing than to say it incorrectly. The opinion of others and the stark warning against heresy paralyzes the expression of creative interpretations. We are always looking over our shoulder to determine the opinion and accept-ance of others; the dark cloud of censorship is a continual threat.

"A heavy personal investment in the good opinion of others can cause people to misinterpret the Scriptures. . . . The brave souls who dare to challenge the theological tenants of the church may suffer ostracism for their interpretive insights."[17] People move between the fears of too much necessity or too much possibility in the process of biblical interpretation. The independent person is unheeding of any need or opinion but his or her own. A dependent person, on the other hand, is too much bogged down in the opinion of peers. We do not work in a vacuum. Interdependence between the believer and the church pro-vides space for creative interpretation and application in the context of love and responsibility.

Integrity in biblical application is a creation, not an imposition; a call to con-tinually create, not simply to adapt and adjust. It will lead to the creative and purposive act, an investment in the future of life, even though we may not be around to see it unfold. The integrative act in the life of the believer will bring startling new creative interpretations. You can count on it. No feedback in expe-riential Bible study groups is more important than continual and consistent encouragement. Each one of us must take the responsibility to "publish" (declare) our considered interpretations, using all the rich resources both internally and externally that God has given us. It is a freedom we take for ourselves and give to others. What happens to you when you are confronted with God's word? After you have done the experiential work on the text, listen to the text again, listen to your group, listen to the church, but never forget to follow the leadings of your heart, hands, and feet.

Practices

All of these activities, events, and practices have the possibility of being filled with the knowledge of God.[18] What movements are we making, what words do we say, what gestures do we make, and what relationships do we enter? All these actions result in specific behaviors of walking, talking, singing, eating, telling stories, blessing children, caring for the sick, burying the dead, breaking bread, and keeping Sabbath. Perhaps practicing hospitality to strangers is the most powerful but also the most difficult. The practice of Christian faith is physical and embodied—the movement of feet to specific places and the movement of hands in giving and receiving with a "priest at every elbow."

There will always be those among us who are concerned that these actions are done appropriately, so we must practice them so they are done correctly. I don't think so! Many times they are not done properly, and so what? Sometimes the awkwardness and vulnerability of the practices make them more memorable and meaningful. But over time, odd and improvised acts will bring a knowing. All the people of God need to do is smile and wink at one another. We know!

Since my early thirties, I have experienced a malady of trembling hands, or "essential tremor." When I held out my hands to show a doctor this problem, he simply said, "Stop holding your hands out like that." I assumed it wasn't serious, and it wasn't, for it hasn't changed in more than thirty-five years. Still, it created an incessant watching of hands, my own and others, and has led me to believe that hands tell the story of Christian behavior and practice.

Practice brings us to specific behaviors. Some things in the Christian life can only be done—not simply studied, examined, or interpreted, but practiced in active participation. Otherwise, we miss most of what is important. The strange reticence of many who resist active, embodied learning is puzzling. We are more self-conscious in activity. When some are watching rather than participating, we are aware of their eyes making judgments about the gracefulness of our actions. Perhaps it is because church actions and practices are distinct and intimate, somewhat strange and odd, peculiar and bold. They are unusual enough to be watched closely and critiqued carefully, making us vulnerable to others' observations. Shaking hands are hard to hide!

As a child, I watched my mother bathe my invalid father's paralyzed left side, carefully washing his hand, arm, leg, and foot. It seemed natural for me to want to bathe the brows and foreheads of the desperately ill whom I visited in hospitals. In performing baptisms, I almost always thought of my mother bathing my father and the countless hours we prayed that he would be resurrected to new life. Pushing the hair back and wiping the foreheads of the newly baptized made me aware of how my hands were shaking uncontrollably.

I can go on with simple practices done with shaking hands: holding a hymnal rather than watching words on a screen and holding a Bible in one hand and gesturing with the other. The impossible task of holding a microphone without trembling. Pouring water over the feet and the enormously intimate act of drying feet with a towel. Wrapping my hands around the clasped hands of a person sitting next to me, saying, "May the peace of Christ be with you," and hearing back, "And also with you." Locking fingers and hands with grieving wives, husbands, sons, and daughters at funerals. Trying, and always failing, to pass communion trays without causing the cups to rattle. Taking bread from hands that have sifted, stirred, and kneaded, and breaking it, saying, "This is Christ's body broken for you. Take and eat and may it feed the hunger of your soul."

As a reflective practitioner, I must always ask, "What is it I am doing when I do these things?" And I must answer, "I don't know!" In order to get the answer, I must think about what I am doing each time and observe myself doing it. It is Christ's spirit and, may I say, John Dewey's spirit (exploration, action, reflection) moving among us. We practice with one another. We are all doing the same thing, perhaps all of us with trembling hands.

Our son, Jud, as a three-year-old, said it best. While watching his mother dress one morning, he brought her to quick awareness by saying, "You know, Mom, skin is very important." I should have known. The thing I miss most about pastoring is the touching. I miss the children hanging on, the horseplay with teenagers, the firm handshakes and the soft hugs (not gender-specific) of men and women of all ages, the hands on other hands, heads, faces, shoulders, arms, and feet.

Through the primal act of touch, we finally see and understand. Touch is the "contact lens" through which we apply, practice, and actively experiment with the faith. Jesus says to the disciples, "Look at my hands and my feet: [no clothes to cover] see that it is myself. Touch me and see" (Luke 24:39).

NOTES

[1] Allen Wheelis, *How People Change* (New York: Harper & Row Publishers, 1973), 102.

[2] Thomas Groome, *Sharing Faith* (San Francisco: HarperCollins Publishers, 1991), 271.

[3] This is a major point in the prophetic work by James Smart, *The Strange Silence of the Bible in the Church* (Philadelphia: Westminster Press, 1970), 28-38.

[4] Wheelis, *How People Change*, 106-107.

[5] A summary of this work is found in Jack Mezirow, *Transformative Dimensions of Adult Learning* (San Francisco: Jossey-Bass Publishers, 1991), 177-80.

[6] Groome, *Sharing Faith*, 197.

[7] Wayne Robinson, *The Transforming Power of the Bible* (New York: Pilgrim Press, 1984), 86.

[8] Ibid., 86-87.

[9] Avery Brooke, *Learning and Teaching Christian Meditation* (Cambridge: Cowley Publications, 1990), 48-51.

[10] Ibid., 51.

[11] Hank Karp, "The Lost Art of Feedback," in *The 1987 Annual: Developing Human Resources*, ed. Pfeiffer (San Diego: University Associates, 1987), 237-46.

[12] Elisabeth Kubler-Ross, *Death and Dying* (New York: Macmillan, 1970).

[13] David Kolb, *Experiential Learning: Experience as the Source of Learning and Development* (Englewood Cliffs NJ: Prentice-Hall, Inc., 1984), 222.

[14] Donald Schon, *The Reflective Practitioner: How Professionals Think in Action* (New York: Basic Books, 1983).

[15] David Kolb, *Experiential Learning*, 225.

[16] Smart, *Strange Silence*, 15.

[17] Cedric B. Johnson, *The Psychology of Biblical Interpretation* (Grand Rapids: Zondervan Publishing House, 1983).

[18] Jossey-Bass is publishing "The Practices of Faith Series." See Dorothy C. Bass, *Practicing Our Faith: A Way of Life for a Searching People*, 1997; and *Receiving the Day: Christian Practices for Opening the Gift of Time*, 2000. Also, see Stephanie Paulsell, *Honoring the Body: Meditations on a Christian Practice* (San Francisco: Jossey-Bass Publishers, 2000).

Come and Die: Leadership

Let the same mind be in you that was in Christ Jesus, who, though he was in the form of God, did not regard equality with God as something to be exploited, but emptied himself, taking the form of a slave, being born in human likeness. And being found in human form, he humbled himself and became obedient to the point of death—even death on a cross. (Phil 2:5-8)

We may have trouble identifying the problem in the Philippian church. It may not have been a big problem at all—just little problems stacking up. However, the Philippian church was in distress. One sure sign of stress is that the little things begin to get to us. We encounter pettiness, small-mindedness, magnifying differences, and concentrating on trivial matters. The little deals suddenly become big deals. People become more aloof and insulated. All the energy goes down the drain of more "oughts" and "shoulds."

Paul's answer to littleness was a big answer. The greatest christological statement ever written seems to be a response to small-mindedness and degrading meanness. But the problem may have been bigger than that, and one we know well. The problem was individualism, a selfish eye, a pompous mind, an aloof spirit, an ear hungry for praise and adoration, and a hand that served self.

All of us are trained in individualism. We have been taught to be independent, competitive, and aggressive. Our minds are filled with perceptions of ourselves as individuals. Our relationships with others, even our own kin, are marked by distance and suspicion, concealed by the respectable cover of reserve. We are isolated, insoluble, unblendable, and incompatible, like oil and water.

Paul's answer to individualism is this: "Make my joy complete, be of the same mind, having the same love, being in full accord and of one mind. . . . Let the same mind be in you that was in Christ Jesus." What is this mind? This is the mind of the Christian educator. From Philippians 2, I would like to describe the mind of Christian educators and, by implication, the leaders of experiential Bible study.

First, this mind becomes a learner; there's a willingness to give up what we know. Jesus Christ came into this world as a learner. He was born of a human mother and developed in the same way as all infants develop. He ate, drank, slept, cried, and learned to walk. Philippians 2 says that he emptied himself, taking on weakness. What did he know? He knew the same things that children of his age knew. He came as a helpless infant, not as an adult, born into a humble family in a conquered and subjected land. Most of his life was spent as a child and youth.

He was not born with knowledge of language or culture. He learned language from his parents. He learned to play from his peers. He learned a trade from his father. He learned to party from his community. He studied the Scriptures like all in his time studied. He went through the world in wide-eyed wonder and profound gratitude, learning from all that he observed.

Hebrews 5:8 says, "Although he was a Son, he learned obedience through what he suffered." Through "obedient learning," Jesus accepted death. For him, death is the result of learning obedience. For the rest of us, death is a necessity. That is one of the significant differences between Jesus and the rest of us.

During our brief one-year excursion on the mission field, Lela and I began picking up the phrase "incarnational missions." The missionaries in West Africa taught by example the meaning of this phrase. Whatever else it may mean, it carries the idea of beginning to learn all over again, much like a helpless infant. We were immersed into a different world and a different culture. Like children, we were seeing everything new, learning to see, hear, speak, eat, and play like newborn infants.

This drastic personal reorientation of becoming ignorant of everything is repugnant and repelling to most of us. The discarding or setting aside of our intellectual identities is almost sacrilege. After all, we have made many personal sacrifices of time, energy, and money to get where we are educationally. People will give up money, positions, and status but will cling doggedly to what they know!

Second, this mind is like-minded with others through identification. Philippians 2 says that Jesus took the form of a servant and became like us. Taking the form of a servant is a distinct form of teaching. Walter Wink in *Transforming Bible Study* said that the leader willingly sacrifices what she or he has learned in order to discover a fraction of it in others.[1] Those who are rich in information and training are invited to become poor so that we might make others rich. But servanthood is only half of the Philippians phrase. Without identification, servanthood comes to a dead end.

Jesus was not only found to be a servant. He was found to be "like us." Those who came into contact with Jesus "found" him to be like they were. The miracle of the Christian faith is God becoming like us. John 2:25 says that Jesus did not need anyone to tell him what we were like. He had an "experiential knowledge" of what was in everyone.

To be liked-minded is to find our lives centered in compassion. Compassion is a different form of love seen only in identification. It is the way I see weakness and deficiency in another person. The opposite of compassion is lack of connectedness between ourselves and the vulnerabilities in others. This aloofness inclines us toward a dwelling on differences. "I am somehow different than they are." The Pharisee stood in the temple and prayed, "God, I thank you that I am not like other people" (Luke 18:11). This was the big problem in the Philippian church—lack of a connectedness and dwelling on difference. If we are looking for it, we can find it in a hundred different ways.

But Jesus is "God with us." He is one of us. Hebrews describes Jesus as becoming like us in all ways, "yet without sin" (Heb 4:15). He does not merely sympathize with us. He does not simply stand beside our sickbed. He takes our sicknesses upon himself. No matter how much he abhors our sickness, he refuses to dissociate himself from us.

A story tucked away in 1 Chronicles 11:17-19 gives us a beautiful picture of identification. It is repeated again in 2 Samuel 23:15-17 and must be a narrative indelibly impressed on the memory of Israel. The Hebrews loved to tell this story! The Philistines were encamped at Bethlehem and Jerusalem. David, engaging in guerrilla warfare, whimsically asked (longed for) the cool water found in Bethlehem's deep well. He was not dying from thirst. He just wanted it! Three of the men broke through the ranks of the Philistines, risked their lives, and brought the water to him. David held the water and responded, "The LORD forbid that I should do this. Can I drink the blood of the men who went at the risk of their lives?" He would not drink it. That water from Bethlehem's well had suddenly become holy water. David poured it out as an offering to the LORD.

If ministry is only seen in servanthood, then disdain and despair are soon to follow. You serve and they do not respond. You plan and no one comes. They seem to be indifferent, unresponsive, and apathetic. "Look at all we have done for them." But, what if you mix servanthood with identification? There is the story of Damien, burning out in ministry to lepers. After a futile day of evangelizing, he returned home, put a foot in hot water, and felt nothing—the first unmistakable sign of leprosy. That Sunday he got in the pulpit and did not begin with the customary "you lepers." Now it was "we lepers." From that point on, his heretofore unsuccessful ministry was electric and fruitful beyond his wildest dreams. He was their story, and once more the word was made flesh, even leprous flesh, and dwelt among people.

Attitude

There are many books on good group leadership methods, but I am not concerned about group methods here. A Bible study group takes on the same characteristics of other groups and is subject to the same principles of group process. The same kinds of communication problems and possibilities occur in Bible study groups as in other groups. Experiential Bible study is a group situation, and the principles of good group work apply.

Here, I am concerned with attitude. Attitude has to do with the way we place ourselves in the group context. It has to do with where we sit, not so much physically, but emotionally and mentally. We are initiated into this process by the statement of Paul in Philippians 2:5, "Let the same mind [attitude, way of thinking] that was in Christ Jesus . . . ." Attitude is a way of placing oneself, a positioning of mind, body, and emotion. Positioning ourselves is the way we find our bearings, much like ancient navigators oriented themselves by observing the sky and stars. Attitude is an orientation that shapes perspectives, a way of seeing and hearing everything that goes on around us. From Philippians 2, we get the attitudes that shape leaders for experiential Bible study.

Presence and Identification

The first dimension of attitude is the sense of presence. Whatever the condition of people, we find ourselves to be with them. Presence with people prepares us for the broader framework of presence with Scripture. Presence is a form of compassion, a call that goes against the grain of our life, in some sense, turning our standing and sitting around, so that we see and hear from a different viewpoint.

Our calling to compassion is a calling from a compassionate God. God has chosen to be God-with-us. All critical situations in life call for the sense of a presence of someone who cares. So we sit in a group with the attitude of being present to each other. Paul said to the Thessalonians that he was among them, like a mother nursing her children (1 Thess 2:7). There is someone there, alongside us. Being "with" someone is not as easy as it sounds. Being with someone is sharing vulnerabilities, weaknesses, powerlessness, feelings of uncertainty and inferiority. Those who have stayed "with us" know our anguish, our spiritual darkness, and the uncharted places in which we wander.

Presence is willingness to give up distinctions, comparisons, and differences. Defining ourselves can either create connections or maintain distance. Competition keeps the dividing lines distinct, while presence connects solidarity and likeness. Our identity in Jesus Christ brings us into likeness with others where distance and fear of likeness is overcome. In Jesus Christ we follow one who gave up distinctions to be born in our likeness. Instead of following someone who does not face the same problems as we do, we follow one who has become as we are, knowing the same difficulties we face.

Jesus knew what we were like because he had become one of us. As long as the assistance we offer and the teaching we give are motivated primarily by the changes we see, our service will not last long. This is the paradox of learning. Learning is change, but our leadership cannot be motivated by the changes we see in people. What happens when results do not appear, when success is absent, when people remain uninformed and shallow, or when we are no longer praised by what we do? We lose the strength and motivation to continue. Only identification and "being one with" save us from disappointment and resentment.

Presence is willingness to become obedient to the group process. The word *obedience* is derived from the Latin word *audire*, which means to "listen to." When Jesus was obedient to God, he was in a position of listening and attending, of being "all ears." Jesus is set apart because of obedience and attentive listening. Jesus' death becomes his ultimate act of obedience and listening. "He humbled himself and became obedient to the point of death" (Phil 2:8).

Identification and presence are a way of being together. Philippians 2 expresses the powerful movements of encouragement, consolation, fellowship, affection, and compassion. There is not a more powerful word in the New Testament than *splancha* (compassion), originally a physical term encompassing all the vital inner organs. *Splancha* is an emotional word calling for the total involvement of one's being at the deepest levels. This is essential to all significant group life—the capacity to feel with others, to be moved by their concerns, and to care about what is happening to them. When Paul exhorts the Christians at Philippi to live a life of identification with the mind of Christ, he describes it in graphic terms. "Do nothing from selfish ambition or conceit, but in humility regard others as better than yourselves. Let each of you look not to your own interests, but to the interests of others" (Phil 2:3-4).

In community, God's compassion reveals itself. Identification is not an individual accomplishment. It is difficult to enter into the lives of others by ourselves.

> But in the community gathered in Christ's name there is limited space into which strangers from different places with very different stories can enter and experience God's compassionate presence. It is a great mystery that compassion often becomes real for people not simply because of the deeds of one hospitable individual, but because of an intangible atmosphere resulting from a common life.[2]

Displacement

People sitting in a circle take on an atmosphere of voluntary displacement. Displacement means a shift from the ordinary or customary place. A leader sitting in the midst of a circle or around the middle of the table among people is an example of displacement. Leaders are usually seen standing or sitting at the head of the table. This is clearly seen in the placement of people away from the centered lectern or distancing from the "head chair." In displacement, the leader is often difficult to find. But voluntary displacement brings us into deeper solidarity with our fellow human beings. Part of what it means to be church is to be "called out" of the traditional patterns and familiar places that have become comfortable but meaningless.

The incarnation is the greatest example of displacement. "Who, though he was in the form of God, did not regard equality with God as something to be exploited, but emptied himself, taking the form of a slave, being born in the human likeness" (Phil 2:6-7). God must have known that the proper place would not do. There Jesus would be, standing at the front of the room or sitting at the head of the table. All the rest of us would be staring at him in rapt attention, backs straight, eyes glazed over, lips compressed in a tight smile. We would act like we were supposed to act in the presence of a great leader. We would put on a show just to make a good impression. No real relationship, just honor and admiration. There must be another way. God sent his son wrapped in swaddling clothes and laid (displaced) him in a manager because there was no room for him in the inn.

The life and ministry of Jesus is the story of displacement. As a child, he is displaced in Egypt, away from the threats of Herod. As a young boy, he gets lost in the temple. He is initiated into ministry through the solitude and loneliness of desert living. He continually moves counter to popularity and success. Among crowds, he withdraws to lonely places. He tells the disciples intentionally to choose the last places. He avoids the well-to-do and has dinner with sinners and lunch with tax collectors. He wastes time blessing children when there are hundreds of more important people waiting to see him. He focuses attention on losers and failures and ignores high achievers. His is a displaced life, the life of a vagabond. Finally, his displacement leads him to a cross on a lonely hill outside the city walls. He is buried in a borrowed tomb. Jesus is the displaced Lord. In spite of the fact that "at the name of Jesus every knee should bend," he was completely at home in an ordinary way of life, away from the "centers" of attention.

But displacement is an attitude before it is a physical movement. It is a refusal to place oneself as an object of interest on which others focus attention. It is a vastly different form of leadership, a giving up of a concern to be "interesting" or "inviting" or "compelling." The movement toward compassion and identification begins by distancing ourselves from all those who want to make us the centers of interest and attention.

Grounding

Part of the meaning of the incarnation is the grounding of Jesus. Incarnation means he walks on the ground. He is not a "star." He does not take on the role of the super-hero, performing great feats that no one else can imitate. He is the obedient one whose courageous response leads him to suffering and death.

The superstar teachers, sometimes called the "master teachers," create more fascination with themselves than with the body of teaching. Superstars are not down to earth. They are distant, somewhere up in the heavens, to be admired but not touched. Wise leaders are grounded, having gravity, weight, and stability. They can work with a variety of group situations, without flying all over the place. When leaders are grounded, they are fully present, offering balance to otherwise erratic situations.

A graphic story of grounding is illustrated by Philips Petit, a high-wire artist.[3] At the close of his act on the steel wire stretched between two towers, he began to walk down a wire string between one of the towers and the sandy ground. Everyone was so engrossed in the act that no one realized that for several seconds he had been walking on safe ground. Only after he looked down at the ground with a puzzled face and then up to the stands with a happy, surprised look did the crowd catch the true artistic moment. This is something all of us can do! Leadership as an art reveals a deeper level of sameness, not individual distinctiveness. What separates us is not as important as what unites us. Groundedness reveals sameness, something characteristic of all of us. Paul saw this sameness: ". . . of the same mind, having the same love, being in full accord and of one mind" (Phil 2:2).

The Downward Pull

Leadership, then, does not provide an upward push but a downward pull. Leadership does not lift us out of our ignorance and incompleteness. Leadership becomes one with our fears, uncertainties, incompetence, and lack of completeness. Instead of standing above those who are lacking, the group leaders sit in the middle of what is not known, experiencing the unknowing. Power, knowledge, and competence are concealed and hidden away through an intentional act of becoming little, last, and least.[4] Donald McNeill called this our "second nature," the nature we receive in and through Christ—our "natural" way of being in the world.[5]

This downward pull runs counter to all the identifiable objectives we see in most group leadership goals. The group leader is to "lift us out" with objectives that "inform," "explain," and "interpret." How different are the leadership objectives that "pull us down," such as "empathize," "identify with," or "respond emotionally."

Lifting us out shows particularity by describing, explaining, categorizing, defining, differentiating, setting apart, specifying, diagnosing, and explicating.

How different are the movements that pull us down—being in one accord and of the same mind, being in communion with, catching the spirit of, being moved by, caring about, and entering into fellowship with. This attitude violates our most basic instincts.

Slowness

Almost everything about experiential Bible study is slow. Learning is a process—sometimes a long and tedious one. When someone says, "It's time to get on with it," we have probably lost an important dimension of the group's life. Silence, space, and the open places between movements are significant moments. What is happening when nothing seems to be happening in a group? People's speech and actions are crucial group events. The silence and empty spaces, however, reveal moods and provide a context for everything that happens.

The movements in experiential Bible study (experience, exegesis, reflection, and application) are significant, but so are the transitions. Recent architectural design shows the importance of passageways from one place to another. The dramatic effects of large rooms are amplified by the narrowness of halls that lead into large spaces. The passageways slow down movement and we get the panicky feeling that nothing is happening. But we know that "nothing never happens" in a group.

Good group leadership is a call to patience, a slowing down of process. Roberta Hestenes reminded us of this important principle:

> Often we "know" much more than we live. If we slow down our pace of study in order to concentrate on "learning to live" from the Bible, instead of rushing to study new verses in the Bible, our lack of serious discipleship may be revealed, as well as the very real problems that Christians encounter. The desire in this method is not to "know" more but to be transformed from within as our lives are submitted to God and to each other as we encounter the Scriptures.[6]

Patience is an overused, unpopular word. We conjure in our minds a frozen ability to act, a passive and dependent approach to life. But patience connects closely with compassion and identification.

> Patience is the capacity to see, hear, touch, taste, and smell as fully as possible the inner and outer events of our lives. It is to enter our lives with open eyes, ears, and hands so that we really know what is happening. Patience is an extremely difficult discipline, precisely because it counteracts our unreflective impulse to flee or to fight. . . . When someone approaches a sensitive issue, something in us tries to change

the subject. When a shameful memory presents itself, something in us wants to forget it. And if we cannot flee, we fight. We fight the one who challenges our opinions, the people who question our power, and the circumstances that force us to change.[7]

Group leadership is slow cooking. Stir lightly and delicately. Allow the natural juices to do their work. Don't bother the pot too much. Take a deep breath, relax, and wait. Stirring things too much releases the forces before their time. When things emerge "in the fullness of time," they cannot be pushed. The significant issues come out of hiding naturally, and they resolve themselves naturally when the time is right.

The Scriptures teach us that God's time is not our time. In our fast world, God is slow. "The LORD, a God merciful and gracious, slow to anger, and abounding in steadfast love and faithfulness" (Exod 34:6). The parable of the vine growers in Mark 12:1-11 reveals the slowness of God. The master sends the servants to receive some of the produce of the vineyard. He sends them one by one. He sends many of them, and they are all beaten and killed. Finally, he sends his son and he, too, is beaten and killed. Does God's patience finally run out? That is not for us to know.

Courage

Leaders show courage in vulnerability, admitting failures and losses, and risking the boundaries of their limitations. They are willing to confront others, following their hunches and intuitions, even if eventually they are proven wrong. They are open to being touched by others through empathy and identification. They are continually in the process of examining their own growth edges—things that seem to be personally threatening and anxiety producing. They are willing to express their fears, expectations, and hopes about the group process. They do what they expect others to do—an honest and direct interaction with themselves and others in the group.

This courageous self-examination brings power and vitality. Leaders have it when they know who they are. Life is an expression of what they espouse and believe. Group members have a confidence that the person knows what he or she is doing. Power is revealed in how we show ourselves, a fearful but honest self-examination. Powerlessness is revealed in defense of self-knowledge. There is vulnerability without one's knowing it or one's refusal to face it. Vitality is drained through spending energy in concealing vulnerabilities from oneself and others. Leaders with dim self-awareness and blinded for fear of what they may discover in themselves are dangerous people in a group.

Good group leaders go about their business of self-examination with stout-hearted assurance. Communication is a look directly in the mirror, meeting all situations face to face with what they see. Those who lack courage feel unequal to this task. Courage is always a process of self-examination, an issue of the heart and of one's confident relationship to God. "Wait for the LORD; be strong, and let your heart take courage; wait for the LORD!" (Ps 27:14). Our courage to take the tough self-look comes from God, whose grace and love will "comfort your hearts and strengthen them in every good work and word" (2 Thess 2:17).

Preparedness

Only well-prepared people can give away leadership with grace. This is perhaps the most difficult leadership task of experiential Bible study. Let us do our homework on the text, using all the skills of biblical exegesis available in our repertoire. Then, let us give up some of our knowing for the sake of the group. Let us become poor so that others may have an opportunity to be rich. Preparedness frees us for spontaneity with the group. A thorough familiarity with the biblical text frees the leader for participating with and attending to the group. When the leader is fully prepared, packaged techniques and programmed interpretations can be avoided. New methods can be invented on the spot. Leaders who are good at discovering new ways of evoking responses and who are willing to risk the suspension of established techniques are unlikely to grow stale.

Again, let us emphasize the importance of the leader using knowledge as leaven in the group. The more the group leader becomes the focus of attention and the object of interest in the group, the less time there is for attending and listening. The spotlight brings preoccupation. We wonder how we are doing, how we are looking, and how we will respond to the next comment. Hiding our knowing in the group frees us from the constant need to respond.

Surprisingly, research points out the paradoxical role of leader competence while remaining "just one of the group." Robert Wuthnow's voluminous study of groups and leadership roles points to this double-edged role: "Leaders . . . generally function best when they are sensitive to the dynamics of the group, steer the discussion, encourage members to participate, and help to keeps things running smoothly rather than dominating the discussion themselves. But some members also look to leaders for advice. They want them to be more experienced, more knowledgeable, better informed."[8] Although most people in Bible study groups do not learn best through lecture, they still want their teachers and leaders to be good lecturers. Good lecturing—the coherent understanding of information—assures people of a competence that will be available when needed or wanted.

Abundance

When we take our rightful place on the ground among God's people, we finally see the abundance of resources that surrounds us. Walking on the ground does not suppress unique talents but calls them forth in fruitfulness. Attending to others with a desire to make them the center of attention and making their interests ours is a form of self-emptying in order that others may be fulfilled.

As long as we magnify difference and competition, competence and quality are in short supply. We live under the illusion of scarcity. Only a few people have real potential and never enough to get the job done. The view "from the top" never sees the overflowing of resources. Through the process of identification, we finally understand the meaning of education—to draw out, to evoke, to awaken, to give birth, and to become the midwives of abundance.

Walking on the ground, we finally see the abundance of resourceful people. They are everywhere, ministering to individuals, families, and structures. They go places where professional ministers have never set foot. They speak to people professional ministers never see. But without the process of identification, the church never really sees them, never acknowledges them, never equips them with this ministry, never supports them in it, never commissions them to it, and never holds them accountable for it. Ultimately, we are all impoverished for our lack of seeing.

In making others' interests our own, we finally see the enormously diverse ways people learn and know and the remarkable adventure required of the human spirit to emerge—insight, analysis, appreciation, enthusiasm, creative energy, intuition, hands, heart, signs, symbols, metaphors, colors, tastes, textures, form, contemplation, and engagement. There is abundance beyond our imagination to conceive. Parker Palmer has reminded us that only through prayer do we see gifts most clearly.[9] In prayer we find our rightful place in God's order of things where position, knowledge, and status take on much lesser importance. Only in prayer do we see that the world's illusion of scarcity is a snare, and God's promise of abundance is possible all around us and in us.

Balance

The longest step most group leaders ever face is the movement from a controlling to facilitating style. With our feet firmly on the ground, we search for balance for the group and ourselves. Balance is knowing when to intervene and when to sit back. There are times when groups need direct intervention. Group leaders should have needed information available from their accurate exegesis of Scripture. When and how that information is shared is a question of intervention. Group leaders intervene in setting boundaries, asking questions, summarizing discussions, seeking different viewpoints, probing for common understandings, and suggesting alternative processes.

However, group leaders do not intervene unnecessarily. The leader's presence and support are felt, but a group often runs itself. In facilitation, we are evoking another person's growth processes. We are assisting in someone's birthing of new learnings. I never think of this *maieutic* (midwifery) method of teaching without recalling Lela's birthing of our children and our daughter Melissa's and daughter-in-law Lori's birthing of our grandchildren. Of all the events of life, these are the most memorable. What is birthed has form, but it is fragile and can die in a moment. Those fleeting insights have been in silence and darkness for months, and the labor is often uncomfortable and painful. We seek to do good without show or fuss. We carefully attend to the others' knowing. We work with what is actually happening rather than what we think ought to be happening. If we must lead, let us lead so others still feel in control of their own learning and birthing.

The control of a group is difficult to give up. The facilitative leader is more in control when the group process is flowing freely and unfolding naturally. Expecting people to say what you want them to say often runs into stark resistance. When the leader sits back, the resistance usually relaxes. In most group situations, a little bit of control is plenty. Issues that emerge naturally in the course of a group's life usually find a way of resolving themselves naturally.

The dilemma of balance for most group leaders is this: how much of what we know do we tell? We are personally responsible for discovering how our personal biases distort our understanding of Scripture and our insight into group life. Sometimes our love for truth overcomes our love for group. At other times, our love for group keeps us silent when we would have much to say. The trick is in finding the right balance.

H. G. Wells in *Country of the Blind* told of people in South America cut off from civilization by a natural disaster.[10] Through many generations they became less sighted. After a period of time, the entire group was blind. They adapted so well to the blindness that eventually no one noticed the loss of sight. One day a mountain explorer named Nunez was caught in a landslide and landed in the valley of the villagers. Nunez thought he was in a superior position and attempted to get the villagers to acknowledge his leadership. He asked the leader of the people, "Has no one told you in the country of the blind that the good-eyed man is king?" The blind leader responded, "What is blind?"

When Nunez fell in love with one of the young women in the valley and wished to marry her, he was faced with a life decision—have himself blinded or give up his love. With his sight he was a misfit. He wanted to marry his love and also be accepted as a part of the community, but the value system of the community dictated that sightedness was the same as sickness. Nunez made the most difficult decision of his life. He left the community and his love in order to retain his sight.

Some choose to retain their sight. Others allow their eyes to be put out for the sake of being part of a people. Many people make that choice unconsciously. There are a few that make that choice intentionally; they will have to determine their motives for making the sacrifice.

Staying Alive

When I look back at the things I wrote about leadership several years ago, I am alarmed at the distance I have strayed from these concepts. My deep gladness has come from being a facilitator of small group processes and gradually coming to a point of disappearing as far as being an object of interest. This is as much self-protection as it is personal conviction. I have never done well being close to the center of attention. I like it too much. Every day I want people to sing, "O Come, Let Us Adore Him," meaning me. Being a catalyst and facilitator of learning makes it easier to turn people toward one another. I have always been at my best in facilitating multiple small groups and creating community out of a company of strangers.

For most of my life, I have worked in large institutions buffeted away from the centers of power. There is a certain freedom of expression in running in the middle of the pack. What I had to say mattered, but it didn't matter much because it was part of a chorus of responses that most of the time eventually found a way of harmonizing.

Thirty years ago a Catholic nun called forth my gift as a "catalyst of contingencies." That was a fancy way of saying that the possibilities for change are lying around dormant all over the place until someone stirs them up and calls them out. In trying to be faithful to that calling, I have been guilty of throwing things out of balance and challenging what people hold dear, offering little more than the potentials for something different. Difficult issues and disturbing news are not things people take easily, but constant debriefing in small group processes helps modify and dilute the most painful aspects. This is no promise that things are going to be better; betraying deep attachments and committing to new loyalties is tough work. Being the leaven in the lump rather than the top chef was a freedom I took for granted, and carelessly at that. I was not successful with that as pastor and fell into the trap of being too much front and center.

I agree with Heifetz and Linsky that the most difficult work of leadership involves learning to experience distress without numbing, experiencing a thousand little deaths but somehow managing to stay alive. They reminded us that, "Even the word lead has an Indo-European root that means 'to go forth, die.'"[11] History is full of those standing at the front of the line, leading the charge, and ending up that way. But once we can fully experience the little deaths, feeling it all without letting go of any of it, we may understand the impact of the losses and little deaths other people experience with our ideas.

In the middle of trying to discern if I was to become a pastor for the first time as a sixty-year-old, I had a dream. The dream came as a result of several insistent expectations that I would wear a clerical robe during Sunday morning worship. This was not appealing to me, but some people made it quite an issue. In my dream, I was the pope being vestured for my first appearance before the people. The robe was of various pieces and lengths, with many different shades of deep red. As the pieces were added, they became more awkward and heavy. In spite of the difficulties, I knew my task was to bless the people, and when the huge doors swung open, I stepped out into a crowd of people down a long corridor that divided them. I moved down the corridor between the people, blessing each one by pointing my index finger at them and winking—not exactly the traditional for-mula for blessing! The dream left such a powerful impression that it became a primary impetus in the decision to become a pastor. I could do this! Eight years later, I see the dream in a much different light. Although clerical robes fit others well and appropriately, they were too much for me. I now see the dream as a warning more than a blessing. For me, the robe became a symbol of position and privilege. It was too much, creating distance rather than intimacy. A long flowing robe had a way of keeping me "out of touch" and emotionally tripped me up many times. I have often told that dream story, and it is still funny!

Humor

Finally, humor will save us. I have never been a part of a healthy group where humor was absent. Let's face it—groups are funny. Humor breaks the logjams, stirs the imagination, provides creative interpretations of Scripture, and connects the Bible with our modern situation. A healthy church is a laughing church, with an ability to see the ridiculous in human dilemmas. Humor is the universal med-icine, an elixir of the spirit, helping things go down easier and minimizing pain. Something funny happens that erases or transforms what was embarrassing, oppressive, or painful. Humor is the breath of fresh air the group needs. Whatever else the spirit of God brings to a group, humor must be one of the things God loves, laughing at our ritualized, predictable behavior, hoping we can do the same.

Much humor will flow naturally from the group's life. By being sensitive to the needs of the group, leaders can see in almost any situation an underlying well of humor to tap. Humor is not the same as joy, but it is an integral part of joy. Joy seems to come spontaneously in the group's life just as sadness, anger, and fear occur. These are common human characteristics that all people understand in their essence. By looking closely at the process of a group, we can always find opportunities to cultivate humor. The paradoxical, ironic, unpredictable, unanticipated, and absurd provide a constant source of humor.

Groups that are able to laugh at themselves are more able to take risks together, tend to communicate more openly and without threat, and will be more receptive to change. These "laughing matters" are generated spontaneously, flowing from the natural development of the group. Order and predictability are the biggest enemies of humor. The funniest things spring from uncertainty, discomfort, and disorder.

> In reality, a marvelous source of humor that is readily available to any group member is the group itself. . . . People attempt to maintain their personal sense of integrity, to look "good" rather than "foolish," to walk away wanting to return, and knowing they are wanted. The constant struggle within any group of individuals attempting to meet their own needs as well as those of the group creates marvelous dynamics and is a never-ending source of humor.[12]

Satire and irony are a part of the biblical revelation that need to be exploited in bringing legitimate humor to the group's life. Satire exposes human vice and folly, making "jabs" in a number of directions. "It is a convention of satire that satirists feel free to exaggerate, overstate, and oversimplify to make their satiric point. Satire is a subversive form. It assaults the deep structures of our thinking and aims to make us uncomfortable. It questions the status quo and unsettles people's tendency to think that their behavior is basically good."[13]

In irony, the readers have an advantage over the characters in the story. The readers know some things that the actors don't know, and the smiles and laughs come quickly when we know the "tricks." In Judges 3, Ehud informs the king that he has a word from the LORD for him. The king thinks that the word is coming from the oracle, but the reader knows that the "word" is a dagger hidden beneath Ehud's coat.

The book of Job is full of irony. Job offers sacrifices in Job 1:5, fearing that his children are not "blessed" but "blessed out" by God. Job takes a "jab" at his friends in 12:2, saying all wisdom will surely die with them. He was saying that his friends were not nearly as wise as they thought they were. It seems that the unexpected contrasts make us laugh. We expect one thing and get another. Humor in the Bible usually exists at the expense of God's enemies. Note Isaiah's descriptions of the manufacturing of idols in Isaiah 40:18-20; 41:5-7; and 44:9-20. Jesus exposed the Pharisees in a humorous and ironic way in Matthew 23.

Paul used a similar approach in making fun of the "super apostles" in 2 Corinthians 11. Can we see the humor in Paul's discourse against the super apostles? These "most eminent apostles" are a pain to Paul, so he makes fun of them. They alleged that he was an amateur, unskilled, and untrained in comparison to the "professionals." After all, the professionals were trained in rhetoric—the art of public speaking (11:5-6). They would do anything necessary in order to maintain their advanced spiritual condition (11:12). While they found ways of boasting of their successes (11:18), Paul never seemed to have the nerve to boast of his. Their "successes" included exercises of tyranny over the people, making slaves of them, fleecing them of their money, and humiliating and demeaning them (11:20). Paul confessed, "To my shame, I must say that we have been weak by comparison" (11:21). Paul did not have the advantage of the traditional mantle laid on him by those in powerful positions as did Hebrews, Israelites, and descendants of Abraham (11:22). We can almost see Paul laughing at the incredulity of it all. The tragedy is that the super leaders are oblivious to what is happening, for the rest of us are laughing at them, too.

NOTES

[1] Walter Wink, *Transforming Bible Study* (Nashville: Abingdon Press, 1980), 95.

[2] Henri J. M. Nouwen, Donald P. McNeill, and Douglas A. Morrison, *Compassion* (New York: Doubleday, 1982), 57. I am indebted to these authors' book for their interpretation of Philippians 2.

[3] Ibid., 77.

[4] Robert Farrar Capon, *The Parables of Grace* (Grand Rapids: Eerdman's Publishing Co., 1988), 32. Capon said that the parables of grace are preoccupied with the notion that the work of the Messiah will be accomplished not by winning but by losing. The catalogue of losing categories are the "last," the "least," the "lost," the "little," and the "dead."

[5] Nouwen, McNeill, and Morrison, *Compassion,* 30.

[6] Roberta Hestenes, *Using the Bible in Groups* (Philadelphia: Westminster Press, 1983), 86.

[7] Nouwen, McNeill, and Morrison, *Compassion,* 93.

[8] Robert Wuthnow, *Sharing the Journey: Support Groups and America's New Quest for Community* (New York: Free Press, 1994), 267.

[9] Parker Palmer, *The Active Life* (San Francisco: Harper & Row, 1990), 121-38. Also see Palmer's *The Promise of Paradox: A Celebration of Contradictions in the Christian Life* (Notre Dame: Ave Maria Press, 1980).

[10] Cedric B. Johnson introduced me to this story in his *The Psychology of Biblical Interpretation* (Grand Rapids: Zondervan Publishing House, 1983), 117-18.

[11] Ronald A. Heifetz and Marty Linsky, *Leadership on the Line: Staying Alive through the Dangers of Leading* (Boston: Harvard Business School Press, 2002), 227 and 208.

[12] Rodney W. Napier and Matti K. Gerschenfeld, *Groups: Theory and Experience* (Boston: Houghton Mifflin Company, 1993), 417.

[13] Leland Ryken, *Words of Delight* (Grand Rapids: Baker Book House, 1987), 329.

CHAPTER EIGHT

Rearranging the Furniture of the Mind: Preaching

> The self persuading preacher must keep in mind that such previous self-schemata (personal items in the house) cannot be reordered by force—no one breaks into someone's home to rearrange the furniture. So the self persuading sermon asks to be invited in. . . . The room may need to be straightened, an extra chair may need to be brought in, or the door may need closing, given the private nature of the talk. But every conversation changes the room in which it takes place. Over time, these changes, however slight, change the feeling of the room, and thus, the outlook of the occupant . . . attics are for memories, kitchens for gossip, dens for the signing of contracts and the drawing of wills, and rec rooms for loud jokes, instant replays, and exaggerated tales of athletic prowess. The sermon that can move into a room and rearrange it, or just leave it in a different humor, is a sermon that knows how to make the conversation partners believe that they are responsible for the new design.[1]

I have always been a preacher of sorts. I preached for the first time as an eighteen-year-old and have preached periodically for more than fifty years. For every sermon I preached, I have heard a dozen—a strange combination of listening to myself in both settings. For six years, I pastored a church; I know something of the rigor and discipline of weekly preparations in the incessant return of Sunday. I have heard this comment in various forms many times: "You seem to be an educator. What do you know about preaching?" Somehow, the two don't seem to mix in the perceptions of many people. But when I talk about learning in the classroom, preaching students immediately intuit the connections and generally show the most energetic responses.

Although I have made presentations in almost every imaginable setting, nothing seems to match the mystique of preaching. I am generally seen as a facilitator of process and get my "deep gladness" from the facilitation of learning. My attempt in this chapter is to speak of preaching in terms of learning and education, especially in the little I know from the expanding field of brain research. It seems to me that congregations are nurtured and sustained by what they already know and are always looking for new ways of knowing it. They want to hear how preachers work through their own way of knowing what the congregation already knows. Preaching is much like thinking out loud, and thinking is much like preaching to oneself. There is some kind of connection between the brain, the ear, and the vocal cords. That connection is mysteriously embodied in the congregation.

Experiential Preaching

Experiential preaching is the result of working through cycles and polarities and letting others observe how we are working through the processes. A sermon is the product of a preacher hearing Scripture through experience, exegesis, reflection, and application. The cycles and polarities of experiential Bible study engage the mind in conversation—a talking to ourselves. The congregation hears how the preacher is doing this work.

Experiential preaching also awakens the process in the minds of the listeners. In preaching, we are telling others the secrets of our hearts. Preaching engages the listener in what the preacher has gone through. Preachers also listen, assessing their own work. Preachers who are bored with themselves will bore congregations. But when they carry on fascinating inner conversations, both preachers and listeners experience amazement, alarm, fear, inspiration, and wonder. In hearing themselves, preachers feel anger, sadness, delight, humor, and surprise in what they say and what is happening in them. This is the skill of listening and speaking at the same time. The same process is experienced in the small group, except now it is experienced in a larger public setting with a continual flow of nonverbal feedback. The word that best describes this process is passion. This quality is hard to describe without misunderstanding because it is clouded by many meanings. "It is a word that describes the momentary insanity of criminals as well as the delirium of lovers. It is said to make us interesting on the one hand, dangerous on the other. Without it, life becomes an endless afternoon, a flat, tedious stretch of mindless motion."[2]

Preaching often forgets a basic principle of communication. Learning to communicate with oneself is the first movement in learning to communicate with other people. If preachers listened to themselves, they would not say some of the things they say—a sure sign of the lack of self-awareness. When people talk to themselves, they are honest. They do not waste words, exaggerate, play games of self-deception, or use bloated sentence structure. The messages we give ourselves are simple, clear messages.

Brain research tells us about that inner household of multiple connections, the inner family that we live with every moment of every day. Our brain tells us about this family of inner relatives connected by spirit, blood, and body. We are people with many inner members, all clamoring for a voice. Some will think that talking and listening to yourself is odd, even strange. But when we are honest, we must admit that it is something we all do. Periods of solitude bring talking with ourselves into reality, when at other times, it is smothered by external busyness. We house in our brains the lifelong friends that ultimately are difficult to ignore. These friends are waiting to talk to us if we can open the doors and welcome them into our consciousness. Preaching is a continual process of self-study, inner communication, and honest self-reflection.

Brain-based Learning

All learning is brain-based in some sense; however, in understanding how the brain works, we acknowledge the brain's rules for meaningful learning and organize communication with these rules in mind. Multiple complex and concrete experiences are essential for meaningful learning. The immersion of the learner in both the biblical and modern worlds makes possible a number of rich connections and a grasp of larger patterns of meaning.

Everything happens in a spatial environment. We are always operating in a rich physical environment. Part of the task of preaching is to develop an expanded awareness of the environment so that the consciousness of the worship environment has opportunities to connect with the verbal message. Space in a church sanctuary takes on some of the same connecting dynamics of the doors and rooms in our brains. A congregation takes on "whole brain" characteristics. In other words, think of the congregation as a brain. While being an interim pastor, I reminded the church of the rich imagery of the stained-glass window at the back of the sanctuary. It portrayed the powerful symbolic language of the seven churches of Revelation. They had never "noticed," although the light through those powerful images shone down on them every Sunday. So are our houses full of the furniture we select. The pieces surround us and exist in a precise but ever-changing relationship to us. Regardless of what we are doing, we are always in a physical context, and that context in preaching has specific elements.

Our brains give us the capacity to "navigate" through these spatial maps that we have described as rooms in a house. Maps are constructed within a locale memory system. Being in a strange church can place limiting boundaries on our capacity to see and hear, but from prior experience we know most of the things to do and when to do them. We automatically draw from long-term memory without deliberately rehearsing each step. There are basic features of the locale memory system that help in preaching:[3]

1. Every human being has a spatial memory system.
2. Locale memories are never static, context free-facts. They are records of ongoing life events.
3. Initial maps form quickly. We get an instant sense of the layout of a room and it will stay with us.
4. We update our maps continuously and quickly. We immediately and spontaneously compare our present surroundings with past, similar surroundings.
5. Map formation is motivated by novelty, curiosity, and expectation. We expect this "world" to be a particular way because of memories of similar environments.
6. Locale or spatial memory is enhanced through awareness of all the senses. Some people have unusually well-developed sensory systems.

Mental maps operate in the same way. That is, they exist in mental space and are called thematic maps. That same memory system is engaged in worship experiences where stories, metaphors, celebrations, imagery, word pictures, and music are powerful tools for brain-based learning. Frederick Buechner has seen the connection between our memory systems and these "thematic" rooms in *A Room Called Remember*. "The room called Remember . . . is a room we can enter whenever we like so that the power of remembering becomes our own power."[4]

Using Our Whole Brains in Sermon Design

In spite of notes and careful design, a sermon sometimes unfolds according to brain-based principles. It changes in the process of delivery and finds a new form. We understand it after the fact but cannot capture it in the initial design. Our brain takes over and redesigns the delivery.

Sermons, like lesson plans, are cursed with the technology of "nuts and bolts" and "building blocks." We have been trained to see the essential pieces without seeing the connecting links and the "mortar" between the bricks. In experiential preaching, the connecting links that focus on movement are as important as the substance of the various points. Movement denotes energy, rebels against the more static aspects of "parts," and "points" to a process that is more organic and growing, with a life of its own.

If a sermon is walking through a house with many relatives present, it can walk in a circular or clockwise motion or jump from one room to the other. When people move into rooms of the house that have not been visited for a while (or perhaps closed off for lack of use), there is a sense of strangeness, of not feeling "at home." Against such an analytical wall, often there comes a resolution, a clue that feels revelatory. In it, one senses the missing key that "unlocks" the whole. Until found, the matter seems irresolute; after being found, the matter seems self-evident! In gestalt terms, it is the "Aha!" the one piece that allows the whole puzzle to come into sharp focus.

This is often experienced as a surprise. You didn't expect to find what you found in that room, and it brings the feeling of turning things upside down or of looking at it standing on your head. Unlocking the door to a new room has been identified as the difference between first-order and second-order change. First-order change occurs within a given system that itself remains unchanged. Second-order change alters the system itself. To illustrate the difference, note a person having a bad dream. Many things can be done in the dream, but it still remains a dream. This is a first-order change. Second-order change is a shift from dreaming to waking, an altogether different state of being. The system is no longer the same.

The power of "cognitive ruts," often called common sense, has a firm grasp on our minds. Rearranging brings the unthinkable thought (generally a reversal from common sense), and the intuitive hunch has a chance to break through. The gospel does not parallel mundane human experience.

> It would be closer to the truth to say that the gospel is continuous with human experience after the gospel has turned human experience upside down. The preacher is apt to walk into the pulpit with exegesis and exposition as the initial homiletical approach, only to discover that when the time comes for application the congregation had long since walked out existentially and left him there—standing on his head with the gospel![5]

Conventional wisdom comes from a concentration on one or two rooms in the brain. The surprise of the gospel comes from reversal and reframing, walking into rooms that have been rearranged or remodeled.

Doorways into the Rooms

Howard Gardner introduced the concept of multiple intelligences (types of potentials and abilities) in 1985 with the publication of *Frames of Mind*. According to Gardner, intelligence is the ability to solve problems or create products that are valued within one or more cultural settings. Gardner countered the traditionally agreed upon concept that intelligence is the mind of large general powers pointed in some particular direction. Rather, there are several intelligences that operate independently and do not draw on one intelligence. They typically work in harmony, so the autonomy of each may be difficult to see except when the intelligence appears with clarity in an exceptional individual. An example is Dustin Hoffman's portrayal of an "autistic savant" with high mathematical intelligence in the movie *Rain Man.*

Gardner argued against the concept that intelligence can be measured and reduced to a score on an artificially designed test. In that sense, high intelligence is limited to the "gifted kid down the block." It's like red hair—you either have it or you don't. The biblical concept of intelligence would say that all are gifted and all have their distinct ways of knowing. In preaching, the better we understand these different ways of perceiving, the more likely we are to communicate the message.

Gardner would see communicating with people as a process of walking through seven rooms:[6]

1. *Linguistic intelligence.* Fascination with language and technical facility with words. Sensitivity to sounds, rhythms, inflections, and meters of words. Being word smart in written and speech forms of "finding just the right word."

2. *Musical intelligence.* Like language, not dependent on objects in the physical environment. Sensitivity to the components of pitch, rhythm, and timbre. Failure to understand music seriously limits any understanding of the human condition. Music may be the key that opens all the other intelligences.

3. *Mathematic intelligence.* Confrontation with the world of objects—ordering, reordering, and assessing their quality. Love of dealing with abstractions and long chains of reasoning. The practice of science.

4. *Spatial intelligence.* Recognizing when seen from different angles or from different viewpoints. Understanding through creating a mental image. The photographic ability of the mind to create a mental picture and produce a graphic likeness.

5. *Bodily kinesthetic intelligence.* The control of one's body motions and the capacity to handle objects skillfully.

6. *Personal intelligence.* A core capacity to access one's emotional life and discriminate among feelings.

7. *Interpersonal intelligence.* The ability to notice and make distinctions among moods, temperaments, motivations, and intentions.

Let's not make this difficult. Although Gardner's concept of multiple intelligences is used in many educational settings, we can see through daily experiences that people are smart or "savvy" in at least one of seven ways—words, music, numbers, pictures, body, self, and other people.

Is there such a thing as spiritual intelligence? If there is, wouldn't a church want a preacher with such "splendid isolated" capacities? Do I want to get into this? On numerous occasions, I argued with Jerry Bowling, the writer of a doctoral thesis on Howard Gardner, that spiritual intelligence would be a rich combination of multiple capacities. However, Jerry proposed spiritual insight as a candidate for a distinctive intelligence, suggesting the following, among others, as "artistic judgments rather than scientific assessments":[7]

- Receiving and comprehending symbolic messages that may be pictorial, auditory, gestural, or linguistic.
- Understanding and evaluating the "dances, dramas, and designs" of faith fashioned by a church community.
- Forming, equipping, and healing the human heart. The heart includes everything we ascribe to the head and brain—perception, reason, insight, memory, knowledge, reflection, discernment, and imagination.
- Understanding one's spiritual self that encourages transformation.
- Sensitizing and responding to deeper spiritual wisdom.
- A distinctive developmental history that operates relatively independent of other intelligences. Thus, the spiritual prodigy or "stunning talent."
- A fear of the Lord, incarnate in Jesus Christ. "The fear of the LORD is the beginning of wisdom" (Prov 9:10).

Robert Emmons identified several components of a spiritual intelligence that facilitates everyday problem solving and goal attainment:[8]

- The capacity for transcending the material and physical.
- The ability to sanctify everyday experiences such as work, parenting, and marriage.
- The ability to experience heightened states of consciousness.
- The ability to utilize spiritual resources to solve problems with higher levels of well-being.
- The capacity to engage in virtuous behavior—showing forgiveness, expressing gratitude, feeling humility, and displaying compassion.

Boredom and laziness are the great enemies of preaching, viewing intelligence in a limited number of ways. Boredom is the result of one-dimensional preaching. Preaching should be a respecter of individual styles and an act of stretching into other domains. If our whole beings are not stimulated, exercised, and challenged, we all suffer. If the whole is not addressed, the parts suffer with it. Preaching should be an orchestration of the whole.

All the functions of the seven intelligences are interdependent. You can visualize this interdependence by imagining a large house with seven rooms. When you switch on the light in one room, it clarifies the vision in other rooms. Only the brightness and the intensity of the rooms are different.

The "Seven Doorways Model" uses brain theory in describing ways we learn and compares to Gardner's seven intelligences.[9] Preaching to the whole house means passing through these doors and "rummaging" around in these rooms.

1. *Causation.* A room that processes information that is time-bound, analytical, and requires a logical flow of words.

2. *Intuition.* A room that processes images and spatial relationships with rich connections to affective and memory systems. This room responds to nonverbal cues and metaphoric communication.

3. *Automation.* A room that modulates attention between two polarities: rest and agitation. This room legitimizes information that is new and unusual. It houses long-term physical memory such as bike riding and anything that takes place automatically, such as heartbeat and blinking.

4. *Relation.* A room that houses the emotional life and affective elements in communication. Energy is intensified in this room, depending much on the "like" or "dislike" of the communicator.

5. *Administration.* A room that maintains an orderly environment, balancing and harmonizing life—a clerical room.

6. *Motivation.* A room that channels the goals, drive, will, and motivational energy necessary for action. This is the "executive room" with information from both verbal and nonverbal data in making informed decisions.

7. *Motion.* A room that coordinates small and large muscle movement.

The model will make preaching more alive, especially in areas that seem to be less interesting and more difficult.

Diagram 3: The Seven Doorways

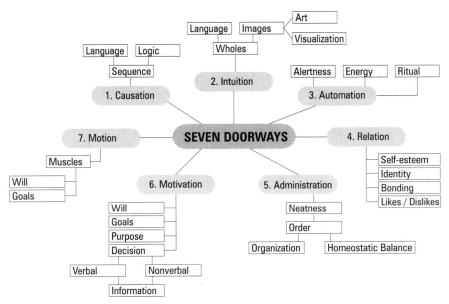

Source: David Lazear, *Seven Pathways of Learning*

Designing the Sermon on Paper

The traditional style of taking notes in linear outline form is an accustomed habit. Although the mind does not work in that fashion, we have used it as a time-honored method. Mind-mapping creates a central image or theme, then uses key words, images, colors, codes, and symbols to create connections between ideas. It is a form of visual note taking, a primitive art form found in the ancient paintings of our ancestors. An adult friend of our preschool son, Jud, sat in church with him, and they "mind-mapped" during sermons for several years. They called it doodling then, but the principle is the same.

A mind map records a great deal of information on a page and shows the connections with other concepts and ideas. It works contrary to outlining. What's Roman numeral one? Now what's the "big" A? The next thought must follow in exact order and follow the rules of outlining, i.e., each subset must have at least two items. We all know our brains don't operate in that manner. We have numerous thoughts, feelings, intuitions, mental pictures, and imaginative ruminations all happening at the same time. The complexities of our thought processes don't fit outlining. Mind-mapping works like our brain works.

Traditionally, the mind has been seen as a storehouse for information and facts. A computer now does what the mind was called on to do and with much more efficiency. Now we are freed to do what the computer can never do—use the information with creativity and intuition. We are better equipped because of the exploding research on the human brain. When mind-mapping, one uses not only words but symbols, images, and drawings, connections with ideas that might not ever connect in linear fashion.

Nancy Margulies in *Mapping Inner Space* identified several steps in mind-mapping that can be applied to sermon preparation and delivery:[10]

1.Select a biblical theme and write the theme in the center of the paper, keeping it fairly small so that there is plenty of room left for other ideas.

2. After you have drawn the central theme and image, move out in any direction from the center in drawing key words, symbols, and pictures. When you draw a symbol or picture, write a word or two after it so you will remember what it represents.

3. After you identify the initial word or symbol, branch out to other ideas in brainstorming fashion. Generate more words until you move out in many directions from the initial image.

4. Try not to judge the images and pictures that come. Simply allow them to happen. Eliminate extraneous data. Key words are the major building blocks. The more creative and unusual the words and images, the better they will be remembered. (This is one reason for the sustaining power of the King James Version of the Bible.)

5. After all the ideas are written, drawn, and recorded, review what you have done and organize the information. Do this by highlighting the significant ideas and drawing lines around distinct branches to define sections. This will begin a process of organizing the "rooms" as a part of the total pattern. Use a clock image for organizing, beginning with one o'clock position and proceeding in clockwise fashion.

6. Make whatever changes seem appropriate. You will probably be left with a messy map. If that bothers you, redraw the map on a clean sheet of paper.

Diagram 4: "Messy Map"

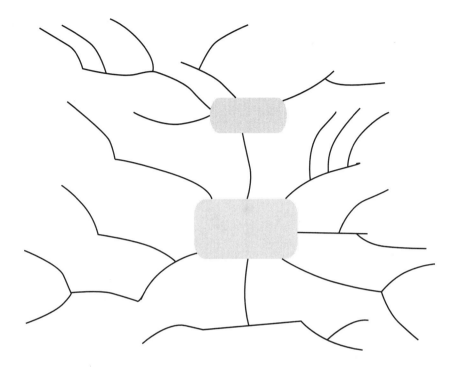

Our brains have many ways to take in information from within our inner spaces and from the outside world. Imagine being in the desert with Jesus during the feeding of the 5,000. Feel the atmosphere of the desert, smell the air and the dryness, see the whole view of the terrain, notice the changing colors of the sun and clouds on the desert floor, identify the people in groups of fifty, see yourself as one person in a group. Part of our brain sees the whole picture, visioning things we don't see but imagine, and experiencing feelings even when we don't have specific words to describe them.

Imagine now that you are in a big building called a library. There are rows and rows of catalogued books on both sides of you. You pull a book off the shelf and you see that it is a commentary on the Gospel of Mark. There is a verse-by-verse exegesis of the feeding of the 5,000. You move down the aisle and go into a room with huge filing cabinets. You open a drawer and there is a neatly typed paper giving accurate information on the passage in Mark. You open another drawer and there are folders on each verse in the Gospel of Mark in ordered sequence. This part of our brain works in ordered, sequential fashion.

What happens when we put the seven intelligences (seven doorways) together with the four movements in the Experiential Bible Study model?

Although the following diagram may appear more complex than it actually is, there is a way of moving through all the rooms when we pay attention to the movements of the experiential cycle.

Diagram 5: Four Quadrants of Experiential Bible Study Model

EXPERIENCE

- Body / Kinesthetic Intelligence
- Motion Room—Muscles, Motor Skills
- Motivation Room—Will, Goals, Purposes, Decision-making
- Connecting mind and body
- Mimetic abilities
- Skill development
- Performance
- Explain orally and written
- Dramatize
- Role-playing
- Interpretive Movement

APPLICATION

- Spatial, Musical Intelligence
- Intuition Room—Wholes, Art, Images Mind Pictures
- Activity (awakening intelligences)
- Imagination
- Forming mental pictures
- Sensitivity to sounds, tonal qualities, pitches, rhythm, harmonies
- Shapes, textures, colors
- Living in different periods of history
- Feelings through sound
- Awareness of environment
- Dreaming

EXEGESIS

- Interpersonal Intelligence
- Intrapersonal Intelligence
- Automation Room—Alertness, Energy
- Relation Room—Self-esteem, Bonding
- Administration Room—Neatness, Order Organization, Balance
- Cooperating with a group
- Seeing from other's perspectives
- Empathy and caring
- Evaluating own thinking
- Aware of and expressing feelings
- Thinking / reasoning at higher levels
- Connecting separate pieces of information

REFLECTION

- Verbal / Linguistic Intelligence
- Logical / Mathematical Intelligence
- Causation Room—Sequence, Language, Logic
- Scientific Investigation
- Outlining, note-taking, study guides
- Recognizing abstractions
- Inductive, deductive, reasoning
- Discerning cognitive connections
- Remembering
- Humor (play on words)
- Explaining, convincing
- Understanding syntax and word meanings

Here Comes Everybody

The purpose of using the senses and imagination in preaching is to create an experience—a life event. Preaching is not merely a process of explaining a text; "If biblical concepts are severed from biblical characters—devoid of taste, touch, sight, smell, and sound—the listener may be stirred to sleepy agreement or polite deference, but there will hardly be any persuasion. Persuasion takes passion, and passion is generated in the presence of something real."[11]

What do we do with all those neurons cascading around and making connections with all those other neurons? What is happening in our brains is constantly interacting with brains of those around us as part of the larger social system. All of it is searching for the familiar as well as the novel and trying to make sense of all our experiences while ignoring meaningless isolated information. We might say, "I don't know what is happening here and I don't want to know." Or, we might say, "I don't know what is happening here but I'm okay with it." Being okay with it may lead us through curiosity to mystery and wonder and finally to gratitude, knowing that every time we speak "The word of the Lord" our eventual response will be "Thanks be to God." If we only get a dribble of consciousness rather than a stream, there are still a lot of neurons working for you in preaching. The eye sends millions of bits and pieces of information to the brain every second, the skin more than a million, the ear and the nose a hundred thousand each, and the taste buds about a thousand. Here comes everybody and everything all at once! If we only get a glimpse, a whiff, and a taste, it might be enough. Thanks be to God!

If I am ever chosen for a pulpit committee to look for a pastor, I will look for those gifted with a spatial and sensory intelligence. What we want in preachers is sensory genius. Without the senses, preaching does not make sense. Where are these preachers, why do we need them, and how will we know when we have found one?

Smell

Perhaps the first thing these preachers will say when they walk into our church is some kind of comment about the "smell" of the church. In spite of all the deodorants, a church, like a house, has a certain smell. A preacher with olfactory gifts knows that when you hit the tripwire of smell, memories explode in a complexity of images. A fragrance needs no interpreter because the memory system is triggered immediately before we have time to sort out all those memories. There are no short-term memories in smells. They are all long-term. Smells are surer than sights and sounds to touch the heartstrings. John Milton in Dante's *Inferno* described the odors that God found pleasing. Satan was a sniffer "of carnage and living carcasses." Preachers who know how to smell can sniff out the scent of love in a church. They know that churches are the training ground in the art of loving and, like the bold and spontaneous act of Mary in John 12, when it all comes together the "whole house" is filled up with the smell of loving. Diane Ackerman asked the big question: "If they can't describe the scent of sanctity in a church, can you trust them to describe the suburbs of the heart?"[12]

Helen Keller could smell where people had been—the kitchen, the garden, or the sickroom. With their eyes closed, mothers can pick out the T-shirts worn by their children. The olfactory tissue is intimately connected to the cerebral tissue of the brain. We smell, therefore we think. If we want preachers who are both thinkers and lovers, we had better check out their smellers. I have often thought that the flowers on the communion table were not for the sight of the congregation but for the smell of the preachers, filling their minds with the long-term memories of Scripture, intoxicating them with the love of God, and fanning the fires of their spiritual fervor. If the first gifts to the Christ child were of incense, then we should "birth" our preachers with scents that awaken their memories of Scripture and life.

Touch

The language of preaching is immersed in the language of touch. We want preachers to "touch us" in powerful ways. Preaching that has a sense of touch has some indefinable skill of execution. Those who don't have that skill leave us with a vague feeling that they are out of touch. Those who have the "touch" can tell us about love, abandonment, anxiety, desire, and perhaps most importantly, pain. We all carry pain (perhaps a sixth sense), and to "make sense" of pain is an expectation we all carry to church.

Preachers with a sense of touch have a love for the etymology of words. They know that words not only stand for something; they stand on something. Behind words is concreteness. You can almost reach out and touch the hair on Esau's arm and feel the trickery in the arm of the old "smoothy" Jacob (Gen 27:11).

Language that stands on concreteness is more like poetry than prose, more often symbolic and paradoxical than logical. Abstract language can communicate facts and information but not come close to human feelings and emotions. "Emotive language" is not merely propaganda. It stirs the imagination of the human heart and cannot be described as either sentimental or even eloquent. It can be described as passionate language. Passionate language is not lacking in precision and factual accuracy. But the precision is the precision of passion. Paul wrote with passionate precision when he spoke of fathers and sons, the body and its members, love poured out in our hearts, sold under sin, engrafted branches, building up people, thieves in the night, trumpets, noisy gongs, and clanging symbols. Who could forget the concreteness of the gospel accounts of the Lamb, the Bridegroom, the Bread of Life, the Door, the Shepherd, the Way, and the Vine?

Basketball players, like our son-in-law Cal, are said to have "touch." The same can be said of preachers. Those who have "lived" the richness and the diversity of their personalities make the best preachers. Some have described them as "characters." A dull personality is the end product of mental laziness, spiritual lassitude, and moral cowardice—a refusal to take risks in relationships. Being "out of touch" shows a lack of curiosity about God's word, God's world, and God's people. Anguish, pain, engagement, sweat, and blood characterize and punctuate the communicative process. It was said of the medieval painters that they cut their fingers and mixed their own blood with the paint in order to get more of their "touch" on the canvas.

Painters have the gifts of sight *and* touch. Preachers have more in common with artists than scientists. The painter must deliberately use symbolism, which conveys how things appear rather than how they actually are, in order to over-come the problem of recording two dimensions of space on the single dimension of canvas.

Preachers can only preach beyond their own experience when they are "in touch" with the church's experience. Is there anything that people have experi-enced that the church has not known? The church has lived through the totality of human experience.

Hearing

Of all the senses, hearing is most crucial to worship. At least, Martin Luther believed that. We depend on hearing to help us communicate with the world around us. A sensitive preacher can hear the heartbeat of the congregation, sensing the discordant breathing or the breathing in unison and in harmony. The rhythm and harmony of the African American church congregational responses can almost be picked up in breathing. The only audible sound in many Anglo churches is laughter. A young pastor said, "Until I hear them laughing I can't quite get into it."

Despite all the folk wisdom about hearing, most people would rather lose their hearing than their sight. We really don't believe the old axiom: "God gave us two ears, but only one mouth, that we might hear twice as much as we speak." But people who are both deaf and blind often feel the deeper loss is hearing. Helen Keller said, "I am just as deaf as I am blind. The problems of deafness are deeper and more complex, if not more important, than those of blindness. Deafness is a much worse misfortune. For it means the loss of the most vital stimulus—the sound of the voice that brings language, sets thoughts astir, and keeps us in the intellectual company of man." Perhaps those who experience its absence can tell us what is most important in preaching. Even for the deaf, the emotion of the "word" somehow gets through with surprising ingenuity, from the outer world of silence to the inner world where the word can be heard.

There is a decided difference in preachers who love to sing and those who don't. When we sing, our vocal cords vibrate along with some of our bones. Music seems to carry throughout the body so we get a chance to hear our whole body tuning up and singing in concert. We don't have to learn a lot about it to understand and appreciate it. If the words we are using don't seem to mean much, put a tune to them and see how they hook you. Many of the great hymns of the church would thrill us even if they didn't have words. But we get a double whammy with words–emotional music tied to emotional messages. "Like pure emotions, music surges and sighs, rampages or grows quiet, and, in that sense, it behaves so much like our emotions that it seems often to symbolize them, to mirror them, to communicate them to others, and thus frees us from the elaborate nuisance and inaccuracy of words."[13] Music is the language that communicates experience. We will carry the old gospel songs to our graves, singing them as we go.

Preaching is a different kind of music, but music nonetheless. The preaching event is filled with tumult, comings and goings, bouts of passion, knots that must be untied, complications and resolutions, abruptness, disorder, and final reconciliation. Analyze a good sermon and you will find the same things in a good musical composition. A good composer knows that emotion can be created with certain sounds. Howard Gardner believes music to be an intelligence that develops in a child about the same time as speech, located in the right frontal lobe of the brain. We seem to be driven to make music. The more preachers see the connection between what they do and music, the more the entire worship experience wraps us all in a cocoon of organized sound. Organized sound takes two forms—words (rational sounds for objects, emotions, and ideas) and music (nonrational sounds for feelings).

Who knows when the sequence started? Music precedes and follows preaching. If there is not music before and after preaching, we feel that something is missing. In a sense, they are one and the same thing. When words and music combine, each enhances the effect of the other. All passionate language takes on a form of music, and when we listen closely, we can hear the passionate sermon taking the shape of song, a form of measured time.

Sight

Sometimes we have to be reminded that the eyes don't see at all. The purpose of the eyes is to gather light. Everything else happens in the brain. In some ways we don't need the eyes at all. We can picture events from yesterday, last year, or even years earlier from the "mind's eye" and can create imaginary events using the same process. Long after events are over, they keep parading before our eyes (or behind our eyes) in the middle of the night, keeping us awake because we can't turn off the pictures behind our closed lids.

I don't know if this is the experience of all preachers, but I will pre-visualize a sermon a dozen different ways before I ever preach it. Sometimes the images come in black and white, sometimes in color. The congregation before me is made up of people present and past, living and dead, friends and enemies. There they all are in full array, responding in much the same way as they did in reality. They provide a framework for practice preaching and their presence is often richer, more scintillating and profound, than in the actual public arena.

This "seeing" is done before the preacher ever steps into the pulpit. "Before a preacher says something a preacher must see something. To be a preacher is to be called to bear a witness, one who sees before speaking, one whose right to speak is created by what has been seen."[14] Because our eyes love novelty, we can get used to seeing almost anything without any of it getting our full attention. This pushing everything to background is magnified by television, which presents every imaginable scene before our eyes without a sense of wonder, astonishment, ugliness, or beauty. But opening our eyes is intended to wake us up so we don't miss the sights directly in our path, the ground under our feet, and the continually changing scenery overhead.

Biblical people seemed to have their feet planted firmly on the ground with their eyes fixed firmly in the heavens. They were constantly "considering the heavens" and the work of God's fingers. They proclaimed the brightness of God's creation—the brightness of the skies, the night as bright as the day (Ps 139:12), the bright and morning star. The early church was born with people gazing into the sky (Acts 1:10). Ackerman said, "The sky is the one visual constant in all our lives, a complex backdrop to our every venture, thought and emotion. Yet we tend to think of it as invisible—an absence, not a substance."[15] Not so with biblical people. To them, the sky was a ceiling with a continual unfolding drama—open-air theater at its best. From the sky came thunder, lightning, fire, voices, and great signs, a vaulted ceiling on which everything imaginable was painted.

Ground was just as important as sky. Some ground was perceived to be holy ground. Stephen's sermon looked back to the holy ground where Moses stood (Acts 7:33). Ground was either rocky or fertile for the growing of seed. The word is seen as a lamp to the feet and light to the path.

In some way, the preacher is there to connect us with both places. The Bible proclaims that we begin with ground and return to ground, but we picture the sky as the final resting place of those we love. The preacher is the shepherd of that life cycle, a vicarious visual representation, feet firmly planted on earth, pointed to the sky. The way the preacher stands carries a visual impact that matches anything else seen in worship. So we stand there, "amazed in the presence" of all that is coming at us. I have a longtime habit of preaching on tiptoe.

Color

One of the troubles with print is black on white. Red-letter editions of the Bible help a little but not much. My first memories of Christian faith come from the swing on the long screened-in porch of my grandmother. Swinging lightly, I spent hours with a comic book format of "Picture Stories from the Bible," all in full color. Noah, Moses, Joshua, Ruth, and David were my first heroes. The voice that came from the cloud at the top of the page was a voice that somehow knew me and spoke to me. How much of that I could actually read doesn't matter. The colored pictures carried the message.

Color is not a dominant theme in the Bible. That's too bad. Primitive languages first developed words for black and white, then added red, then yellow and green. Some lump blue and green together. The ancient Greek language had few color words, so my hunch is that when we stumble across color words in Scripture they are there to portray a distinct message. Why would Mark take pains to talk about green grass growing in the desert in the feeding of the 5,000? Why would he describe a white "like no laundered on earth could whiten" in the transfiguration account? I've never seen much of an exegesis on color—the purples, scarlets, crimsons, and violets of the Old Testament nor the greens or whites of the New Testament. I hoped someone would tell me why Mark talked more about color than any other Gospel writer. At the same time, he described the people's response as amazement and astonishment.

Hopefully, this will not be taken in a derogatory manner, but many preachers see like some animals—only in black and white. Our lives are desperate for beauty and wonder. Surely, the psalmist's declaration of "the beauty of the LORD" (Ps 27:4) is not a total abstraction. I can't imagine worshiping the Lord "in the beauty of holiness" without color. My hunch is that imagination is what it takes. The biblical writers left most of it up to us to paint the pictures and to provide the "color" commentary.

Dreams

I had almost decided not to include this section, but an early morning dream changed my mind. I was in an unfamiliar house with family members, friends, and strangers. The main floor was crowded with stored-up furniture and not suitable for conversation. Straight chairs were pushed up against sofas and tables. The chairs and tables were old and had been refurbished and repainted many times. I was playing a game with my grandchildren with the rule of not touching the floor (the danger of alligators), so we had to climb over furniture, dangerously close to tipping over. Finally I found my way to a staircase that led to an upper room or attic where we would be safe from the snapping jaws. When I arrived at the top of the stairs, I was startled at the appearance of the room. This was my new study with all kinds of bright, colorful new furniture, pictures, and lamps. The people who had furnished this room knew my deep longing for a well-ordered room that contrasted with the disordered chaos in the room below.

I have many dreams about preaching. Well, not about preaching, but about not being prepared to preach. The setting is always recognizable as some form of a church where I was previously an interim pastor. The worship service has started and the people are singing, and I am desperately searching for my Bible or sermon notes—somehow a warning that the exegesis of the text or reflection on the text has not been done. This dream has usually occurred on Thursday nights, reminding me that I have only two more days to be ready to say something to myself and others.

Only once did this dream vary. I was not searching for a Bible or notes but for communion trays. I could not find them, and the worship service was moving on without me. I had looked in all of the obvious places but finally, in a far dark corner of the church (or in my brain), there they were, pushed back behind some old furniture, discarded curriculum, and hymnals. However, there were only two small trays holding four to six glasses, possibly enough for a dozen people. Both trays and cups were dirty and broken, but out of the cups were growing an intricate abundance of vines with fruit hanging from every leaf. In waking from the dream, I remembered a similar dream that Lela had during the early years of our marriage as she struggled with calling and vocation. The communion cups were filled with milk and, through some strange configuration of passing, the trays were being kept from her.

Sometimes I try to interpret these dreams as themes of the reality of abundance amid the illusions of scarcity, an important lesson to remember in preaching. Most of the time, however, I simply let them be and hope that the strange workings of the brain will bring me again to awe, mystery, wonder, and, finally, gratitude. Thanks be to God!

Do you seek to understand these strange nighttime visions and visitors? Do they seem to work with the unresolved events of the day, all those pieces of unfinished business? The hole in the top of the head will find our brain never completely at rest, always active, an electric storm like no other, rearranging the furniture of the previous day. What you see is what you get, although it may not be what is actually out there. The brain has a unique talent for making pictures and telling stories, writing the screenplay for the movies in your mind.

If you think all of this is pure gibberish, take a good look at Matthew 2. Joseph has five dreams that result in some action on his part and all with a background of human conversation. All shaped decisions, prompted actions, and served as preludes to the acts of God. Joseph seemed to be walking in two worlds: a world of keeping his fragile life together and an enchanting world of strange and novel visions. Are we not like Joseph? We try desperately to keep our act together during the day. But the night comes. We close the blinds, lock the doors, check the alarm system, and slip under the covers all safe and sound, but somehow the thief in the night from the Gospel of Matthew finds the way in. If we had known the thief was coming we would have stayed awake and kept the house from being invaded but we did not know, so we dream. In Matthew, the whole story depends on Joseph paying attention to dreams. If Joseph believes his dreams are visions from God, the whole drama will continue. If Joseph does not believe, the whole story comes to a screeching halt.

Why does any of this surprise us about Joseph? He comes from generations of dreamers–from Abraham's fire pot to Jacob's ladder and the other Joseph with his sheaves of dreams. Dreams shaped them as a people and called them out as a peculiar people. What would have happened to us if they had written them off as neurons bouncing around in the head or pizza rolling around in the stomach?

Lela has a framed poster in her study: "I'm not just a dreamer; I'm a wild dreamer." Her dream journal lies on her bedside table, somehow giving permission for the thief in the night to come visiting. But what about the rest of us? I'm warning you not to be surprised when the hole in your head is left unlocked, when that soft, velvety curtain of sleep slowly rises, when you begin to see something where there was nothing and the brain wakes up and, like Jacob, we sleep at the gate of heaven.

NOTES

[1] Robin Meyers, *Ears to Hear: Preaching As Self-Persuasion* (Cleveland: Pilgrim Press, 1993), 101-103.

[2] Ibid., 4.

[3] Renate Caine and Geoffrey Caine, *Making Connections: Teaching and the Human Brain* (Alexandria VA: Association for Supervision and Curriculum Development, 1991), 41-42.

[4] Frederick Buechner, *A Room Called Remember* (San Francisco, Harper & Row, 1984), 5.

[5] Eugene Lowry, *The Homiletical Plot* (Atlanta: John Knox Press, 1980), 60-61.

[6] Howard Gardner, *Frames of Mind: The Theory of Multiple Intelligences* (New York: Basic Books, Inc., 1983), 60-61. Gardner's other works include *The Unschooled Mind: How Children Think and How Schools Should Teach* (New York: Basic Books, 1991); *Creating Minds: An Anatomy of Creativity Seen through the Lives of Freud, Einstein, Picasso, Stravinsky, Eliot, Graham, and Gandhi* (New York: Basic Books, 1993); *Extraordinary Minds: Portraits of Exceptional Individuals and an Examination of Our Extraordinariness* (New York: Basic Books, 1997).

Gardner's most recent research suggests two more intelligence candidates: Naturalist—learning through recognizing patterns in nature—and Existential—talent for grappling with big questions like the meaning and life and death. See *Intelligence Reframed: Multiple Intelligences for the 21st Century* (New York: Basic Books, 2000).

[7] Jerry Bowling, "An Examination of Spirituality Based on Howard Gardner's Theory of Multiple Intelligencies," Ph.D. diss., The Southern Baptist Theological Seminary, 1998.

[8] Robert A. Emmons, "Spiritual Intelligence: Toward a Theory of Personality and Spirituality," in *Psychology of Ultimate Concern* (New York: Guilford, 1999). See David Myers, *Intuition: Its Powers and Perils* (New York: Yale University Press, 2002), 244-45.

[9] David Lazear, *Seven Pathways of Learning* (Tucson: Zephyr Press, 1994), 26-42.

[10] Nancy Margulies, *Mapping Inner Space* (Tucson: Zephyr Press, 1991), 16-22.

[11] Meyers, *Ears to Hear*, 77.

[12] Diane Ackerman, *A Natural History of the Senses* (New York: Random House, 1990), 18.

[13] Ibid., 206-207.

[14] Thomas G. Long, *The Senses of Preaching* (Atlanta: John Knox Press, 1988), 4.

[15] Ackerman, *A Natural History of the Senses*, 235-36.

CHAPTER NINE

Reading from the Margins: Cross-cultural Bible Study

*In life one must forever choose between being one who tells stories
and one about whom stories are told.*[1]

When we move away from those who are skilled in the tools of biblical interpretation, we find a different reading and study of the Bible. This difference may be described as cultural—a pattern of living that includes thought, speech, action, and other diverse ways of communicating. These "people groups" provide us with another perspective on experiential Bible study.

The people groups interpret the Bible in much the same way they interpret their lives. They do not read the Bible through the lens of scholarship and commentaries. Scholarship usually seeks to alter and shape the people's vision rather than using that vision as a starting point. When the people's vision of the Bible is lost, something vital is lost. Many peoples of this world discover in the Bible the same living conditions that they find in their own lives, experiencing the same injustices and at the mercy of the same forces. Significant issues that have been hidden from the learned and the clever have been revealed to the "little ones" (Matt 11:25-26). Paul saw the difference between the early church's work with Scripture and that of the professionals: "For the written letter kills, but the spirit gives life" (2 Cor 3:6).

The people discover themselves and something of their own experience. For many it is experienced as an event, a happening, a revelation—the power of the spirit acting in the vision of the person who reads the text. The Bible reveals a dimension of human life that cannot be seen by exegesis, just as the conversion experience cannot be described by factual accounts. This tension between accurate exegesis and the subjective interpretations of the world's peoples will continue to be one of the largest issues in biblical interpretation.

What is awakened in the subjective experience of the believer is a longing and a memory for a better way of life. Unless something is awakened in the believer, the information in interpretation remains a lifeless, "dead" letter. What they discover are the formulations of their deepest aspirations and the reformulations of their lost hopes. Their identity as a people is restored and a sense of mission rejuvenated. Suddenly, the light comes out of darkness. The exegesis of the text is needed, but no one has a corner on the action of the spirit. This comes only through reflective silence and listening, with our ears close to the ground and our elbows close to the people. Beginning with experience gets us on the same road with the people, so the map that is now drawn corresponds more closely with the features of the land on which the people walk.

The people's reading of the Bible follows no fixed pattern, but several processes seem to emerge spontaneously. People begin with a real-life situation. The reading of the text follows. However, the reading of the text is not enough. The attention of the people is not captured until it is told in the form of a story, as if the text is spoken in the readers' own words. Following the reading or narration of the Bible, questions start the discussion. Around this basic pattern many variations may occur, some more detailed and searching, others more simple and superficial. Sometimes the real-life situation is stated in the form of a case study or story. At other times, the experience is taken from the events of the past week. The starting point is crucial—a reflection on a real-life incident. The biblical text may be chosen in advance or in response to the issues raised by the group. The text that emerges out of the group's life seems intuitively to meet the needs of the group. Understanding seeks to channel everything into community activity.

Meeting times are varied. Orderly time sequence is not an issue. The group may meet every two weeks or every week. If there is a widespread issue confronting the people, then two or three times a week may not suffice. Groups come into being around a variety of issues and seasonal events. Groups have a variety of labels, but one thing is common: reading the Bible and reflecting on it in the context of life.

Sometimes the groups use prepared leaflets. Once in a while a Bible dictionary or commentary is available. For the most part, however, commentary is "live," with reflection combined with discussion, exchange of ideas, dramatizations, role-plays, prayers, meditation exercises, songs, music, poetry, and proverbs.

The process does not run smoothly. The people do not always succeed in making a firm connection between the Bible and their lives. Some connections are made that have no basis in the text or in life's realities. But that does not diminish the profound intuitive gifts that see life mirrored in the biblical text. The Bible is read and interpreted in order to understand more clearly the present situation.

Our lives are reflected in the gospel and the gospel is reflected back into our lives. Our first and foremost use of the gospel is to compare it with our world in order to get a better idea of the shape of our lives. Once you've discovered the gospel, life joins in a duet with it, harmonizing even in the most trivial details.[2]

Some would call this only the product of one's imagination. But it is hard to explain away the profound changes in the lives of people who have little understanding of the exegetical tools of Scripture, yet live their beliefs with firmness and conviction. The vision is not something taught but, rather, something discovered, emerging from within the people and from their way of living the faith. This comes from congenial interests and problems with those mentioned in the text, being open to its parallel issues.

Culture

Edward T. Hall in *The Silent Language* identified ten primary message systems found in every culture:[3]

1. Language (spoken, written)
2. Temporality (time, routine, schedule)
3. Territoriality (space, property)
4. Exploitation (method of control, use, and sharing of resources)
5. Association (family, kin, community)
6. Subsistence (work, division of labor)
7. Bisexuality (modes of speech, dress, conduct)
8. Learning (observation, modeling, instruction)
9. Play (humor, games)
10. Defense (health procedures, social conflicts, beliefs)

Hall defined culture as "the way of life of a people. The sum of their learned behavior patterns, attitudes, and material things. . . . It is not innate, but learned; the various facets of culture are interrelated."[4] Culture is often equated with nationality but has a much broader scope. Almost any country has various cultural groups with distinctions in race, ethnicity, religion, region, and gender.

Eugene Nida has defined culture as "all learned behavior that is acquired, that is the material and nonmaterial traits which are passed on from one generation to another."[5] Culture is the totality of what a persons learn, what they see and hear, how they live in a specific period of time, and how they pass on that heritage to future generations.

Biblical Culture

Without seeking to describe all aspects of biblical culture or even seeking to do an overview, let us work with Hall's categories in describing that strange and alien life we find in the Bible.

1. *Language (spoken, written).* Biblical language was a combination of Hebrew, Greek, and Aramaic. The Old Testament was written in Hebrew, with the possible exceptions of Ezra and Daniel. The New Testament was written in Greek, although Jesus and the early believers probably spoke Aramaic. Hebrew can convey abundant meanings though a few words, focusing on action verbs. Aramaic was the spoken language of Palestine after 600 BC. The Greek language spread throughout the Mediterranean world following Alexander's conquest in 335 BC. Some Aramaic and Latin forms are found in the Greek language. Greek was an easy language to speak, and it swept across cultures. The Greek language of the New Testament (*koine*) was the common language of the people. Paul was probably multilingual, knowing all three biblical languages and Latin as well.

2. *Temporality (time, routine, schedule).* The biblical writers did not see God as being governed by time or organized by special events and seasons. People encountered God in each moment and in the awakening of a new day. They did not fill their days with tightly scheduled agendas. Days were sometimes counted and years were counted by the cycles of the seasons. By far the most important unit of time was the day, the basic unit of intuitive experience. But days were not simply counted. They were identified by their most significant event. Throughout the Scriptures we read "day of rejoicing," "day of trouble," "day of salvation"—expressions that commemorate a given day's experiential quality.

3. *Territoriality (space, property).* There is not much private space in the Bible, although withdrawing to a "quiet place" seemed to be a must in the ministry of Jesus. Biblical people knew private ownership and private enterprise, but as the monarchy developed, bureaucracy took more and more control of land and economic activity. Foreign control by Assyria, Babylon, and Rome continued the domination by external forces. Throughout much of the Bible the people live under heavy submission to foreign powers that control through heavy tax burdens (Matt 22:17-21). Most people were limited in travel. Jesus' range of ministry never took him far from home, although there was not a permanent place "to lay his head." Travel was on foot through a rugged geographical landscape of "rough ways."

4. *Exploitation (method of control, use, and sharing of resources).* Slave labor was an outgrowth of urbanization, but laws regarding slaves were quite stringent (Exod 21:1-11, 20, 26). Most landowners hired day laborers (Matt 20:1-5). The leasing of land to tenant farmers became common in the New Testament period (Matt 21:33-41).

5. *Association (family, kin, community).* The tribal unit was the basic social and political formation of Israel. In biblical times, a nation was referred to as a people. The people of Israel saw themselves as the people of God. Nations had tribes and tribes had clans. A clan was a cluster of families or households with common ancestry. A traditional family pattern as we know it (four and no more) is difficult to find in Scripture. The composition and practice of family life changed radically from Old Testament to New Testament. In the Old Testament, family referred to the larger patriarchal clan, which included people related by blood, marriage, slavery, and even strangers and sojourners. The family centered on the oldest male, viewed as father, master, and ultimate authority, signifying the family as "the father's house." The authority of the father was powerful, and the family was held together by this central figure. The importance of lineage shifted in the New Testament from ancestry to lineage from God—from earthly father to God the Father, accessible to anyone through Jesus Christ. The roles of men and women were transformed through the love of Christ. The father was no longer the central figure of the family but was replaced by God the Father and faith in Jesus Christ. The authority of the male became like the sacrificial servant authority of Jesus Christ (Eph 5:25-34). Both men and women gave themselves voluntarily and sacrificially to each other (Eph 5:21), and mutual submissiveness was another way of making all things new.

Closely tied to concern for family was love for neighbor. After the love of God, the Bible's main concern was how we treat the neighbor. Refusing to respect the rights of neighbors brings moral disintegration and punishment of the nations (Isa 3:5, Jer 9:4-9). Leviticus 19:18 defines neighbor as "any of your people," one of your own kind and one who believed as you did. By Jesus' day, neighbor had been further restricted to those who observed Jewish law. Other people were enemies (Matt 5:44). However, Jesus broadened the concept of neighbor to include enemies. The parable of the Good Samaritan (Luke 10:30-35) saw the neighbor as any person in need. Since all have some kind of need, neighbor would include everyone. Neighboring is done as we show mercy (Luke 10:37).

6. *Subsistence (work, division of labor).* All things belonged to God, but land possession was strictly a business matter. Land could revert to the king if not used (2 Kgs 8:1-6). The kinsman-redeemer (Lev 25:25) protected the land against

those who would try to steal an inheritance. Private lands were subject to seizure by a ruler. Ground and people were intimately connected. God chose dry, loose material on the surface of the ground from which God, like a potter, formed humankind. God is a vital connection between land and people, and the land is fruitful if people are faithful to God (Deut 28:1-14).

7. *Bisexuality (modes of speech, dress, conduct)*. Biblical writers are ambivalent about sex roles and sexuality. Sex was both good and bad—a contrast of equality and dominance/submission. Patriarchal over-lording by males was a result of sin and a distortion of God's plan. Before the fall and after the coming of Christ, man and woman are set forth as equals. Modes of speech, dress, and conduct come from the shame of nakedness. Clothing creates jealousy in the Joseph conflict with his brothers (Gen 37:3-4). The purpose for clothing was its practical use as a night covering (Deut 24:13), a "handbag" for travel (Isa 3:22), a veil (Gen 24:65), and as a protective garment against the sun. Although much of the clothing of men and women appear to be the same from our horizon of the biblical picture, wearing clothes of the opposite sex was forbidden (Deut 22:5).

8. *Learning (observation, modeling, instruction)*. Much learning came from observation, modeling, and instruction. Two methods with cultural significance are mentioned here. Dreams were real. God used dreams and night visions to communicate. Dreams ranged from simple messages in Matthew 1 and 2, to symbolic dreams in Genesis 37, to complex dreams needing interpretation in Daniel 2 and 4. God revealed his will through dreams, but the prophets also warned against that method in knowing the will of God (Jer 23:28; Zech 10:1-2).

The home was the primary agency for learning. The ordinary activities of life were filled with faith meanings, and teachings about God flowed naturally from these activities (Deut 6:7). The traditional teachings of the priests in the synagogues were often ineffective, and Samuel attempted an educational reform through the school of prophets (1 Sam 19:19-20). No formal educational approach is described in the New Testament. Jesus taught through all the experiences of life, using stories, parables, and action parables to communicate the love of God.

9. *Play (humor, games)*. References to sports (2 Sam 2:14-16) and allusions to child play (Isa 11:8 and Zech 8:5) are brief biblical descriptions. The Bible is almost silent about the nature of play. Public games took on the spectacle of current games, and Paul used them as metaphors of the Christian life (Gal 2:2; Phil 3:13-14; 2 Tim 2:5; 1 Cor 9:25-27).

10. *Defense (health procedures, social conflicts, beliefs).* A meager understanding of the human anatomy limited the ability to combat disease and to enjoy healthy living. Illness was often attributed to sin or to a curse by an enemy. Most people were born and died without trained medical attention. Some sought physicians but went without healing (Mark 5:25-34; Luke 8:43-48). Folk remedies were used for most illnesses. Infection, nutritional deficiencies, birth defects, and injuries were common. Preventive health was unknown since the cause of illness was unknown. Regardless of the illness, people found that Jesus could truly help.

Famine and drought caused by lack of rain, locust, wind, and the enemy were constant fears. The best defense against famine and drought was obedience to God. The productiveness of the earth was related to the people's obedience. When the people obeyed God, the land was productive (Deut 11:11-14). Famine will be a part of God's coming judgment of the earth in the last days (Matt 24:7; Rev 6:8). God protects his faithful ones in times of famine (Ps 33:18-19).

Cross-cultural Learning

Cross-cultural learning is difficult because people come from vastly different value systems. There are differences in social values and learning styles even among cultural groups. Edward Hall has developed a concept that is useful in understanding the unique individual differences in and among cultural groups.[6] He placed cultures on a continuum from high to low context. Context refers to environmental, social, and cultural conditions that surround and embody the life of an individual, organization, or community. In a high-context culture, what is happening at the moment in and around us influences everything. In a low-context culture, these dynamics are filtered out for more long-range goals. High-context communication takes time where trust, personal needs, and attention to nonverbal communication play into the interaction. In low-context cultures, the immediate circumstances are ignored, and the parties focus on objective facts and ideas. Interactions are based on speed and efficiency. Witness the popularity of any kind of interaction that will only take "one minute." It would be useless to attempt a listing of all the "one-minute" books.

High-context cultures focus on community rather than individual concerns, the importance of process and relationships in tasks, communication as an art form, and a perception that for everything there is a time. Learning takes place in practicing and rehearsing concepts. A task should not be accomplished at the expense of relationships and community-building. High-context structures tend to be egalitarian with flat, rather than hierarchical, organizational models.

Again, we must warn against placing people in "cultural boxes." Every person is a complex mix of cultural influences determined by the amount of time spent in different cultural settings and the comfort or discomfort with the learning styles of a culture. People seem to relate to different cultural learning environments by adopting the cultural patterns, fitting in when it seems to be necessary, or choosing to remain alien and a stranger.

Learning Orientations

We will seek to identify several different orientations based on traits and contexts among cultures with attending learning possibilities and processes.[7]

1. *Word Orientation (oral and written).* In oral orientation, wisdom is a perception and vision of the daily life. Education is a full-time process with global aims and approaches. Processes are full of tradition and repeated time and time again. Communication is direct, immediate, group-oriented, and given "all at once."

In written orientations, wisdom is the amassing of empirical knowledge and objective detail. Education is selective, specialized, and scheduled. Approaches are based on individual pursuits following a cumulative model. Communication is indirect, individual, and given "piece by piece."

2. *Temporality Orientation (event and time).* In event orientations, there is a time for everything and everything in its time. Time is not easily scheduled, and circumstances and needs of people will interfere with set times. The details of the event are more important, regardless of time. All events must have exhaustive consideration, in spite of perceived time restraints. Present experience is valued rather than past or future events. Meetings begin when the last person arrives and end when the last person leaves. Baseball is event-oriented. "It's not over till it's over!" One hour late might not be late!

In time orientations, things are scheduled to be done at particular times, and one thing at a time. Efficiency is as important as getting the task done. Punctuality is valued, and time is carefully allocated to achieve the maximum within set limits. The past is valued with references to dates and history. Basketball and football are time-oriented, following "clock time." Five minutes late is late!

3. *Learning Orientation (inclusive and exclusive).* In inclusive orientations, knowledge is embedded in the situation. All things are connected, and judgments are open-ended with "all things considered." Multiple sources of information are valued and used. Thinking is deductive, proceeding from the general to the specific. Learning occurs by observation, demonstration, and practice. Group and multiple interactions are preferred for problem solving. The quality of learning is

valued, regardless of time. Information and experience are seemingly disorganized, based on stories, activities, and events independent and complete in themselves. Learning follows the Hebrew pattern of stories, life histories, prophecies, and proverbs. Learning is perceived in whole units, like checkers and chess.

In exclusive orientations, knowledge is fragmented and compartmentalized. One or two sources, intelligences, and senses are used to develop knowledge. Specific criteria are involved in right/wrong, black/white thinking. Information and experience fit into categories and are systematically organized. Learning occurs by following explicit directions and explanations of others. An individual orientation is preferred for learning and problem solving. Speed is valued. Learning follows a Greek pattern of systematized thinking. Learning is perceived in the understanding of parts, similar to Scrabble, crossword puzzles, phonetics, and sentence diagramming.

4. *Handling Crisis Orientations (crisis and non-crisis)*. In non-crisis orientations, the possibility of crisis is downplayed with a focus on "come what may" and actual direct experience. Attitudes are basically optimistic, but decision and action are delayed. Change is slow. Things are rooted in the past, stable, and slow to change. Solutions have many options and are taken from many sources. Expert, "professional" advice and counsel are not trusted.

In crisis orientations, problems are anticipated and proper planning is valued. Change is fast; one can make a change and see immediate results and quick resolution. Operation manuals have correct procedures and should be read before beginning a procedure. Expert advice is valued and sought.

5. *Goal Orientation (person and task)*. In person orientations, the focus is on relationships and the satisfactions achieved in face-to-face interaction. Relationships are sought with people who are group-oriented. Relationships build slowly and are stable. One distinguishes between people inside and outside one's circle. How things get done depends on relationships and attention to group process. One deplores loneliness and will sacrifice personal achievements for group interaction. Work life includes friends and intimate relationships. Social structure and authority are centralized for the good of the group.

In task orientations, the focus is on a task and principles, and satisfaction is achieved in reaching goals. Friendship is sought with people who have similar goals. Relationships begin and end quickly. Many people can be inside one's circle, and boundaries are unclear. Things get done by following procedures and paying attention to goals. Loneliness and deprivation are accepted for the sake of personal achievements, and identity is rooted in one's accomplishments. Significant relationships are outside work environments.

6. *Communication Orientation (nonverbal and verbal).* In a nonverbal orientation, there is high use of voice tone, facial expression, gestures, and eye movement in conversation. Nonverbal messages are implicit; the context (situation, people, and environment) is more important than words. The nonverbal message is indirect, with narrative and embellishment. Communication is seen as art form—a way of engaging people. Disagreements are personalized, and conflict must be solved before work can progress or avoided because of personal threat.

In verbal interaction, the message is carried more by words than by nonverbal means. The verbal message is explicit. Context is less important than words. The verbal message is direct and spelled out in specifics. Communication is a way of exchanging information, ideas, and opinions. Disagreement is personalized, with the focus on "getting on with the task" and rational solutions. One can be explicit about another's bothersome behavior.

7. *Self-worth Orientation (status and achievement).* In a status orientation, prestige is ascribed. Formal credentials of birth and rank determine identity. Titles are important and permanent. The amount of respect one receives is permanently fixed with high social status, in spite of personal failings. People are expected to play out status roles. People associate with social equals.

In achievement orientations, prestige is attained and identity determined by achievement. Achievement comes and goes quickly. The amount of respect received varies with accomplishments and failures and depends on personal performance. Individuals are self-critical and will sacrifice to accomplish greater achievement. People associate with those of equal accomplishment, regardless of background.

8. *Vulnerability Orientation (openness and concealment).* In openness orientations, space is communal. People stand close to each other and share the same space. There is relative unconcern about error and failure. People are willing to push beyond limits and enter the unknown with openness to alternative views and criticism. People talk freely about personal lives and readily admit culpability and shortcomings. People will try things even if they look foolish.

In concealment orientations, space is compartmentalized and privately owned. Privacy is important and people are further apart. Self-image is protected at all costs, and errors and failures are avoided. People are reluctant to go beyond recognized limits and alternative viewpoints, and criticisms are devalued. People are vague about personal lives and deny guilt. They tend to withdraw from activities that reveal limitations.

One of my most stimulating writing assignments has been in designing simulated life on the streets of five major world cities: the complex family networks of Hong Kong; the sensory experiences of traffic noise, loud music, strong smells, and strange foods in Dhaka, Bangladesh; the language barriers in Moscow, Russia; the extended family systems in the garbage dumps and tombs of Cairo, Egypt; and the sports activities on the crowded streets of Buenos Aires, Brazil.[8] Immersion into different cultural contexts, even though they are simulated, invigorates the learning environment in an unusual way and reveals the polarities of learning orientations.

Nonverbal Communication

While it may be difficult to describe all the nonverbal details for every language, we can still describe the emotional impact of nonverbal dimensions. These dimensions of nonverbal communication exist in every culture. At least five of these dimensions can be described.[9]

1. *Kinesics*–movement of the body (head, arms, legs, fingers).
2. *Phonemics*–use of interpersonal space (the distance between people when standing, sitting, or talking).
3. *Chronemics*–timing of verbal exchanges during conversation (the period of silence between statements and response).
4. *Oculesics*–eye-to-eye contact (patterns of contact or avoidance in speaking and listening).
5. *Haptics*–tactile forms of communication (where, how, and how often people touch each other when conversing).

These five dimensions are not exhaustive and may include such things as dress, posture, smell, colors, time, and a various number of intricate mannerisms. Education and training in nonverbal communication patterns has always been treated in a haphazard manner. Some would consider nonverbal communication to be of little importance. They indicate this view by a lack of awareness of their own body language. The designing of learning experiences along any of these dimensions usually results in emotional responses similar to those occurring in actual intercultural situations. Learners can then practice new simulated behavior until it becomes a more natural part of their repertoire of communication skills. Dyadic encounters seem to be one of the most effective training methods. One member of each dyad acts in a prescribed nonverbal manner that elicits a response from this "strange" behavior. A "participant observer" creates a triad and adds the dimension of debriefing.

This methodology attempts to sensitize learners to many other behavior patterns of nonverbal communication by using an "informed" partner and a "control" partner in a pattern of strange nonverbal behaviors. Discussions following the training exercises can pick up other dimensions of messages communicated cross-culturally. The introduction of nonverbal communication patterns brings activities and discussions that are both interesting and fun and, at the same time, enhances communication and perception skills. One of the most energetic training sessions in a church occurred in a two-hour Sunday evening session. The "morning" English-speaking church met with the "afternoon," Korean-speaking church in a series of dyadic encounters with the only instructions being to "communicate in any way you can." Usually, these sessions will increase awareness of nonverbal behaviors that have remained unknown and oblivious for years, even though people have been surrounded and exposed to them daily.

Nonverbals in the Bible

Nonverbal communication includes all the movements of the body that communicate thoughts and emotions. The piercing look of Jesus in Luke 22:61 is an example of nonverbal communication. Many gestures are expressions of life and customs of a culture and are visual symbols of communication. The ancient Near Eastern culture had many ways of bodily expression that would be difficult for us to interpret today. Kneeling and bowing expressed honor and devotion in worship (Isa 45:23; Rev 4:10). Dancing was a way of expressing joy and celebration before the Lord (Exo 15:20; 2 Sam 6:16). The tearing of one's clothes and heaping ashes on one's head were expressions of deep grief (2 Sam 1:11) and sudden alarm (Matt 26:65).

Head movements in modern American culture are interpreted quite differently from what might have been interpreted in biblical times. Shaking one's head communicated scorn and reproach (Psa 22:7, Matt 27:39). Lifting one's head could mean exaltation (Ps 27:6) and contempt (Ps 83:2).

Eye-to-eye contact has different meanings across cultures. Winking the eye may indicate deceit and trouble (Prov 6:13; 10:10). Jesus, looking at Peter at the time of his denial, showed both hurt and disappointment (Luke 22:61). The lifting of eyelids expresses pride (Prov 30:13). Eyes can show the expressions of anger (Mark 3:5). Jesus, lifting up his eyes upon the disciples, shows his personal regard and affection for them (Luke 6:20). Mouths show happiness and joy as well as scorn (Ps 22:7; Mark 5:40) or rebuke (Ps 2:4). Pursing the lips can show contempt (Ps 22:7). Kissing, a sign of affection, is used to hide Judas's real intentions (Matt 26:48). Spitting is a way of showing contempt (Matt 26:67).

Inclining one's ears is a way of intensely listening (Ps 45:10). An outstretched neck reveals haughtiness (Isa 3:16).

Perhaps the most revealing nonverbal expressions come through the hands. The hands are the visible expressions of the heart. The hands are raised in prayer (Ps 141:2), an act of blessing (Luke 24:50), or an act emphasizing an oath (Deut 32:40). Covering the mouth with the hand indicates silence (Job 29:9). Touching someone with the hand can give all sorts of mixed messages. In Genesis 37:22, it is an indication of violence, or it can mean a form of blessing (Gen 48:18) or healing (Luke 4:40). The clapping of hands can be confusing. In Job 27:23 and Nahum 3:19, it is a sign of contempt. In Isaiah 55:12, it is an indication of joy and celebration. The waving of hands beckons (Luke 5:7) or calls to silence (Acts 12:17). The pointing of fingers can show ill favor (Prov 6:13) or accusation (Isa 58:9).

Shaking the dust off one's feet is a call to separating and distancing (Matt 10:14). Washing the feet of another is an act of servanthood (John 13:5-12). Uncovering one's feet is an act of grief or repentance (2 Sam 15:30; Isa 20:2). When Boaz uncovered his feet (Ruth 3:4), he was indicating his willingness to marry and protect Ruth.

The prophets were the masters of nonverbal communication. In Isaiah 20:3, Isaiah walked barefoot and naked for three years, expressing the humiliation of Egypt and Ethiopia when Assyria defeated them. In Jeremiah 27:1-7, Jeremiah wore a yoke of wood around his neck, symbolizing the domination of the Babylonians over Judah. Ezekiel lay on his side for many days (Ezek 4:4-8), indicating a year for each day of iniquity. His lack of eating in Ezekiel 4:9-17, the cutting of his hair (Ezek 5:1-17), and setting his face toward the mountains of Israel (Ezek 6:1-7) were nonverbal expressions of the judgment of God.

West Africa

In 1989, I was invited by a mission board to do a curriculum workshop for the churches of West Africa. The Baptist Association Press of West Africa (BAPSWA) met me in Lome, Togo, for a four-day workshop. I carried with me the experiential Bible study model and two commentaries on the Gospel of Mark. Missionaries and local West African leaders had been given specific texts for preliminary work before coming to the workshop. Following a brief introduction to the model and a couple of practice sessions, each writer went off to design and write with two directives—stay close to the West African experience and close to the integrity of the Markan text. Each lesson followed the circular motion of experience, exegesis, reflection, and application (or "hook," "book," "look," "took.") After several hours, each writer brought back a session plan and engaged the group in a lab experience with the text. Suggestions and debriefing followed.

This process continued for four days: a brief lecture twice a day introducing different aspects of experiential Bible study, design and writing, practice sessions, lab experiences using the creations of writers, clarifications, suggestions, and debriefing, and back to more design and writing. At the end of four days, we had an experiential study guide on the Gospel of Mark, later published by BAPSWA and distributed to the churches of West Africa.

I left West Africa with two strong impressions. The West Africans knew some things about the Gospel of Mark that I did not know and had a clarity of vision that I did not have. They knew the meaning of traveling by foot and by boat. They had experienced a vulnerability to the elements of wind and storm. They saw clearly the focus of Mark more in action than in word. They had insight into the storytelling genre of the Markan Gospel that provoked powerful images in the mind of the reader. They heard the language that was simple and to the point, using common patterns of speech. They played with the theatrical aspects of the Gospel, with its flair for the dramatic and its eye for detail. They felt the desert heat, hard soil, and thorny bushes on their feet. They feared the demonic powers that could cause people to lose their rightful minds. They saw and heard the importance of gesture and emotion, the power of word and action to bring cleansing, healing, and cursing. They felt the ominous shadows of illness, suffering, and death as daily experiences.

It is true that some of this was mixed with African traditional religion. When that happened, we went back to the text for clarification and correction. But the experiential model wrapped us all in a web close to life and text, a related but disciplined thinking, feeling, and doing process.

There was another strong impression. The experiential process that seemed to pose the "yes, but . . ." ambivalence on the Western mind came easily to the West African mind. I suspected that this was the way they had always done Bible study when left to their own ministrations. I had only brought clarity and perhaps legitimacy to a process that they knew intuitively. I needed to know more, so I asked permission from the trustees at Southern Seminary to spend my sabbatical in West Africa during the 1989–1990 school year.

Our first Sunday in Liberia during late summer 1989 provided a symbolic action parable of my internal fascination with West African Bible study. We arrived for Sunday school at the Providence Baptist Church in downtown Monrovia during a torrential rainstorm characteristic of the rainy season. Shuffling Bible, umbrella, and more than a little anxiety, I stepped out of the car and dropped my Bible on the street pavement. It was immediately picked up by the current of rainwater and swept down the street. I caught up with it a half-block later, dropped it soaking wet in the car, and went on to church. My Bible took three days to dry. This was my study, teaching and preaching Bible with an accumulation of fifteen years of notes in margins. Most of my notes had been washed away in Liberian rainwater, and those that had not were blurred beyond recognition. The insight came sharp and clear. If I was going to live in West Africa for a year, I must learn to read the Bible, in spite of all my limitations, with West African eyes.

During my first semester at the Liberian Baptist Theological Seminary, our class in experiential Bible study designed, wrote, and published a Bible study guide on the Gospel of John. During the spring semester, the students in a course on Hebrews were writing a faith development study guide from Hebrews 11:1–12:3. The civil war that began in Liberia in December 1989 finally closed the seminary in mid-semester of 1990. Those manuscripts are tucked away for a better day. Much of our published works on Mark and John were destroyed during the civil war that has raged in Liberia since 1990.

I would not claim that the experiential model has started a revolution in curriculum development in West Africa. Like most other places, it has a committed following of people who find in this simple process a depth of meaning for themselves and with others. I know a group of thirty to forty seminary students and graduates who understand the process and use it weekly in the churches, villages, and refuge camps of the West African nations. I received a draft of an experiential Bible study guide on the book of Galatians from a pastor in Sierra Leone who was one of the original designers in the workshop at Lome, Togo. His purpose was to issue a clarion call to the churches of beleaguered West African countries, "For freedom Christ has set us free."

I am far from being an expert in cross-cultural Bible studies. Most of what I know comes from hunches and the good fortune of stimulating student bodies that were fearless and courageous in working with the biblical text. Our products were not high-tech, color-coded, age-graded learning outcomes with focused or taxonomy-oriented designs. Rather, they were simple, two-page mimeographed movements of experience, exegesis, reflection, and application, putting our ideas and inspiration into movement and motion. Here are some tentative proposals of building homegrown curriculum models starting from an experiential base of the local cultural setting.

1. Local creativity and self-expression can be tapped in an energetic and celebrative atmosphere of community design, stories, and writing.

2. A new generation of indigenous curriculum builders is waiting to be born, coming from every cultural setting, calling the name of Christ.

3. Learning style is a larger umbrella, organizing principle rather than specific cultural and ethnic values. All types and modes of learning styles can be found in all cultures.

4. Cross-cultural curriculum design explores and uses all the senses.

5. Mind-mapping, both in simplicity and complexity, is a process that indigenous cultures understand. A culture map will identify each individual in a center circle. This is the person within his or her culture. Working out from this person are the various elements in the culture: the individual, masculinity, femininity, freedom, wisdom, death and dying, time, work, modesty, humor, violence and terror, abortion, justice, problem solving, the future, and so on. Discussion will follow around the unique attitudes within the culture about any one particular element.

6. Traditional learning objectives are linear and digital. In many cultures, objectives are more global and holistic. Analytical, logical progression starts with pieces and seeks to build a whole. Global objectives start with the whole and move to pieces, with the whole seen from many different perspectives.

Text-specific Interpretation

What the people of the Bible saw and heard and how they lived is not just another problem of interpretation for us. It is our primary source of identification and empathy. The more we search the culture, the more we discover that they were like us. We would call the biblical world primitive in comparison to our modern culture. But letting the biblical world be primitive does not mean that it was crude, unlearned, and aboriginal. By primitive we would mean original, primary, and basic, that which is of the essence and substantial, having an inner coherence. Midwifery would be considered a primitive form of giving birth. But midwifery is in contact with the essence of life, in touch with blood, water, sweat, and tears, supporting the fragility of life without denying the labor and pain of it all. Finding ourselves back in the primitive culture of the Bible is to find ourselves in that which is basic and essential. We cannot make the Bible say what we want it to say. We must let it say what it says with the presupposition that what it is saying is essential and basic to what God wants us to know.

The answer to cultural relativism and many forms of contextualism is a return to the specificity of the text. This is the point that Walter Brueggemann made so well in *Texts Under Negotiation*. The specificity and oddity of the text focus on the little story the text has to tell rather than the "great story" spoken of only in generalities. The little story that contains strange, odd, or even offensive material needs to be examined and honored like Paul's "lesser members of the body." We cannot deny or ignore that which is unacceptable to the modern consciousness. By accepting that which is contextually relevant, we might miss that which is most interesting, most poignant, and most "disclosing" in the text. Selective reading violates the text but also denies a serious access to the oddity and strangeness of the text, which denies the importance of the Christian's "oddity" in the world.

Brueggemann proposed a fresh honoring of the ambiguity, oddity, and "embarrassing" aspects of the text. This is why some biblical material is never covered in Sunday school lessons. Selecting and censoring of texts are ways of censoring and selecting what God would say to us. The resurfacing of buried, subversive texts creates a rereading in light of the newly recovered material.

> In parallel fashion, in Bible reading new texts require us to reread everything of God, self, and neighbor in light of neglected texts. Note well that texts, like recovered memories, do not want to be contextualized, placed, or interrelated. They need only to be voiced. When voiced, they linger a while, with power, in our imagination.[10]

Ezekiel Will Be a Sign to You

"Thus Ezekiel will be a sign to you; you shall do just as he has done. When this comes, then you shall know that I am the LORD God" (Ezek 24:24). Ezekiel was a sixth-century BC priest and prophet caught up in a whirlwind of changing times. He was a character, an imaginative artist, flamboyant preacher, ecstatic prophet, and sympathetic pastor. He had an amazing arsenal of communication strategies, a storehouse of information about historical events and geography, composition of armies, and political intrigue. He has been charged with psychotic and schizophrenic behaviors because his bizarre actions are foreign to the Western mind. But to the Near Eastern culture, his behavior is not so strange. Much of his behavior hardly stirs the people at all. Chapters 4 and 5 of Ezekiel provide adequate examples of Scripture that must be seen and interpreted from a multicultural perspective.

Ezekiel's behavior in chapter 4 has been described as symbolic action, role-playing, and pantomime methodology. He creates a stage in the center of a city street. He tells his story through powerful expressive movement. Inspiration is both verbal and nonverbal where God inspires both word and act. Word and action are closely related, giving the sense that "these things really will happen."

Ezekiel presents four action parables. In verses 1-3, he acts out the roles of the enemy. He shapes the image of Jerusalem on clay bricks and builds a siege against it. God, who has been the iron defense, is absent, and the ominous "iron curtain" of the enemy surrounds the city. In verses 4-8, Ezekiel plays the rebellious people of Jerusalem. He reclines on his left side for 390 days and on his right side for 40 days. During this period, he eats and drinks only enough to keep alive. In verses 9-17, he dramatically portrays the people besieged.

The people get the picture. A besieged people, surrounded by the enemy, are weakened by starvation and death and perish from lack of water. Starvation, plague, sickness, death, and despair produce withered bodies and broken spirits. Bread is baked on fire made from human excretion because customary fuels are no longer available. With emotions drained, supplies exhausted, and defenses destroyed, the spirit of the people is gone and they waste away.

The fourth action parable is described in Ezekiel 5:1-6. Ezekiel cuts his hair and beard and divides it into three parts. One part is burned, one is cut up with a knife, and one is scattered to the winds. Only the merest remnant of hair is left—the fate of the people of Jerusalem.

The book of Ezekiel illustrates many of the cultural values that seem foreign to us today. Communication is an art form rather than the processing of information. Symbolic communication is used to touch many of the dimensions of learning—rational, emotional, and intuitive. We will find his bodily movements, dress, posture, mannerisms, and sense of appropriateness not to our liking. We find him in an exhaustive time frame, detached from schedules and any sense of clock time. For Ezekiel, time seems to stand still. We can't imagine him "watching the clock." The immediate environment takes on ultimate concern. The message is communicated nonverbally (4:1 to 5:6) but is interpreted verbally (5:5-17). Ezekiel is totally vulnerable, with no sense of privacy and no concern for saving face.

Reading from the Margins

I have spent enough time in West Africa and in Indian and Hispanic cultures of New Mexico to know that they read and hear Scripture differently. I never heard the "silent themes" of rape, physical torture, malnourishment, infertility, and the lack of education of women in the Bible until I heard them from women. Students who were "challenged" in some way had interesting perspectives on Scripture in seminary classes. It startled me when I heard "Exodus in reverse" from the Indian culture of the southwest, describing land taken from them rather than land given to them. The minority peoples of the world could tell some of the same stories. "We had the land and you had the Bible. Now you have the land and we have the Bible." These are some examples of "marginal" readings from people who tend to be "invisible."

We don't have a single word of Scripture written by an American. I can hear you saying, "We know that." The nature of the American presence in the world and the extension of power, authority, and influence may lead us to think that we can remake the world in our own image, including our understanding of biblical texts. There is a long history of the Bible being read to "civilize the natives."[11] There is also the subversive resistance to that kind of reading when the people discovered their power in reading for themselves. This is illustrated in a brief encounter of one "learned in Scripture" and one unlearned.

"Who taught you the gospel?"

"Luke."

"Luke who?"

"The writer of the Gospel Luke."

What else is to be done? We have filled our libraries with an exhaustive number of commentaries, much of which now can be accessed with the flip of a computer switch. We will continue to produce translations, revisions of translations, and argue over the revisions of revisions. We will continue to produce learner and leader guides and a host of sophisticated helps. There is something else we can do. We can listen to the readings of indigenous communities, maybe among those marginal people on the edges of Asia where it all began in the first place.

NOTES

[1] R. S. Sugirtharajah, *The Bible and the Third World* (New York: Cambridge University Press, 2001), 244.

[2] Carlos Mesters, *Defenseless Flower: A New Reading of the Bible* (Maryknoll: Orbis Books, 1991), 99.

[3] Edward T. Hall, *The Silent Language* (Garden City: Doubleday Publishing Co., 1959).

[4] Ibid., 16, 20.

[5] Eugene Nida, *Customs and Cultures: Anthropology for Christian Missions* (New York: Harper & Row, 1954), 220.

[6] Hall, *The Silent Language*.

[7] Some of these categories are suggested in Sherwood G. Lingenfelter and Marvin K. Mayers, *Ministering Cross Culturally* (Grand Rapids: Baker Book House, 1986).

[8] John Hendrix, *Harvest of the City* (Birmingham: Women's Missionary Union, 1995).

[9] Melvin Schapper, "Nonverbal Communication and the Intercultural Encounter," in *The 1975 Handbook of Group Facilitators*, ed. Jones and Pfeiffer (San Diego: University Associates, 1975), 155-59.

[10] Walter Brueggemann, *Texts Under Negotiation* (Minneapolis: Fortress, 1993), 60-61.

[11] The perils and promises of Scripture reading in precolonial, colonial, and postcolonial period of the Third World are recounted in R. S. Sugirtharajak, *The Bible and the Third World*.

CHAPTER TEN

The Seed Finders: Curriculum

In an important departure from older traditions, the crops we now grow in the United States are extremely uniform genetically, due to the fact that our agriculture is controlled primarily by a few large agricultural corporations that sell relatively few varieties of seeds. Those who know the seed business are well aware that our shallow seed bank is highly vulnerable; when a crop strain succumbs all at once to a new disease . . . researchers must return to the more diverse original strains for help. So we rely on the gigantic insurance policy provided by the genetic variability in the land races, which continue to be hand-sown and harvested, year in and year out, by farmers in those mostly poor places from which our crops arose.[1]

I have great faith in a seed. Convince me that you have a seed there, and I am prepared to expect wonders. —Henry David Thoreau

Perhaps the most important work to be done today in curriculum development is in the restructuring of curricular language. Most of us involved in curricular development are pragmatists, constantly at work in the practical, concrete, ever-changing tasks of development, design, implementation, and evaluation. Metaphorical thinking is an attempt to talk about curriculum in new ways. The purpose of metaphor is to understand, to test our most sacred assumptions, and to find our way back to root meanings.

The Metaphorical Roots

Several themes seem to dominate the metaphorical roots of curriculum design. One theme is technological, with emerging patterns of industry and production. The other theme is biological, emphasizing living organisms and growth. Herbert M. Kliebard has provided a helpful analysis of the metaphorical roots of curriculum design.[2] He identified three metaphors that have influenced the thought and practice of curriculum-making in both general and Christian education. These three metaphors are production, growth, and travel.

In the metaphor of production, students are the raw material that has the potential of being transformed into a finished and useful product under the control of highly skilled technicians. Production is carefully plotted in advance, according to specific outcomes. Production has the feel of a factory and the dominant image of an assembly line. Technical accuracy, systematic control, long-range planning, and prediction are emphasized. Although there is some variation, most products come off the assembly line looking alike. Education changes from a process to a commodity that can be produced and sold. Teaching is viewed as a science that specifies, measures, and evaluates both content and methodology to maximize its impact in the lives of students. The four basic steps of this rationale are familiar to all of us. They are: identifying educational objectives, selecting appropriate learning experiences, organizing learning experiences, and evaluating the learning.

The second metaphor is the metaphor of growth. The curriculum is the routine care provided in a "garden" situation where students grow and develop to their full potential under the watchful eye and patient care of teachers. The plants that grow in the garden are of every variety, but the gardener values each plant and wants them all to blossom and come to full flower. Using a garden as a metaphor for learning creates all kinds of interesting images. Is a curriculum best described as a carefully cultivated, groomed garden that makes use of all the technological advances and identifies distinctions between types, classes, and groupings? Or, does the natural environment know things we don't know about uniqueness and distinctiveness? Nature has not clustered people into well-defined groups corresponding to our value-laden labels. We, not nature, decide what is a flower and what is a weed. To paraphrase Ralph Waldo Emerson, a weed is a flower that someone decides doesn't belong in the garden.

A friend and I had yearly arguments about our lawns in Louisville, Kentucky, and Jeffersonville, Indiana. He has a beautiful stand of fescue that he fertilizes, waters, manicures, and mows to a scientifically prescribed height. He is sure to win a prize from Lawns Beautiful in Jeffersonville. But every blade of grass in that lawn looked the same. He had fescue; I had fescue. I also had blue grass. I also had purple, yellow, and white wildflowers. I also had bentgrass, St. Augustine, dichondra, carpet grass, and clover. One summer I had a cornstalk growing in the middle of my front yard. My neighbor called it a weed. But most of the peoples of this world could not imagine a more valuable plant.

The third metaphor is the picture of pilgrimage. Teaching is related to a journey in which leaders are expected to make crooked ways straight and rough places smooth. Each traveler, or student, will be affected differently by the journey. Great effort is made to plan the route so that the mind is imprinted with the journey in such a way that stories can be told. Curriculum design seeks to shape a "mind map," providing useful and practical knowledge. The teacher has been this way before and is the guide and fellow traveler who has experienced some of "the way" and knows the pitfalls and dangers.

Curriculum Theory and Biology

Curriculum theory got a good start when the images came from the discipline of biology and the emphasis on living organisms and vital processes. Biology is a life science providing a sense of vitality and aliveness. Our curriculum language would be limited without the help of the biological sciences. A group of courses is described as a "field" of study. Fields are cleared, enclosed lands used for cultivation and pasture. Fields imply the territorial imperatives of departments and divisions. To "field test" something is to examine it in its natural environment.

A "core" curriculum has a vital center that shapes the heart and nucleus of the organism's life. To find the core of a curriculum is to find its nerve center. The core is the "nitty gritty" center where sap, marrow, heart, soul, and spirit come together. People who are doing well in learning are flowering, blooming, blossoming, flourishing, and taking root. People doing poorly are "dying on the vine." We could go on: paper comes from plants, ideas germinate, people grow like weeds, institutions have branches of learning, information is broadcast like seeds in all directions, and seminal ideas are sown.

The Historical Roots

These metaphorical roots can be traced in the cyclical nature of curriculum development through human history.[3] Education began in primitive societies with an emphasis on the life of the culture—heritage, skills, beliefs, and actions needed to survive as an intact group. From the eighth to sixth centuries BC, bodies of knowledge were imparted in formal education rather than immersion in daily experiences. The development of schools organized knowledge into subjects of instruction. By the fourth century BC, courses of study were organized into steps rather than simply divided into subject areas, and "plans" for learning were introduced.

These patterns can be seen in biblical life. As with other primitive cultures, pre-exilic education was part of daily life—not preparation for life but synonymous with life. Education was characterized by participation in ritual, knowing and telling the story of your people, and the maintenance of group identity. Post-exilic Hebrews became students of the law, and a body of knowledge became more defined and elaborate. The early church had an organized body of knowledge in the reinterpretation of Jewish Scriptures, the Gospels, the teaching of Jesus, and the Christian way of life. A "plan" was not recognizable until the fifth century AD, when an organized, sequential content was organized for new members.

It took twelve centuries or more to complete the first cycle: pre-exilic people experiences; a post-exilic body of knowledge; the early church organization of knowledge; and the catechetical application plan for instruction of content.

During the Middle Ages, the pattern was repeated with a narrowing of each definition. Keep in mind the four movements—experiences, body of knowledge, organization of knowledge, and application to life. People experiences were introduced through the apprenticeship system. Charlemagne's court schools offered selected knowledge limited to the Bible. The late Middle Ages introduced the historical, allegorical, topological, and ethical meaning of the Bible. The development of detailed textbooks soon followed. Comenius designed goals for each day, month, and year, along with ways of recalling these goals.

In the eighteenth century, the cycle began again. Locke and Rousseau offered ordered and controlled experiences. The nineteenth century saw Pestalozzi, Froebel, and Spencer emphasizing methods of interaction and "maps" for instruction. By 1827, the Uniform Lessons Series formed a pattern that took five years to complete. By the twentieth century, curriculum development had become a science with specific learning objectives. The pattern of the cycle can be seen clearly—curriculum as experiences, curriculum as useful and valued subjects, and curriculum as a plan of uniformly prepared lessons.

In the 1920s, the cycle began all over again. John Dewey reasserted freedom from plans and maps, with the present experiences of the learner as the starting point. In the 1940s, Ralph Tyler established the formative curriculum design for the rest of the century—objectives, content, teaching methodology, arrangement of material, and means of evaluation.[4] Tyler's proposal for a rationally developed curriculum was raised to the status of revealed doctrine. When D. Campbell Wyckoff emerged as a leader in the curriculum field, Tyler's theory reached its apex as a blueprint for an educational program with a context, scope, purpose, process, sequence, and means of organization.[5] When I went to the Baptist Sunday School Board (now LifeWay) in 1966 as a curriculum designer and editor, this was the first process to know and implement. When I left in 1984, this process was still in place.

From the 1960s to the present, curriculum as experience, organized knowledge, and blueprint or plan all became evident, with a narrowing of each definition. We seem forever doomed to draw and redraw these patterns for use in local churches. Why have these patterns of conceptual tightening occurred? What are the forces that drive us into these patterns? Is it possible to loosen the conceptual tightenings so that their controls over us are not such dominating forces?

Bible Study Curriculum

Without going into great detail, I will attempt to sketch a way of using the movements of the experiential cycle (experience, exegesis, reflection, application) as a way of describing how a Bible study curriculum is developed and practiced. The four movements provide a continuum of simplicity to complexity. Joyce and Weil suggested a simple formula for identifying simplicity and complexity: a need for and tolerance of structure and a need for and tolerance for task complexity.[6] Structure refers to the number and degree of prescribed processes. The greater the structure, the more detailed the plan and dependence on the plan. Do this, do this, do this, and in this order, like a recipe. Task complexity refers to the intricacy of the process. More complex tasks require higher degrees of skill and competence on the part of the learner.

1. *Bible Study with a Focus on Experience (low structure, low task complexity)*. We have all engaged in this type of study in one form or another. The text is read, with personal interpretations following. Anecdotes, stories, and analogies are used freely. A general familiarity with Scripture is assumed. A relaxed, informal group atmosphere is encouraged. This "commonsense" approach to the text assumes that the group knows and agrees with the intended meaning of the author. People may paraphrase or "free associate" around the text. Personal problems may be explored in light of the text. The text evokes a memory of other texts or events in Scripture or reminds learners of past events in their lives. Curriculum materials are used sparingly, even if they are available. The teacher gently guides the process and may have leaders' guides and commentaries available for "snippets" of interpretation. Additional teaching methods and materials are scant and seldom used. Time is variable—from fifteen minutes to an hour.

2. *Bible Study with a Focus on Exegesis (high structure, high task complexity)*. A focus on exegesis will emphasize the mastery of subject matter. Learning may be inductive, deductive, or guided discovery. Inductive Bible study will emphasize the collecting and organizing of information and the forming of concepts. Deductive learning will focus on an organized presentation of the biblical material. Guided discovery will guide the learner through a step-by-step series of interpretive tasks. Biblical learning demands tough, demanding practice of cognitive processes, the ability to make inferences, to remember, extrapolate, and categorize; thus, the four rules of curriculum planning—practice, recency, frequency, and intensity. The teacher presents information in an ordered and organized way, defines problems, and provides guidance. The learner is expected to conceptualize, analyze, locate relevant resources, make applications, and evaluate. Study may focus on chapters,

books, themes, topics, or words. Careful attention is given to the text, providing a common base of knowledge before moving to diverse interpretations. A working knowledge of the biblical languages is useful, but not essential. Curriculum materials are multiple and varied, taking on a "textbook" format. Adequate time blocks are essential—a minimum of one hour.

3. *Bible Study with a Focus on Reflection (low to medium structure, high task complexity).* A focus on reflection will emphasize personal meaning and an integration of emotional and intellectual personal development. Stimulating individual creativity and self-expression are encouraged. Motivation comes from the inside rather than the outside, and personal frames of reference shape the nature of knowledge. The focus is on "people investment," which emerges out of sympathetic interaction with people rather than published routines and tasks. The teacher is a catalyst, providing a climate and environment that can nurture interaction among texts, interests, and experiences. The teacher models transparency through the expression of personal vulnerabilities and "stories." The expression of feelings and emotions is encouraged. Drama, role-playing, guided imagery, imagination, and psychological interpretations of the text are accepted by the group. Agreement and consensus of interpretation are not deemed to be necessary. Curriculum materials may be many and varied, including multimedia resources and worship guides. Leadership in the group may change according to the resources used. Time is needed and protected—one to three hours in length.

4. *Bible Study with a Focus on Application (high structure with medium to high task complexity).* Curriculum is often seen as the mechanism for meeting personal, group, denominational, or publishing agendas. Goals and purposes are clearly defined and even measured in terms of goal achievement. In order to meet goals, objectives are clearly specified, and efficiency and effectiveness are accomplished by the creation of routines. Everyone knows what they are expected to accomplish. Each task builds on what preceded and prepares for that to come. The teacher is a designer of precise action strategies, providing workbooks of sequential materials. The study of Scripture is to lead somewhere—action plans for confronting issues such as drug and alcohol abuse, sex education, parenting, racial issues, abortion issues, political action, multicultural studies, sexism, peace-making, evangelism, church growth, and numerous other concerns. Students are expected to meet all requirements and may receive certification. Curriculum materials focus on the biblical text's application to the group's agenda and motivating people toward action and "doing the word." Time is needed for work and ministry projects outside of meeting times.

The Four Orientations

Each curriculum orientation carries a concept of learning style and Scripture interpretation. A group's use of Scripture boosts certain purposes and outcomes and diminishes others. Rarely do they guarantee some results and obliterate others. Ideally, they will be used in concert and will be more productive than if used in isolation from other movements.

Biblical content interacts powerfully with a personal style of learning and the teaching methodology. The methods will determine what aspects of the biblical revelation are highlighted—the implications for living, the retention of information, the growth in self-understanding, or the way it speaks to modern issues. A focus on one aspect of the experiential cycle will bring out different views of how people learn.

The way people use intelligence, solve problems, analyze information, develop creativity, organize the inner self, face complexity, develop warm, affective responses, draw personal meanings, and respond aesthetically through artistic expression all have a power to integrate the biblical material into new forms. This may sound complex, but it actually operates simply and naturally. This coming together is revealed through reflection and debriefing. How did I come up with that? Where did it come from? How committed am I to it? Eventually, all of these ideas and commentary reside increasingly in the hands of the scholars and designers of curriculum materials. Even the intuitive, imaginative work of the people eventually becomes a reservoir of information available to the designer of curriculum. What they do with these messages is another story.

Any attempt to break out of these powerful historical and cultural forces is close to impossible. Yet, many are trying. The number of publishers using different interpretive tools and learning styles expands yearly. The focus of this book is to find our way back to the more basic, "primitive" forms. In other words, curriculum theory can find its roots in the images of biblical revelation.

The Seed, the Sower, and the Soil

If metaphors help us see and understand curriculum in a new and helpful way, let us seek to find those metaphorical roots in Scripture. In keeping with our emphasis on the primitive (primary), let us look at one of the first of the teaching parables found in Mark 4.

Jesus begins a fairly simple story about a farmer who randomly broadcasts (scatters) seeds. The seeds fall into four different environments: the road, the rocky ground, among thorns, and good ground. If we are like the disciples, we have no idea what he is talking about. We have heard this parable so often that we immediately begin to rehearse the interpretation. But we would be wiser to try to hear it, as if for the first time, and readily admit with the disciples that we do not know what Jesus is saying.

He tells the disciples that they have been given the secrets—the hidden, unobservable workings of the kingdom of God. This revelation, which God gives through Jesus, is revealed to babes and hidden from the wise (Matt 11:25). All of those who have that understanding will be given more, and the little understanding others have will be taken away. Such a statement should immediately make us suspicious of any educational theory with observable, predictable outcomes.

The seeds that we sow randomly and everywhere are small compared with what they will eventually produce. I remember the sensation clearly as a small boy taking my first lessons in the family garden plot. The seed seemed magically to disappear as soon as it was dropped into a furrow. You might as well have planted nothing, for all you could observe.

As educators, we long to see more than that—evidence that our efforts are producing an outcome through knowledge, attitude, or skill. But the parable issues a warning. Even if you can observe the growth, it doesn't look like much, and when it does finally get around to doing its work it is unrecognizable. The work of the kingdom proceeds as the work of the seed. Something is happening that is quiet, fragile, and beyond notice.

John Dewey taught us many things, but none more important than this statement: "Perhaps the greatest of all pedagogical fallacies is that people learn the thing they are studying at the time they are studying it."[7] As with seed, the moment of emergence has an inner requirement, occurring in its own time, and not on any controlled or predictable schedule. Emergence happens silently, and one acts violently in pulling up the plant to see if the roots are growing.

The seed that is sown does its work. We can trust it. Even the seed falling on the road is distributed abroad by the birds. And whether on rocky ground, in the thorny underbrush, or in the well-prepared soil, most of the seed does emerge and often goes beyond our most hopeful expectations.

The response to the sowing is the most mystifying yet. For we do not insure its growth through haste, quick helps, and easy fixes, but through patience and noninterference. This should be a motivating message to every writer, editor, artist, manuscript assistant, printer, and publisher. Keep on sowing! In spite of deep uncertainty and numerous severe hazards, a sower went forth to sow.

The real point of the parable is the sureness and inevitability of growth far vaster than anything that could be organized. This should be a great word of encouragement and hope and an answer to impatience, discouragement, and swifter and more sophisticated methods. The conversion that takes place between the planting of the seed and the ripening of the grain does not lie within the sower's domain; it is God's mysterious work. In Mark 4:27, the farmer sees the growth but knows not how it happens. Jesus seems to be saying, "Are you getting the picture of what I am trying to tell you? Do you think you can put all this together in a way that makes the communication of God's word effective?" The parable is trying to teach us things about God's word that are essential for experiential Bible study.

1. God's word is for the whole world, all-inclusive and all-embracing. The seed is sown randomly in every earthly place and every earthly condition. It is not limited to any particular group or audience. There are no favorite conditions, climates, or peoples.

2. God's word has already been sown. We are to go find it. It is paradoxically and frustratingly hidden and not easily observed. We will need to go looking for it in remote corners, among indigenous peoples. It will be living and growing naturally in environments native to the local soil.

3. Even though you can't see it, God's word is working now, in the present moment, and not at some future time when conditions are just right.

4. God's word operates amid every kind of resistance imaginable. Although different soils cause different responses, God's word does spring up. Our task is to evoke the response. Not haste, but careful waiting. Not the quick helping hand, but patient noninterference.

Seed and Curriculum as Industry

A parable concerning the dilemmas in curriculum development comes from some of the most recent developments in the seed industry.[8] Early in this century, one-fourth of the 250,000 plant species may vanish, victimized by deforestation, shifts to monocultures, water control projects, and urbanization. The loss of genetic diversity escalated with the "green revolution" of the 1960s. (The 1950s and 1960s also were the decades of the most powerful centralized producers of Christian curriculum materials.) During the 1960s, new miracle seeds were produced through crossbreeding to increase food processes. Uniformity was bred into crop production. This resulted in increasing yields but made each plant identically vulnerable to disaster.

This demand for growth had a great price. The growing organisms had less resistance to pests, disease, and drought, and less quality in taste and preserving entities. Do you get my drift? Increased production (more of the same) carries with it the backlash of uniformity, vulnerability, and redundancy. The promises of difference and improvement in quality never quite materialize.

The search is on for unique genetic strands that grow wild in primitive settings. In that critical vocation are the seed hunters, searching old fields, rocky hillsides, abandoned farms, and dark corners of dilapidated barns. They are looking for the same thing that curriculum designers look for—the preservation of uniqueness and originality. Amid massive uniformity we seek to find unique strands in the dark corners of human lives where we discover God working in a quiet, hidden, unobservable way. These strands provide the new seed for designing educational experience.

What is happening in the seed industry provides some of the best insights into the continuing problems of curriculum development. Let us imagine some of the connections.

1. Many economic forces seek to take over the seed industry and throttle diversity. In the same way, modern curriculum industry reflects the disappearance of diversity and variety. In both curriculum and seed development, variety is the spice, the stuff and the staff of life.

2. Diversity in seed life, like curriculum, is quirky, idiosyncratic, and spontaneous, with unpredictable shifts. All true gardeners prize diversity. They look over in other gardens like we look at other churches. "What have you got growing over there?"

3. Curriculum development, like seed life, is threatened by the loss of distinctiveness. Everything begins to look, sound, and taste the same. The diversity of Christian experience loses out to uniformity. New life comes to both seeds and curriculum in much the same way—by focusing on the "originals."

4. Curriculum, like seed, thrives on the natural environment. The more mechanical and technical the production becomes, the less nutritional food value is available. Thus, the same strange dilemma confronts food production and Bible study curriculum. More food is produced, but more people are hungry. Curriculum production, like food production, develops an inverse correlation between yield and nutrition. Nutrition, quality, and taste become less important than yield, weight, and quantity. "Perhaps the biggest single environmental catastrophe in human history is unfolding in the garden. The loss of genetic diversity in agriculture—silent, rapid, inexorable—is leading us to a rendezvous with extinction, to the doorsteps of hunger on a scale we refuse to imagine.[9] The mass

of Bible study materials multiplies yearly. Yet, the people remain unsatisfied, longing for something different, but unable to describe their hunger.

5. Curriculum materials, like food production, lose nutritional value in the same way. Uniformity, ease of mechanical production, adaptability for shipping, and emphasis on cosmetic appearance take precedence over nutritional value.

6. The introduction of hybrids (a composite of artificial rather than authentic factors) causes the elimination of many endemic (belonging or native to a particular people) varieties that have served people for centuries. Artificiality in curriculum development has many causes, most of which center on the loss of connection with the vast range of people's experiences.

7. Distributing curriculum design decisions and development among many hands encourages diversity through homegrown curriculum. "Homegrown" is a way of overcoming redundancy and repetition. Centralization in curriculum exceeds what is needed and necessary. Local visionaries can see the excesses. There is much that can be eliminated without loss of nutritional value.

8. Like seed, much of the diversity in Christian faith is unexplored, subtle, and hidden. Innovative curriculum comes from the indigenous—belonging to specific places where people live, love, study, and worship.

A Primitive Curriculum

I have chosen the metaphors of seed, sower, and the soil as a way of emphasizing the need for a primitive curriculum. What do I mean by a primitive curriculum? A primitive curriculum is one stripped of its distractions. It is stripped of videotape, audiotape, fancy books, plush buildings, colorful workbooks, and elaborate packaged teaching aids. A primitive curriculum is stripped of all the clothing we drape around ourselves to keep us from seeing and hearing, listening, and speaking.

What is curriculum when it is stripped of all the accessories? Simply stated, it is experience. Curriculum comes from the root word *currere*, meaning "to run." It describes a race, not only in terms of the course and the readiness of the runner, but also in terms of the running of one particular runner on one particular track on one particular day in one particular wind. "The track around which I run may be inalterably forced, but the rate at which I run, the quality of my running, my sensual-intellectual-emotional experience of moving bodily through space and time: all these are my creations; they are my responsibilities."[10] This information I have belongs to everyone, but my experience belongs only to me. It is this dialogue between each person's idiosyncratic history and one's situation, place, people, and ideas that we call educational experience.

On the whole, curriculum often is taken to refer to materials, intended learning outcomes, and experiences—experiences from the point of view of the developer, designer, or teacher. For example, it is said that one organizes experiences for one's students. If the world were experienced in discretely organized units by people who could isolate emotional responses from intellectual ones, past from present, present from future, I from me, me from us, in a divide-and-conquer approach to learning, we might justify an objective approach. Life is not experienced this way, and further fragmentation of human experience distorts and estranges us not only from each other, but from ourselves as well.

Experience is what one senses, feels, thinks; it is living through one's life. It includes physical sensations, as how your back feels in that chair at this moment or the temperature of the room on your face; emotional, in that you may have a feeling about me, about the person seated next to you, or about this reading; and mental, in that you recall the thoughts about breakfast this morning, or you think about with whom you are to have dinner or about those at home. It is private, although you can make it public; it is individual, although you can share aspects of it with others and be influenced by others, but wonderfully and wholly it is yours. I cannot design it for you. Your experience of me and this environment is yours, and it is your own. Thus, the first step in a primitive curriculum requires the safe discovery or return of one's own voice. Curriculum begins with autobiography—one's own personal history.

There is a parallel to the state of affairs in clinical medicine. After treating an ailing patient with drugs, and additional drugs to counter the effects of the initial prescriptions, and still other drugs to counter the effects of the antidotes, the physician, trapped in a web of treatment, must remove the patient from all other drug therapy and start once more from the beginning by taking a history. Our current responsibility is to rescue our patient from our massive technological attentions. This is what we mean by a primitive curriculum.

A Primitive Reading

One could make a clear argument for the paralleling movements in curriculum development and biblical interpretation. The same cultural and historical forces impacted both disciplines in similar ways. The return to more basic and "primitive" forms can be illustrated through the work of one man.

Søren Kierkegaard was a nineteenth-century philosopher and writer who left his imprint on biblical interpretation. Kierkegaard used the experiences of his life as the grist for shaping his thought. The unstable relationship with his father, aborted love relationship with Regina, continuing literary war with a publisher, and conversion experience during Holy Week in 1848 informed most of his writings and shaped his perspective on Scripture.

Kierkegaard saw the academic and scholarly study of Scripture as a hindrance in the people's human reading of the text. By "human," Kierkegaard would mean "primitive," a stripping away of those things that clouded reading the Bible on its own terms. He suggested reading the New Testament without a commentary and asked rhetorically, "Would it ever occur to a lover to read a letter from his beloved with a commentary?"[11] Kierkegaard suggested a subjective reading of Scripture through imitation, imagination, identification, and immersion. His life experience is seen and interpreted through his daily exposure to Scripture. Kierkegaard persisted in seeking Scripture through imagination and total immersion in its content. It was more important for Scripture to interpret the reader than for the reader to interpret Scripture.

Kierkegaard was not the first, nor will he be the last, to emphasize the "primitive" reading of Scripture. But scholarship often blinds the eyes of the people to finding their own lives in the biblical text. The depths of the biblical text remained unexplored and its deep secrets untold. Like Kierkegaard, our personal need drives us to the deeper dimensions of the text.

Do you know these feelings? Our experiences are varied, but we all have basic needs for nourishment, stimulation, courage, affection, shifts in perspective, and ways of interpreting difficult situations. Meeting the text at an original and essential level gives us freedom to express confusion, uncertainty, wonder, or any of the stark feelings the text evokes. Reading primitively is reading in the language we know best—the language of personal experience. Staying in touch with our experience helps us avoid whatever it is that distances us from the text or shields us from its most intense impact. This primitive reading is what H. A. Nielsen called "entering at ground level and walking on foot."

> If the rule in reading primitively is to enter into the Scriptures at ground level and on foot, it goes without saying that the reader had better travel light, leaving behind the high-powered lighting equipment and special lenses coated against glare, that may be indispensable to other ways of reading the Bible. To read humanly is to read with our natural organ of sight, the naked eye, which can sometimes be dazzled and also now and then find that it is completely in the dark. The naked eye is a primary spotter of texts that bear on personal needs.[12]

Remembering life experiences as we read opens us to surprise. The text suddenly appears in a new light. We see things that we have never seen before. The text does things to and with our life experience, helping us see life in new ways. Try reading the text in a different language—like the language you use when you are talking to yourself. Stay in touch with the spontaneous responses that are created. Open the Bible like you would an anticipated letter from a friend, where everything you have ever read or heard about the text plays into the relationship—even the footnotes in the margins. Try reading from a "pre-Christian" viewpoint, before you knew what you know now about the Christian life. In this way we find the truth about ourselves. The text looks at us and turns a finger, pointblank, in our direction.

There is nothing else in the world that knows us in this way. In more sophisticated curriculum designs we are seen as types, the things we have in common with others, grouping and grading us in categories. But Scripture reveals us as originals, knowing us in the privacy of minds and hearts, and it is in this originality that Scripture searches us out.

The Discovery of Voice

If *currere* is giving attention to the idiosyncratic history of one particular person, then the silence of people in churches is deafening. The research of Belenky, Clinchy, Goldberger, and Tarule in *Women's Ways of Knowing* described the powerlessness of many in hearing their own voices.[13] The silent are characterized by obeying external authority, keeping particular places, and remaining passive and subdued. Their sources of self-knowledge lodge in others and not in themselves.

The recovery or discovery of one's voice includes the ability to put together one's life story. Life story is foundational to the scope of any Christian curriculum. But it is an essential part of any curriculum format, regardless of content and subject matter. Narrative is the form most related to the way people maintain a sense of continuity through time and a primary form in which they share experience. When a person describes an experience in story form, the detail of the story often reveals the attitudes, feelings, and habits of responding to life's experience. The story discloses the teller's "point of view." Story allows others to share the unique way a person experiences life. We organize our lives through stories.

A central feature of a primitive curriculum will be designing processes that assist in listening for the experiential, which is often hidden underneath the categorical and conceptual. One of the first steps in moving out of this experiential silence is for leaders to keep asking, "What has happened to you that has caused you to say that, or believe that, or think that?"

William James, in *Varieties of Religious Experience*, sought to help people move closer to the primary issues—to establish contact with the concrete world of human experience.[14] He distinguished between knowledge about things and knowledge by direct experience of these things. This "clearing of the field" moves us toward primitive experience, prior to interpretation. Rather than telling what we mean, a story formed from experience will lead people to relive the events through memory and imagination so that some primitive contact with the experience may be rediscovered. A layperson in a "ministry group" described this process:

> We live in an environment which silences the sharing of the events of our lives. Our personal experiences are labeled as unimportant, or, even worse, as a hindrance to our common growth. . . . Eventually at the most basic level, I begin to use non-critical but active listening in order to hear the events of my own life. I begin to do this almost without realizing I am doing it. I begin to see how critical I am of my own story and how this critical eye silences much of its meaning and renders it useless for my future growth as a person.[15]

A good test for any curriculum design is in how well it does this "story weaving." Each one of us is a subplot of the great epic story of history. For centuries the church has told and retold the stories through Scripture and the church's faith. The patterns of God's grace are woven together in the unique stories of what each of us knows and how we have learned it. We design curriculum for people with the hope that the biblical story will mesh with our own personal stories in such a way that our lives and our worlds will finally make sense.

In simpler terms, let us note a conversation between a musician and a mathematics teacher. The musician speaks first.

> "Oho, I know what you are. You are an advocate of Useful Knowledge."
> "Certainly."
> "You say that a man's first job is to earn a living, and that the first task of education is to equip him for that job?"
> "Of course."
> "Well, allow me to introduce myself to you as an advocate of Ornamental Knowledge. You like the mind to be a neat machine, equipped to work efficiently, if narrowly, and with no extra bits or useless parts. I like the mind to be a dustbin of scraps of brilliant fabric, odd gems, worthless but fascinating curiosities, tinsel, quaint bits of carving, and a reasonable amount of healthy dirt. Shake the machine and it goes out of order; shake the dustbin and it adjusts beautifully to its new position."[16]

If a many-layered subject matter (like soil) is taken as a principle, it expands and deepens the meaning of curriculum. This is the understanding of human beings as subjects—as subjects who matter—in ways taught by the Brazilian educator, Paulo Freire. Freire believed that, for human beings, the essential decision is between speaking or remaining embedded in a culture of silence, between naming ourselves or being named by others, between remaining an object or becoming a subject. The heart of his vision is that every human being has an ontological vocation to be a subject, namely someone who can separate from the world in his or her consciousness, be critical of it, act on it, and transform it, in the process making the world a subject, too. Such a rich conception of subject matter can only further renew curriculum understanding.

The Making of Bread

The vocation of the sower in relation to the seed and the soil is to provide food for the people. The eventual outcome of the fragile seed, the tender shoot, and the ripening grain is to provide bread. Bread making is one of the most primitive of all the arts and, to this day, is the most universal "stuff" of life. As a child, the bread that I ate was almost always homebaked. By the 1950s, about 95 percent of all bread was baked commercially. There is no food industry any larger, with great mixers, large fermentation rooms, huge dough troughs, and ovens that can bake thousands of loaves at one time.

But I still longed for the homebaked and, almost by accident, became a bread baker. The reason it is such a satisfying experience is that it reminds me of who I am and what I do. As a curriculum builder for almost forty years, most of the time I am reminded of making bread. In one of our earliest curriculum producing projects at Southern Seminary, I wrote these words in the introduction:

> And so we offer you homemade bread. You cannot buy it in the supermarkets of curriculum production. We have blended in the ingredients that seemed to be nutritious, stirred it with vigor, and plopped it out on a table. We pushed, pulled, plied, and prodded it with a dozen pairs of hands. At times it looked like it would fall apart. So we would knead it some more, hoping for a feast day, when we could feed 5,000 but fearing that there wouldn't be enough for 12. Now we cast our bread on the waters, hoping that you will at least nibble. Perhaps there will be groups of you who will take it, break it, and satisfy your hunger, and it will be enough.[17]

NOTES

[1] Barbara Kingsolver, *Small Wonders* (New York: HarperCollins Publishers Inc., 2002), 100.

[2] Herbert M. Kliebard, "Metaphorical Roots of Curriculum Design," in *Curriculum Theorizing: The Reconceptualists*, ed. William Pinar (Berkeley: McCutchan Publishing Corp., 1975), 84-85.

[3] See Pamela Mitchell, "What Is Curriculum? Alternatives in Western Historical Perspective," *Religious Education* 83 (1988): 349-66.

[4] Ralph W. Tyler, *Basic Principles of Curriculum and Instruction* (Chicago: University of Chicago Press, 1949).

[5] Wyckoff greatly influenced the work of Howard P. Colson and Raymond M. Rigdon in *Understanding Your Church's Curriculum* (Nashville: Broadman Press, 1981).

[6] Bruce Joyce and Marsha Weil, *Models of Teaching* (Englewood Cliffs NJ: Prentice-Hall, Inc., 1986), 418.

[7] Quoted in Elliot Eisner, *The Educational Imagination* (New York: Macmillan, 1979), 74.

[8] See Robert E. Rhoades, "The World's Food Supply at Risk," *National Geographic* 179/4 (April 1991): 75-105.

[9] Cary Fowler and Patrick R. Mooney, *Shattering: Food, Politics, and the Loss of Genetic Diversity* (Tucson: University of Arizona Press, 1990), 176.

[10] William F. Pinar and Madeleine R. Grumet, *Toward a Poor Curriculum* (Dubuque: Kendall/Hunt Publishing Co., 1976), vii.

[11] Joey Rosas, *Scripture in the Thought of Søren Kierkegaard* (Nashville: Broadman & Holman Publishers, 1994), 45.

[12] H. A. Nielson, *The Bible As If for the First Time* (Philadelphia: Westminster Press, 1984), 21.

[13] Mary Belenky, Blythe Clinchy, Nancy Goldberger, and Jill Tarule, *Women's Ways of Knowing* (New York: Basic Books, 1986), 23-34.

[14] William James, *The Varieties of Religious Experience* (New York: New American Library, 1958).

[15] John Patton, *From Ministry to Theology* (Nashville, Abingdon Press, 1990), 49.

[16] Robertson Davies, *Tempest-Tost* (New York: Penguin Books, 1980), 182.

[17] John Hendrix, "Preface," in *Once Upon a Time: A Guide to Spiritual Formation in Community* (Louisville: Curriculum Theory and Design Seminar of The Southern Baptist Theological Seminary, 1987).

Bibliography

Abernathy, William Beaven, and Philip Joseph Mayher. *Scripture and Imagination*. New York: Pilgrim Press, 1988.

Ackerman, Diane. *A Natural History of the Senses*. New York: Random House, 1990.

Ausubel, David. *Educational Psychology: A Cognitive View*. New York: Holt, Rinehart and Winston, 1968.

Babin, Pierre. *The New Era in Religious Communication*. Minneapolis: Fortress Press, 1991.

Banks, Robert. *Redeeming the Routines: Bringing Theology to Life*. Wheaton IL: Victor Books, 1993.

Bass, Dorothy C. *Practicing Our Faith: A Way of Life for a Searching People*. San Francisco: Jossey-Bass Publishers, 1997.

Bass, Dorothy C. *Receiving the Day: Christian Practices for Opening the Gift of Time*. San Francisco: Jossey-Bass Publishers, 2000.

Belenky, Mary, Blythe Clinchy, Nancy Goldberger, and Jill Tarule. *Women's Ways of Knowing*. New York: Basic Books, 1986.

Boomershine, Thomas E. "Biblical Megatrends: Toward a Paradigm of the Interpretation of the Bible in Electronic Media." In *The Bible in the Twenty-First Century*, ed. Howard Clark Kee. Philadelphia: Trinity Press International, 1993.

Bowling, Jerry. "An Examination of Spirituality Based on Howard Gardner's Theory of Multiple Intelligencies." Ph.D. dissertation, The Southern Baptist Theological Seminary, 1998.

Brooke, Avery. *Learning and Teaching Christian Meditation*. Cambridge: Cowley Publications, 1990.

Brown, Colin, editor. *The New International Dictionary of New Testament Theology*. Volume 1. Grand Rapids: Zondervan Publishing House, 1979.

Brown, Robert McAfee. *The Bible Speaks to You*. Philadelphia: Westminster Press, 1965.

Brueggemann, Walter. *Texts Under Negotiation*. Minneapolis: Fortress Press, 1993.

———. *The Bible Makes Sense*. Winona MN: Saint Mary's Press, 1997.

Buechner, Frederick. *A Room Called Remember*. San Francisco: Harper & Row, 1984.

———. *The Son of Laughter*. New York: HarperCollins Publishers, 1993.

Caine, Renate, and Geoffrey Caine. *Making Connections: Teaching and the Human Brain*. Alexandria VA: Association for Supervision and Curriculum Development, 1991.

Capon, Robert Farrar. *The Parables of Grace*. Grand Rapids: Eerdman's Publishing Co., 1988.

Carruthers, Mary. *The Book of Memory: A Study of Memory in Medieval Culture.* Cambridge: Cambridge University Press, 1990.

Coalter, Milton J. Jr. "The Craft of Christ's Imperfect Tailors." *Theology Today* 50/3 (October 1993): 389.

Colson, Howard P., and Raymond M. Ridgon. *Understanding Your Church's Curriculum.* Nashville: Broadman Press, 1981.

Dale, Edgar. *Audio-visual Methods in Teaching.* New York: Holt, Rinehart and Winston, 1954.

Davies, Robertson. *Tempest-Tost.* New York: Penguin Books, 1980.

Dewey, John. *How We Think: A Restatement of the Relation of Reflective Thinking to the Educative Process.* New York: D. C. Heater and Co., 1933.

———. *Experience and Education.* New York: Scribner Reprint, 1997.

Diehl, William E. *Christianity and Real Life.* Philadelphia: Fortress Press, 1976.

———. *The Monday Connection.* New York: HarperCollins Publishers, 1993.

Dow, Robert. *Learning Through Encounter.* Valley Forge: Judson Press, 1971.

Driver, Tom F. "Performance and Biblical Readings." In *Body and Bible*, ed. Bjorn Krondorfer. Philadelphia: Trinity Press International, 1992, 165.

Eisner, Elliot. *The Educational Imagination.* New York: Macmillan, 1979.

Elbow, Peter. *Embracing Contraries: Explorations in Learning and Teaching.* New York: Oxford University Press, 1986.

Emmons, Robert A. "Spiritual Intelligence: Toward a Theory of Personality and Spirituality." In *Psychology of Ultimate Concern.* New York: Guilford, 1999.

Fowler, Cary, and Patrick R. Mooney. *Shattering: Food, Politics, and the Loss of Genetic Diversity.* Tucson: University of Arizona Press, 1990.

Friere, Paulo. *Pedagogy of the Oppressed.* New York: Continuum, 1981.

Gadamer, Hans Georg. *Truth and Method.* New York: Crossroad, 1975.

Gardner, Howard. *Frames of Mind: The Theory of Multiple Intelligences.* New York: Basic Books, Inc., 1983.

———. *The Unschooled Mind: How Children Think and How Schools Should Teach.* New York: Basic Books, Inc., 1991.

———. *Creating Minds: An Anatomy of Creativity Seen through the Lives of Freud, Einstein, Picasso, Stravinsky, Eliot, Graham, and Gandhi.* New York: Basic Books, Inc., 1993.

———. *Extraordinary Minds: Portraits of Exceptional Individuals and an Examination of Our Extraordinariness.* New York: Basic Books, Inc., 1997.

———. *Intelligence Reframed: Multiple Intelligences for the 21st Century.* New York: Basic Books, 2000.

Gendlin, Eugene. *Focusing.* New York: Everest House, 1978.

Goldberg, Rabbi Nathan. *Passover Haggadah.* New York: KTAV Publishing, 1984.

Goldberg, Philip. *The Intuitive Edge: Understanding and Developing Intuition.* Los Angeles: Jeremy P. Tarcher, Inc., 1983.

Green, Thomas F. *The Activities of Teaching.* New York: McGraw-Hill, 1971.

Groome, Thomas. *Sharing Faith.* San Francisco: HarperCollins Publishers, 1991.

———. *Educating for Life.* New York: Crossroad, 2001.

Hall, Edward T. *The Silent Language*. Garden City: Doubleday Publishing Co., 1959.

Heifetz, Ronald A., and Marty Linsky. *Leadership on the Line: Staying Alive through the Dangers of Leading*. Boston: Harvard Business School Press, 2002.

Hendrix, John. *To Thessalonians with Love*. Nashville: Broadman Press, 1982.

———. "Preface." In *Once Upon a Time: A Guide to Spiritual Formation in Community*. Louisville: Curriculum Theory and Design Seminar of The Southern Baptist Theological Seminary, 1987.

———. *Harvest of the City*. Birmingham: Women's Missionary Union, 1995.

Hestenes, Roberta. *Using the Bible in Groups*. Philadelphia: Westminster Press, 1983.

James, William. *Principles of Psychology*. Volume 1. New York: Dover Publications, 1890.

———. *The Varieties of Religious Experience*. New York: New American Library, 1958.

Johnson, Cedric B. *The Psychology of Biblical Interpretation*. Grand Rapids: Zondervan Publishing House, 1983.

Johnson, Paul G. *Grace: God's Work Ethic*. Valley Forge: Fortress Press, 1985.

Jones, John E., and J. William Pfeiffer. *The 1975 Annual Handbook for Group Facilitators*. San Diego: University Associates, 1975.

Joyce, Bruce, and Marsha Weil. *Models of Teaching*. Englewood Cliffs: Prentice-Hall, Inc., 1986.

Kaiser, Walter C. Jr. *Toward an Exegetical Theology*. Grand Rapids: Baker Book House, 1981.

Karp, Hank. "The Lost Art of Feedback." In *The 1987 Annual: Developing Human Resources,* ed. J. William Pfeiffer. San Diego: University Associates, 1987.

Kelly, George A. *A Theory of Personality: The Psychology of Personal Constructs*. New York: W. W. Norton, 1963.

Kierkegaard, Søren. *Either/Or (Part 1)*. Princeton: Princeton University Press, 1987.

Killen, Patricia O'Connell, and John de Beer. *The Art of Theological Reflection*. New York: Crossroad, 1994.

Kingsolver, Barbara. *Small Wonders*. New York: HarperCollins Publishers, Inc., 2002.

Kliebard, Herbert M. "Metaphorical Roots of Curriculum Design." In *Curriculum Theorizing: The Reconceptualists*, ed. William Pinar. Berkeley: McCutchan Publishing Corp., 1975.

Kolb, David, Irwin W. Ruben, and James M. McIntyre. *Organizational Psychology: An Experiential Approach*. Englewood Cliffs NJ: Prentice-Hall, Inc., 1971.

Kolb, David. *Experiential Learning: Experience as the Source of Learning and Development*. Englewood Cliffs NJ: Prentice-Hall, Inc., 1984.

Kubler-Ross, Elisabeth. *Death and Dying*. New York: Macmillan, 1970.

Laeuchli, Samuel. "The Expulsion from the Garden and the Hermeneutics of Play." In *Body and Bible*, ed. Bjorn Krondorfer. Philadelphia: Trinity Press International, 1992.

Lazear, David. *Seven Pathways of Learning: Teaching Students and Parents about Multiple Intelligences*. Tucson: Zephyr Press, 1994.

Lewin, Kurt. *Field Theory in Social Science*. New York: HarperCollins, 1951.

Lewis, C. S. *Pilgrim's Regress*. Grand Rapids: William B. Eerdmans, 1992.

Lingenfelter, Sherwood G., and Marvin K. Mayers. *Ministering Cross-Culturally*. Grand Rapids: Baker Book House, 1986.

Loder, James E. *The Transforming Moment*. San Francisco: Harper & Row, Publishers, 1981.

Long, Thomas G. *The Senses of Preaching*. Atlanta: John Knox Press, 1988.

Lowry, Eugene. *The Homiletical Plot*. Atlanta: John Knox Press, 1980.

Maas, Robin. *Church Bible Study Handbook*. Nashville: Abingdon Press, 1982.

Margulies, Nancy. *Mapping Inner Space*. Tucson: Zephyr Press, 1991.

May, Rollo. *The Courage to Create*. New York: W. W. Norton and Co., 1975.

McCartney, Dan, and Charles Clayton. *Let the Reader Understand*. Wheaton IL: Victor Books, 1994.

Messer, Donald E. *A Conspiracy of Goodness: Contemporary Images of Christian Mission*. Nashville: Abingdon Press, 1992.

Mesters, Carlos. *Defenseless Flower: A New Reading of the Bible*. Maryknoll: Orbis Books, 1991.

Meyers, Robin. *Ears to Hear: Preaching as Self-Persuasion*. Cleveland: Pilgrim Press, 1993.

Mezirow, Jack. *Transformative Dimensions of Adult Learning*. San Francisco: Jossey-Bass Publishers, 1991.

Miller, George. "Thirteen Maxims of the Mind." In *Embracing Contraries: Explorations in Learning and Teaching*, ed. Peter Elbow. New York: Oxford University Press, 1986. 254.

Mitchell, Pamela. "What is Curriculum? Alternatives in Western Historical Perspective." *Religious Education* 52 (1988): 349-66.

Moore, Mary Mullino. *Teaching from the Heart: Theology and Educational Method*. Minneapolis: Fortress Press, 1991.

Moore, Thomas. *Soul Mates*. New York: HarperCollins Publishers, 1994.

Myers, David. *Intuition: Its Powers and Perils*. New York: Yale University Press, 2002.

Napier, Rodney W., and Matti K. Gerschenfeld. *Groups: Theory and Experience*. Boston: Houghton Mifflin Company, 1993.

Nida, Eugene. *Customs and Cultures: Anthropology for Christian Missions*. New York: Harper & Row, 1954.

Nielson, H. A. *The Bible As If for the First Time*. Philadelphia: Westminster Press, 1984.

Nouwen, Henri J. M., Donald P. McNeill, and Douglas A. Morrison. *Compassion*. New York: Doubleday, 1982.

Palmer, Parker. *The Promise of Paradox: A Celebration of Contradictions in the Christian Life*. Notre Dame: Ave Maria Press, 1980.

———. *To Know As We Are Known*. San Francisco: Harper & Row, 1983.

———. *The Active Life*. San Francisco: Harper & Row, 1990.

Patton, John. *From Ministry to Theology*. Nashville: Abingdon Press, 1990.

Paulsell, Stephanie. *Honoring the Body: Meditations on a Christian Practice*. San Francisco: Jossey-Bass Publishers, 2002.

Peterson, Eugene. *Working the Angles: The Shape of Pastoral Integrity*. Grand Rapids: Eerdmans Publishing Co., 1987.

———. *Reversed Thunder: The Revelation of John and the Praying Imagination*. San Francisco: Harper & Row, 1988.

Pfeiffer, William, and Arlette C. Ballew. *Using Structured Experiences in Human Resource Development*. San Diego: University Associates, Inc., 1988.

Pinar, William F., and Madeleine R. Grumet. *Toward a Poor Curriculum.* Dubuque: Kendall/Hunt Publishing Co., 1976.

Reinhart, Peter. *Brother Juniper's Bread Book.* Cambridge: Perseus Publishing, 1991.

Ricoeur, Paul. *Freud and Philosophy.* New Haven and London: Yale University Press, 1970.

Rilke, Rainer Maria. *Letters to a Young Poet.* New York: Norton Publishing Co., 1954.

Rhoades, Robert E. "The World's Food Supply at Risk." *National Geographic* 179/4 (April 1991): 75-105.

Robertson, A. T. *Word Pictures in the New Testament.* Volume 2. Nashville: Broadman Press, 1930.

Robinson, Wayne. *The Transforming Power of the Bible.* New York: Pilgrim Press, 1984.

Rosas, Joey. *Scripture in the Thought of Søren Kierkegaard.* Nashville: Broadman & Holman Publishers, 1994.

Ryken, Leland. *Words of Delight.* Grand Rapids: Baker Book House, 1987.

Schapper, Melvin. "Nonverbal Communication and the Intercultural Encounter." In *The 1975 Annual Handbook of Group Facilitators,* ed. John E. Jones and J. William Pfeiffer. San Diego: University Associates, 1975.

Schon, Donald. *The Reflective Practitioner: How Professionals Think in Action.* New York: Basic Books, 1983.

Shaw, Susan. *Storytelling in Religious Education.* Birmingham: Religious Education Press, 1999.

Shea, John. *Stories of God.* Chicago: Thomas Moore Press, 1978.

———. *An Experience Named Spirit.* Chicago: Thomas Moore Press. 1983.

Smart, James. *The Strange Silence of the Bible in the Church.* Philadelphia: Westminster Press, 1970.

Spolin, Viola. *Improvisation for the Theater.* Evanston: Northwestern University Press, 1963.

———. *Theater Games for the Classroom: A Teacher's Handbook.* Evanston: Northwestern University Press, 1986.

Sugirtharajah, R. S. *The Bible and the Third World.* New York: Cambridge University Press, 2001.

Tate, W. Randolph. *Biblical Interpretation: An Integrated Approach.* Peabody MA: Hendrickson Publishers, 1991.

Thomas, Lewis. *The Lives of a Cell.* New York: Bantam Books, Inc., 1974.

Tyler, Ralph W. *Basic Principles of Curriculum and Instruction.* Chicago: University of Chicago Press, 1949.

Wallace, Mark. *The Second Naivete.* Macon GA: Mercer University Press, 1990.

Weber, Hans-Ruedi. *Experiments in Bible Study.* Geneva: World Council of Churches, 1981.

Wheelis, Allen. *How People Change.* New York: Harper & Row Publishers, 1973.

White, T.H. *The Once and Future King.* New York: G.P. Putnam's Sons, 1939.

Wink, Walter. *Transforming Bible Study.* Nashville: Abingdon Press, 1989.

Winquist, Charles E. "Revisioning Ministry." In *Formation and Reflection,* ed. Lewis Mudge and James N. Poling. Philadelphia: Fortress Press, 1987. 32-33.

Wuthnow, Robert. *Sharing the Journey: Support Groups and America's New Quest for Community.* New York: Free Press, 1994.